"For a Vast Future Also"

THE NORTH'S CIVIL WAR
Paul Cimbala, series editor

"For a Vast Future Also"

Essays from the *Journal*
of the Abraham Lincoln Association

Edited by
THOMAS F. SCHWARTZ

FORDHAM UNIVERSITY PRESS

New York

1999

ISSN 1089–8719
The North's Civil War, no. 10

Library of Congress Cataloging-in-Publication Data

For a vast future also : essays from the Journal of the Abraham
  Lincoln Association / edited by Thomas F. Schwartz. — 1st ed.
      p.   cm. — (North's Civil War : no. 10)
  Includes bibliographical references and index.
  ISBN 0-8232-1959-3 (hardcover). — ISBN 0-8232-1960-7 (pbk.)
    1. Lincoln, Abraham, 1809–1865.   2. United States—History—Civil
War, 1861–1865.   I. Schwartz, Thomas F.   II. Journal of the Abraham
Lincoln Association.   III. Series.
E457.8.F66   1999
973.7—dc21   99-36818
                                                                  CIP

03   02   01   00   99   5   4   3   2   1
Printed in the United States of America
First edition

In Memory of T. Harry Williams, John Niven,
and Don E. Fehrenbacher

The struggle of today, is not altogether for today—it is for a vast future also. With a reliance on Providence, all the more firm and earnest, let us proceed in the great task which events have devolved upon us.

—Abraham Lincoln
3 December 1861

CONTENTS

ACKNOWLEDGMENTS

The following selections are reproduced with permission from the Abraham Lincoln Association, the University of Illinois Press, and the *Illinois Historical Journal*, now the *Journal of the Illinois State Historical Society*.

Chapter 1 "Lincoln and the Problem of Race: A Decade of Interpretations," *Papers of the Abraham Lincoln Association*, 2 (1980), 22–45.

Chapter 2 "Lincoln's Constitutional Dilemma: Emancipation and Black Suffrage," *Papers of the Abraham Lincoln Association*, 5 (1983), 25–38.

Chapter 3 "Abraham Lincoln and the Politics of Black Colonization," *Journal of the Abraham Lincoln Association*, 14: 2 (Summer 1993), 23–46.

Chapter 4 "Abraham Lincoln and the Recruitment of Black Soldiers," *Papers of the Abraham Lincoln Association*, 2 (1980), 6–21.

Chapter 5 "Lincoln and Frederick Douglass: Another Debate," *Journal of the Illinois State Historical Society*, 68:1 (February 1975), 9–26.

Chapter 6 "Lincoln's Wartime Leadership: The First Hundred Days," *Journal of the Abraham Lincoln Association*, 9 (1987), 1–18.

Chapter 7 "The Hedgehog and the Foxes," *Journal of the Abraham Lincoln Association*, 12 (1991), 49–66.

Chapter 8 "Abraham Lincoln and the Border States," *Journal of the Abraham Lincoln Association*, 13 (1992), 13–46.

Chapter 9 "Lincoln and Chase, a Reappraisal," *Journal of the Abraham Lincoln Association*, 12 (1991), 1–16.

Chapter 10 "Lincoln and Seward in Civil War Diplomacy: Their Relationship at the Outset Reexamined," *Journal of the Abraham Lincoln Association*, 12 (1991), 21–42.

Chapter 11 "Lincoln and Congress: Why Not Congress and Lincoln?" *Journal of the Illinois State Historical Society*, 68:1 (February 1975), 57–73.

Chapter 12 *Two War Leaders: Lincoln and Davis*, (Springfield, IL: Abraham Lincoln Association, 1972).

Chapter 13 "Lincoln, the Rule of Law, and the American Revolution," *Journal of the Illinois State Historical Society*, 70:1 (February 1977), 10–17.

Chapter 14 "The Use and Misuse of the Lincoln Legacy," *Papers of the Abraham Lincoln Association*, 7 (1985), 30–42.

INTRODUCTION

The following selection of articles comes from presentations made before the Abraham Lincoln Association over the past twenty-five years. Since 1908, the Association has provided a forum for discussion on Abraham Lincoln and his presidency. Believing that these examinations of Lincoln would benefit a larger public audience and support an informed citizenry, the Association began a serious research and publications program in 1924 that continued until 1953. That year, the Association liquidated its total assets to see through to publication all eight volumes of *The Collected Works of Abraham Lincoln* (with the addition in 1955 of a ninth volume, the Index). This remains the definitive compilation of all Lincoln writings and speeches known at that time. Other materials came to light subsequently, and two Supplement volumes were published, in 1974 and 1990.

The Association maintained its charter of incorporation throughout the period 1953–59 even though it never formally met. It reactivated in 1959 at the request of Illinois Governor Otto Kerner to raise money for the restoration of the Old State Capitol, site of Lincoln's famous House Divided Address and where his body lay in state for 75,000 citizens to pay respects before Lincoln's interment at Oak Ridge Cemetery. Meeting the challenge, the Association raised nearly $300,000 for the purchase of period furnishings and artifacts that now comprise the collections at the Old State Capitol.

In 1973, the Association turned its attention back to research and publications. A scholarly symposium became an annual offering, centered around a theme relating to some contested aspect of Lincoln's life or presidency. Also, the Association sponsored an annual banquet featuring leading politicians, cultural critics, historians, authors, and what would now be termed "celebrities." The banquet speakers were not obligated to talk about the sixteenth president, but most did in profound and moving ways.

Beginning in 1973, the Association published the banquet ad-

xiv "FOR A VAST FUTURE ALSO"

dresses in limited numbers for distribution to its members. The supply of these printings was quickly exhausted, and they have since
become difficult to obtain. The Association also paid for a special
"Lincoln Issue" to be added as a supplemental issue of the quarterly
Journal of the Illinois State Historical Society. Most scholars and
members of the Association have long forgotten this brief but vital
publication foray. In 1979, the Association began its own annual publication, initially called the *Papers of the Abraham Lincoln Association*, and in 1987 renamed the *Journal of the Abraham Lincoln
Association*. Given the varied and disparate locations for the Association's publications, it was thought that a one-volume distillation from
the many presentations dealing with Lincoln's presidency would
prove fruitful for scholars and interested public alike. The tone of
these pieces is varied as well. Most of the offerings are scholarly
presentations, appropriately documented. Several of the articles,
however, reflect the familiar tone of after-dinner remarks. Indeed,
these selections tend to date themselves with references to events
such as Watergate and America's bicentennial celebration. The primary criterion was whether the article's content remained of significance in the continuing discussions of Lincoln's presidency. The
selections printed in this volume have been altered only slightly from
their original publications—for clarity and consistency.

Three themes quickly emerged in reviewing the past twenty-five
years of scholarship presented to the Association: Lincoln and emancipation, Lincoln and presidential leadership, and Lincoln's legacy.
The authors are all distinguished historians of the Civil War period.
Many are senior scholars who bring a lifetime of learning to their
work, while others are a new generation of Lincoln scholars. Sadly,
John Niven and Don E. Fehrenbacher, two friends and giants in the
historical field, died during the preparation of this volume.

Nothing is as central to American history as the question of race.
Lincoln was once extolled as the virtuous Great Emancipator, but by
the 1960s his views on black equality were seriously questioned.
Lerone Bennett's 1968 article in *Ebony* set off a heated debate on
Lincoln and race. Arthur Zilversmit carefully examines the historio-
graphical debate following Bennett's damning portrait of Lincoln's
racial views. Written before the findings of the Freedom Project
added yet another dimension to the debate, Zilversmit shows the

fundamental outlines of the problem, arguing that Lincoln as either Great Emancipator or hopeless racist distorts his legacy. Much of what historians use to discern Lincoln's views on race are derived from his actions or inactions as president. The following questions concerning Lincoln's views on race are addressed in this volume: Was Lincoln's reluctant embrace of emancipation and black suffrage largely the result of his own racial fears, or grounded in legal and political concerns (Eugene Berwanger)? Why did Lincoln continue to promote the idea of colonization throughout his presidency if he was committed to a doctrine of equality (Michael Vorenberg)? Was Lincoln's issuing of the Emancipation Proclamation largely as a military necessity to bolster federal forces with a new source of manpower? Or did Lincoln see this as a reflection of the ideals stated in the Declaration of Independence, and a step toward convincing Northerners of the important contributions that blacks made toward preserving the Union (John Hubbell)? How did Lincoln's views and actions on black freedom compare to those espoused by the former slave and the abolitionist editor Frederick Douglass (Christopher N. Breiseth)?

Lincoln has received the highest ranking in every presidential poll conducted among scholars and political writers. But why are historians and students of the political process so interested in, and approving of, Lincoln's political skills? Part of the answer lies in the political and organizational difficulties Lincoln needed to overcome in mobilizing the North for war. The first hundred days of the Lincoln administration, requiring strong and assured decisions, are frequently portrayed by some historians as chaotic, teeming with mistakes and missteps. The late Don E. Fehrenbacher, however, takes issue with conventional descriptions of Lincoln's early leadership and argues that in spite of obvious errors, Lincoln's decisions were significant and decisive. James M. McPherson, borrowing a theme from Isaiah Berlin's classic essay, "The Hedgehog and the Fox," explores leadership strategies of Lincoln, newspaper editor Horace Greeley, and Secretary of State William Henry Seward. Lincoln doggedly pursued a hedgehog strategy of saving the Union while Greeley and Seward acted like foxes who constantly changed strategies to suit changing events. Nowhere were Lincoln's leadership skills put to a greater test than in his dealings with the border states. William Gienapp, in a provocative essay, examines and measures the success of Lincoln's policies in these states throughout the war. Most historians realize that the border states were important early in the war, but they fail to look at Lincoln's policies—especially those regarding arbitrary arrests, elections, party building, and emancipation—when the threat of secession in Missouri, Kentucky, and Maryland eclipsed after 1861.

Leadership is not a solitary endeavor. A cadre of loyal Lincoln men and those who felt superior in ability to Lincoln comprised his cabinet, the Republican Party, and Congress. The late John Niven reflects recent efforts to rehabilitate the reputation and image of one of Lincoln's most capable, but also ambitious, political rivals—Salmon Portland Chase. He was a confirmed abolitionist and a man with an extraordinary legal mind, but vain and hungry for the presidency. Even while Chase devised innovative measures to finance the war as Lincoln's secretary of the treasury, he also allowed his name to be advanced to dump Lincoln as the party standard bearer in 1864. Norman B. Ferris offers a spirited defense of Seward's role in the Lincoln cabinet, claiming that accounts by Gideon Wells, Montgomery Blair, and Chase, all ex-Democrats, distort Seward's character and his famous 1 April 1861 memorandum suggesting that to reunite the country, Lincoln should undertake a war against France, based on French interference in Mexico. Ferris also argues that Jay Monaghan's monograph on Lincoln's diplomacy exaggerates Lincoln's actual role in diplomatic matters. Seward's guiding hand, rather than Lincoln's, set diplomacy. Harold M. Hyman makes a similar point by illustrating how historians naturally assume a relationship between Lincoln and Congress that places Lincoln in supremacy. The dangers of such an assumption lead to distorted understandings, for as Hyman claims, "until we recapture Congress we cannot know Lincoln." The late T. Harry Williams compares the lives and careers of Lincoln and Jefferson Davis as war leaders. Whereas both came from similar geographic, social, and economic backgrounds, they represented different political philosophies and wielded power in very different ways.

Perhaps his legacy is the most elusive aspect of Lincoln—and of Lincoln studies. His own life was cut short from an assassin's bullet, giving rise to images of the martyred president and the Great Emancipator. Merrill O. Peterson has attempted to trace various themes of Lincoln's legacy in his monumental *Lincoln In American Memory*.

Phillip Shaw Paludan deals with one important aspect of Lincoln's legacy, that of preserving and advancing the principles espoused by America's revolutionary generation. Lincoln saw the revolutionary spirit in the laws and institutions governing the country and mediating human interest. Paludan carefully outlines Lincoln's beliefs about the rule of law—peaceful ballots, not bloody bullets—and how they fit with Lincoln's own understanding of the doctrine of equality as stated in the Declaration of Independence.

John Hope Franklin concludes the volume with an examination of the use and misuse of the Lincoln legacy. Among the more benign examples given by Franklin to support special pleadings are women's groups claiming that Lincoln would have supported the Equal Rights Amendment, and beleaguered Richard M. Nixon attempting to draw parallels between the attacks by Lincoln's critics to his own Watergate plight. More disturbing are Franklin's descriptions of Lost Cause writers who distorted Lincoln's record to feed southern resentment toward the Lincoln legacy. Other southern writers, however, embraced Lincoln, claiming he shared their white supremacist views. Black nationalists in the 1960s reaffirmed the myth created by the white supremacists, declaring that Lincoln embodied the American tradition of racism. But Franklin wisely suggests that Lincoln, as well as all great leaders, demonstrated flexibility in his views and had a large capacity for growth. As Franklin concludes, those who purposely distort Lincoln's legacy only reveal how brilliant and instructive it actually remains.

THOMAS F. SCHWARTZ

1
LINCOLN AND THE PROBLEMS OF EMANCIPATION

1

Lincoln and the Problem of Race: A Decade of Interpretations

Arthur Zilversmit

LONG BEFORE ALEX HALEY popularized the idea of "roots," Americans have been concerned with the search for ancestors. The attempt to answer the question, "Who are we?" has often been answered by another question, "Where did we come from?" Although historians have been responsible for drafting answers to these questions, neither the questions nor the answers are exclusively within the domain of historians. Popular culture has its own answers, and we have, in fact, often witnessed a real tension between popular history and professional history in answering vital questions about who we are and where we came from.

In the 1960s, when race was an overriding concern, our search for self-definition through looking at our roots led to a heated controversy over the real meaning of Abraham Lincoln. Lincoln was one in a series of American founding fathers, and his views on slavery and race might provide a guide for those troubled days. The popular view of Lincoln as the Great Emancipator could provide a source for an American commitment to racial justice. Yet, this picture could lead to an obvious question: if Lincoln pointed the way to racial justice, why, in over one hundred years, had we neglected to follow his path? In February 1968, a prominent black journalist, Lerone Bennett Jr., offered an answer to the paradox when he charged that we, in fact, had followed Lincoln's path. Bennett stated that Lincoln's path was itself deeply flawed; Lincoln was the embodiment of the American racist tradition.[1]

According to Bennett, no American story was as "false" as the traditional picture of Lincoln as the Great Emancipator. Lincoln, he charged, was no idealist; he was a "cautious politician" who was never committed to abolishing slavery but only to preventing its extension. He was motivated by a concern for the interests of his white constituents, not the needs of the oppressed blacks. During the celebrated debates with Stephen A. Douglas, Lincoln explicitly supported the doctrine of white supremacy, and he opposed granting civil and political rights to Negroes. As president, he spent the first eighteen months of his administration "in a desperate and rather pathetic attempt to save slavery"; he moved against it only because of circumstances and the pressure applied by a small band of dedicated radicals. The Emancipation Proclamation was not a great charter of freedom; congressional legislation had already gone further, and the Proclamation applied only in areas where Lincoln could not enforce it. Moreover, only a few months before his death Lincoln was still equivocating about immediate emancipation. Lincoln, according to Bennett, never did accept the idea that the United States could be a genuinely biracial society, and to the very end the president supported a policy of colonization. Lincoln's reconstruction policies virtually ignored the needs of the blacks. Therefore, Bennett concluded, "Lincoln must be seen as the embodiment, not the transcendence, of the American tradition, which is, as we all know, a racist tradition."[2]

Bennett's article struck a nerve. His charges were broadcast on radio and television and were debated in newspapers. The issues he had raised were important. For some Americans, Bennett's attack, coinciding as it did with a period of great racial tension, was further evidence of an irreconcilable split in American society. The fact that Bennett was a spokesman for blacks contributed to the article's impact because it had been blacks who had, in large measure, made Lincoln a symbol of liberation in the first place. Bennett's article was a literary equivalent of the Black Power movement, of the split in the civil rights coalition, and of the frightening violence of the summer of 1967. Bennett had not only called into question the reputation of a beloved hero, he had challenged the American picture of our history as the story of measured progress toward liberal goals.[3]

Herbert Mitgang, a member of the *New York Times* editorial board and a Lincoln scholar, was one of the first to reply to Bennett's charges. Mitgang's article asked, "Was Lincoln Just a Honkie?"—and the answer was a resounding "No!" Mitgang was quite explicit about the context of the controversy. The article begins: "One hundred and five years after the Emancipation Proclamation—and, what is far more relevant, five months before the feared summer of 1968, when uptight frustration responding to cries of 'Black Power!' can again enflame American cities in a new civil war—Abraham Lincoln is being called a false Great Emancipator." Mark Krug, a historian who also wrote an early reply to Bennett, pointedly noted: "Only harm can result from this unworthy effort to convince the Negro population, especially its restless young generation, that even Abe Lincoln was just another white supremacist." Both Mitgang and Krug gave the impression that Bennett would be indirectly to blame if racial violence broke out in the summer of 1968.[4]

Bennett's charges against Lincoln were not so easily dismissed by other historians, however. Although they recognized that Bennett's charges were not entirely new (several of them had been anticipated by Richard Hofstadter and Kenneth Stampp), Bennett's picture of Lincoln required careful consideration and measured appraisal.[5] In the historians' dialogue between past and present, the subject of race was increasingly important, and Bennett had been quite correct in his assertion that myths provide little light for present-day problems. Perhaps a reappraisal of Lincoln's views on slavery and race could help us in avoiding the exacerbation of the racial tensions that beset us. In the dozen years since Bennett's article, a number of historians have participated in this reexamination. Where has this reexamination led us? What is our understanding today of Lincoln? Was he the Great Emancipator or merely another white supremacist?

Historians who undertook a reexamination of Lincoln's reputation discussed a large number of issues, but for the purposes of this analysis I deal with four major issues raised by Bennett. First, how can we reconcile Lincoln's popular image with his endorsement of white supremacy during the debates with Douglas? Second, was Lincoln a moral leader in the struggle for emancipation? Third, did Lincoln ever surrender his belief in colonization as the solution to the problem of what to do with the freedmen? And, finally, would he have supported the radicals of his own party in providing for black civil rights and suffrage in a genuinely reconstructed South? The answers to these questions are not, of course, definitive, but a study of recent scholarship will give us a clearer picture of "*where* we are, and *whither* we are tending."[6]

I

Lincoln's speeches in defense of white supremacy during the Lincoln-Douglas debates were an important part of Bennett's charges
and in recent years have become among the most frequently quoted
words of Lincoln. In the following remarks made at the fourth debate, at Charleston, he responded to Douglas's charges that he favored racial equality and amalgamation:

> I am not, nor ever have been in favor of bringing about in any way the
> social and political equality of the white and black races, [applause] . . .
> I am not nor ever have been in favor of making voters or jurors of
> negroes, nor of qualifying them to hold office, nor to intermarry with
> white people; and I will say in addition to this that there is a physical
> difference between the white and black races which I believe will for
> ever forbid the two races living together on terms of social and political
> equality. And inasmuch as they cannot so live, while they do remain
> together there must be the position of superior and inferior, and I as
> much as any other man am in favor of having the superior position
> assigned to the white race.[7]

Those who defended Lincoln attempted to dismiss these remarks
as unimportant. Mitgang, for example, argued that Douglas "had
backed Lincoln to the wall and forced him to temporize," and that
late in his presidential career, Lincoln did, in fact, come out for full
Negro citizenship.[8]

A more fruitful approach is to reexamine Lincoln's words carefully.
George M. Fredrickson points out that although Lincoln argued in
the debate at Ottawa that he agreed with Douglas that the Negro "is
not my equal in many respects," the only respect that he was certain
about was the physical trait of "color." Lincoln was tentative in iden-
tifying ways in which Negroes were "perhaps" not the equal of
whites. Moreover, he avoided using words like "innate" in describing
the inequalities between the races, leaving open the question of
whether those differences were the result of circumstance.[9] Historian
E. B. Smith makes a similar point when he observes that the qualify-
ing words in the Ottawa speech reveal that "Lincoln was obviously
playing to his audience, but . . . was also hedging for the benefit of
his conscience."[10]

Don E. Fehrenbacher, an eminent Lincoln historian, sees Lincoln's statements on race as "essentially disclaimers rather than af-

firmations." According to Fehrenbacher, those statements "indicated, for political reasons, the *maximum* that he was willing to deny the Negro and the *minimum* that he claimed for the Negro. They were concessions on points not at issue, designed to fortify him on the point that *was* at issue—namely the extension of slavery." Fehrenbacher adds that if Lincoln had responded differently to Douglas at Charleston, "the Lincoln of history simply would not exist."[11] Lincoln adopted the least racist position that would not disqualify him from consideration in the context of a racist society.[12]

Professor Fredrickson also points out that we should devote careful attention to what Lincoln claimed *for* the Negro in the Ottawa address. Despite the differences he saw between the races, Lincoln did hold that there was "no reason in the world why the negro is not entitled to all the natural rights enumerated in the Declaration of Independence, the right of life, liberty and the pursuit of happiness." Judged within the context of his own times, Lincoln, as Fredrickson notes, occupied a middle position between those who, like Douglas, would deny the Negro every human right and the small group of abolitionists who supported the radical doctrine of racial equality.[13]

II

Although Bennett's claim that Lincoln was a white supremacist jolted the conventional picture of him, the charge that he was not really antislavery and was, at best, a reluctant emancipator, struck at the very heart of the popular understanding of Lincoln's historic role. If the Emancipation Proclamation was not a charter for black freedom, why were we celebrating Negro History in February? What was the basis for our almost worshipful attitude toward Lincoln?

Stephen B. Oates, recent Lincoln biographer, meets Bennett's charges head on. According to Oates, Lincoln had been consistently antislavery since his earliest days.[14] Yet Lincoln recognized that the Constitution protected slavery in the South, and in the early days of the war both his constitutional scruples and the need for the support of the border slave states prevented action against slavery. Moreover, Lincoln perceived that emancipation would be unpopular in the North. According to Oates, Lincoln feared that an emancipation policy "would alienate Northern Democrats, ignite a racial powder keg in the Northern states, and possibly cause a civil war in the rear."[15] By emphasizing northern opposition to emancipation, Oates is able to depict Lincoln as being ahead of his times when, in 1862, he moved cautiously toward emancipation.

Constitutional historian Herman Belz agrees with Oates that the Proclamation was the product of a genuine ideological commitment to freedom. The military needs of the nation, invoked by Lincoln in justifying the Proclamation, were merely "legal fiction." Belz contends that "the real reason for it, considered in broad historical perspective, was hostility to slavery based on commitment to republicanism and the principle of equality on which republicanism rested."[16]

Moreover, Lincoln rejected the temptation to revoke the Proclamation. Neither northern pressure nor the possibility of making peace led him to abandon emancipation. Lincoln's letter to Horace Greeley is seen by Oates not as proof of hesitation or lack of commitment to emancipation but as part of a strategy of making emancipation acceptable as a legitimate war aim.[17] In that letter Lincoln had said that if he could "save the Union without freeing *any* slave" he would do it, but he went on to say that if he could "save it by freeing *all* the slaves" he would do that. "What I do about slavery, and the colored race, I do because I believe it helps to save the Union."[18] When he wrote the letter to Greeley, Lincoln had already resolved to issue the Emancipation Proclamation (at Seward's suggestion he was only waiting for a Union victory before announcing it), and there is no evidence that Lincoln did not intend to follow through on his resolve. What the letter was intended to do was to make clear that any action to free the slaves should be understood as a measure to save the Union. Unionists who opposed emancipation were being told in advance that they would be fighting not to free the slaves but to restore the Union, with the help of an emancipation policy. Oates, therefore, sees the letter to Greeley as an example of how Lincoln, a shrewd political leader, was preparing the way for the acceptance of a radical new step.[19]

Arguing directly with Bennett and other historians, Oates holds that the Emancipation Proclamation "went further than anything Congress had done." The Second Confiscation Act had not only required extensive judicial procedures but had also exempted loyal slaveowners. "Lincoln's Proclamation, on the other hand, was a sweeping blow against bondage as an institution in the rebel states, a blow that would free *all* the slaves there—those of secessionists and loyalists alike." Lincoln was not a reluctant emancipator, and the Proclamation "was the most revolutionary measure ever to come from an American president up to that time."[20]

The revisionist view of Lincoln as a reluctant emancipator was reinforced by an important article by Ludwell Johnson, published the same year as Bennett's. Professor Johnson argues that as late as February 1865, Lincoln was still equivocating about immediate and total emancipation. According to Johnson, Lincoln told Alexander Stephens at their Hampton Roads meeting that emancipation might be delayed as much as five years and that slaveowners might still receive compensation for the loss of their bondsmen. Lincoln was willing to make such concessions, Johnson speculates, because he saw the need for a quick end to the war lest the South lapse into chaos and anarchy—conditions that would play into the hands of the radical members of Lincoln's party. A quick end to the war would forestall a radical reconstruction of the South.[21]

Johnson's account of Lincoln's position at the Hampton Roads Conference went unchallenged until a recent article by the editor of *Lincoln Lore*, Mark E. Neely Jr., who points out that the only record of what was said there is the account, published five years after the event, by Stephens. Even if Stephens's memory was good, he was by no means an impartial witness. By the time that Stephens wrote, a great deal had happened and there were many reasons why Stephens might cherish the memory of a Lincoln who would have been kinder to the South than the Republicans who eventually took charge of Reconstruction.[22]

According to Oates, Lincoln wavered only once—during the dark days of August 1864, when he considered peace terms that did not include emancipation. "But the next day Lincoln changed his mind. With awakened resolution, he vowed to fight the war through to unconditional surrender and to stick with emancipation come what may."[23] As Lincoln himself put it, once the Emancipation Proclamation had been issued it could not be revoked "any more than the dead can be brought to life."[24]

Finally, even if Lincoln does not deserve the title Great Emancipator for his Proclamation, he is entitled to it for his skillful and determined effort in winning congressional ratification of the constitutional amendment that clearly and unequivocally ended slavery in the United States.[25]

III

Lincoln's attitude toward the future of the newly freed blacks has been a perennial historical question. For many years the dominant school of reconstruction historiography held that radical reconstruction was a grievous and tragic error; moreover, the dominant assumption of that school was that Reconstruction under Lincoln would have been milder and much more protective of white southern rights and sensibilities than was that administered by the Congress.[26] By the time of Bennett's article, however, the traditional interpretation had been all but replaced by the view that reconstruction had been necessary in order to safeguard the results of the war and to provide some protection for the rights of southern blacks and white Unionists. Under these circumstances, the contention that Reconstruction would have been milder under Lincoln depicts the president as unwilling to take the steps necessary to protect the freedom of the ex-slaves; once again, Lincoln was not on the side of those who wanted to further the cause of black rights.

The issues of reconstruction, particularly what to do with the former slaves, had appeared early in the Civil War. One of the solutions promoted by Lincoln was the old idea of colonization, a plan in which blacks would be asked to leave the United States and to establish their own nation. Bennett and other revisionists have charged that Lincoln's continuing support for colonization is further evidence of his refusal to countenance full equality for blacks in this country. An important question for those who study Lincoln's views on race has been: Why did Lincoln support colonization, and did he ever abandon this proposal?

Some of those who defended Lincoln from the charges of racism conceded that he had been a dedicated colonizationist but that he abandoned the position as he evolved "from intolerance to moderation."[27] On the other hand, Oates, who is sharply critical of the revisionists, explains Lincoln's support of colonization as being, in large part, merely a strategy for easing northern fears of the consequences of emancipation. Presumably those who feared that the freed slaves would flock to the North would be pacified by a proposal to resettle blacks elsewhere. Shortly before issuing the Preliminary Emancipation Proclamation, therefore, Lincoln "made a great fuss about colonization—a ritual he went through every time he contemplated some new antislavery move." Once he found another answer to northern fears of black flight—the refugee plan set up under Adjutant General Lorenzo Thomas in the Mississippi Valley—Lincoln dropped his public support of colonization.[28]

G. S. Boritt, who has written a provocative study of Lincoln's ideas, also sees the president's colonization program as motivated in part by strategic interests. Yet, Boritt points out, Lincoln's support for colonization was inconsistent with his deep interest in and understanding of economics. It was clear to anyone who analyzed the question in any depth that the economic resources required to resettle any significant portion of the black population of the United States was simply staggering. Why then did Lincoln support this impractical policy? Boritt draws on the psychological defense mechanism of avoidance as an explanation of Lincoln's behavior. Arguing that the president avoided analyzing the question because he saw no feasible alternative at the time, Boritt concludes, "One cannot escape the feeling that by 1862, even as the colonization fever was cresting, Lincoln began to allow himself a glimpse of the fact that the idea of large scale immigration was [not] realistic." For Lincoln, the idea served a purpose; it helped to "allay his own uncertainties, and more importantly the fears of the vast majority of whites." After emancipation, however, when it was no longer necessary to believe in colonization, Lincoln abandoned it.[29]

Although Lincoln no longer endorsed colonization in public after December of 1863, there is still the question of whether he ever completely abandoned hopes for resettling blacks. Fredrickson, whose account of Lincoln's racial views is generally revisionist, argues that Lincoln continued his support of colonization to the very end. Fredrickson maintains that in April 1865, Lincoln told General Benjamin Butler that he still saw colonization as an important step for avoiding race war in the South. "If Butler's recollection is substantially correct, as it appears to be, then one can only conclude that Lincoln continued to his dying day to deny the possibility of racial harmony and equality in the United States."[30] That contention is directly challenged by Neely, who, after a painstaking evaluation of the evidence, concludes that the interview with Butler could not have taken place when Butler said it did and that there is no reason to believe that Butler's story is anything but a self-serving "fantasy." In the absence of any other evidence, therefore, we must conclude that John Hay was correct in his assertion that the president had abandoned colonization by July 1864.[31]

IV

Once Lincoln rejected colonization he was still faced with the question of determining relationships that would prevail between the freedmen and their former masters. Would blacks have civil and political rights? Should blacks be awarded suffrage? In attempting to ascertain Lincoln's views on these issues, historians have been forced to interpret a small number of documents for clues to what Lincoln would have done had the assassin's bullet not struck him down shortly after the war ended.

Hans L. Trefousse has put Lincoln's reconstruction policy in a new light by pointing out that the traditional picture of Lincoln as a conservative, struggling desperately to control a group of vindictive radicals from his own party, is simply wrong. Trefousse argues that Lincoln's differences with the radicals were often merely matters of timing and that Lincoln was able to make good use of the radicals when creating an atmosphere in which his actions on slavery would be accepted.[32] If we accept such an interpretation of Lincoln's relationship with the radicals, it is easy to believe that he would have continued to lag only a little behind even the most visionary members of the Republican Party as they advocated suffrage and other measures designed to protect the rights of the freedmen.

For the most part Oates follows Trefousse's views on the relationship between the president and congressional leaders, going so far as to avoid using the term "radicals." Oates sees a close relationship between a leading radical, Senator Charles Sumner, and both Mary and Abraham Lincoln.[33] But in describing Secretary Salmon P. Chase's role, Oates comes close to the older view of the relationship between Lincoln and the radicals. Oates charges that Lincoln's reconstruction plan of December 1863 was praised by virtually all congressional Republicans, including Sumner, but that Chase objected to it apparently from purely political motives.[34] On reconstruction, therefore, Oates suggests there was no real ideological split between Lincoln and his critics on the left. Further, Oates maintains that most biographers have misinterpreted the Second Inaugural Address. Although the president did promise "charity for all," he did not mean that he intended to be gentle with the South: "Still preoccupied with the war as a grim purgation which would cleanse and regenerate his country, Lincoln endorsed a fairly tough policy toward the conquered South."[35]

An important document employed by several of those who defend Lincoln from the charges of racism is a letter to General James Wadsworth, said to have been written by Lincoln early in 1864. The letter not only discusses reconstruction but also goes much further than the president's public remarks up to that time. In the letter Lincoln apparently endorsed Negro suffrage: "I cannot see, if universal amnesty is granted, how, under the circumstances, I can avoid exacting in return universal suffrage, or, at least, suffrage on the basis of intelligence and military service."[36] Lincoln's defenders argue on the basis of that letter that Lincoln had moved far beyond the statements he had made in the debates with Douglas when he denied that he favored black political rights.[37] Yet this letter proves to be a very weak reed. Although the original of the letter has never been found, the editors of Lincoln's *Collected Works* lent it apparent authenticity by including it in their publication. As the editors' footnote makes clear, however, the source of the letter is suspect. It was found in the *New York Tribune*, which, in turn, claims to have copied it from a periodical called the *Southern Advocate*. The editors note that "no other reference has been found to the original letter to Wadsworth."[38] Professor Johnson, who conducted a careful study of the letter and the circumstances of its publication, concludes that several paragraphs of that letter are not authentic.[39] I would go further. I can see no reason why we should assume that any part of the letter is authentic—it doesn't sound like Lincoln, and the ideas expressed in it are not consonant with what we know about Lincoln's thoughts at the time he supposedly wrote the letter.

Although Johnson established the dubious nature of most of the Wadsworth letter, those who defended Lincoln's record on race have been able to argue that other evidence substantiates the president's generous views on Negro rights. As the eminent constitutional historian Harold Hyman has put it, "Professor Johnson has wasted . . . his effort to sunder the links that bind Lincoln to the egalitarians of a century past[;] the chain still holds." Hyman rests his case mostly on Lincoln's dealing with the reconstruction of Louisiana. Lincoln not only suggested (in a private letter to Governor Michael Hahn) that some Negroes be given the vote, he repeated the recommendation in his public address; and he further suggested that blacks be provided with public schools. In that final address Lincoln expressed ideas that were not limited to Louisiana, and Hyman contends that Lincoln was moving further along the lines of giving full rights to the freedmen. Although Hyman concedes that it is impossible to say how far Lincoln would have gone, the friends of black rights "shared confidence that Lincoln would keep moving in the happy direction he had already taken."[40]

The contention that Lincoln's policies for Louisiana indicate that he was moving rapidly to a revolutionary policy of reconstructing the South on the basis of black suffrage is the thesis of an exciting new study by Peyton McCrary. McCrary moves beyond a defense of Lincoln from the attacks of revisionists to a new assertion: Lincoln was the revolutionary leader of a revolution in the making. McCrary starts with the assumption that virtually all historians share: Lincoln was a realist. Professor McCrary then goes on to argue that "a radical approach to reconstruction was more realistic than [Nathaniel P.] Banks' moderate policy . . . because the nation was in the midst of a revolutionary civil war, and in such crises only the forceful allocation of governmental power by the victors can produce a stable postwar order." Therefore, Lincoln, as a realist, would have continued to move toward the policies advocated by the radicals.[41]

The evidence that McCrary cites are Lincoln's approval of the Freedmen's Bureau legislation and his last speech, which hint that he might soon announce a new policy. Lincoln's decision to undermine the radicals in Louisiana, by calling for elections before a constitutional convention, was not, McCrary argues, evidence of Lincoln's conservatism but rather evidence that he had been badly misled by General Banks. At last, Lincoln recognized that Louisiana was headed in the wrong direction; he "came to recognize the fragile quality of the Hahn regime's electoral support and became more comfortable with the prospect of Negro suffrage. As a pragmatic politician, if not as a man with a commitment to social justice for the freedmen, Lincoln could hardly have escaped the conclusion that at the end of the war there was nowhere to go but to the left."[42]

Lerone Bennett's article of 1968 was the product of the times. American blacks and members of the New Left were convinced that American society was deeply flawed and that it was the product of a corrupt heritage. Moreover, the radicals of the 1960s were impatient with history; they saw the past as a dead weight that could only limit action in the present—and action was what they wanted. Our golden age lay in the future, not the past.

Yet, if the radicals of the 1960s were impatient with history, they performed a valuable service in leading the reexamination of our past from new perspectives, enriching our understanding of our history. Although most historians have not accepted Bennett's views on Lincoln, we have not merely come back to where we started. We have learned a great deal. We have found out that a number of things probably did not happen—the letter to General Wadsworth, the equivocation at Hampton Roads about emancipation, and the interview with General Butler. Our picture of Lincoln's relationship to the radical wing of his party has also been profoundly altered. We no longer see Lincoln as hapless defender of the Constitution against the onslaught of unprincipled politicians. Lincoln has been put back into the Republican Party.

We also have a new appreciation of the Emancipation Proclamation. The Proclamation, despite its pedestrian language, *was* a revolutionary act that went beyond what Congress had done and that inexorably changed the nature of the Civil War. We also have a new appreciation of Lincoln's reconstruction policies. We no longer see a Lincoln who was hopelessly wedded to the Proclamation of December 1863, but one who was moving with the times and had begun to see, as the radicals had, the need for fundamental social changes in the South.

As we continue to study Lincoln we continue to define ourselves. Most historians have discarded the myth of the saintly Great Emancipator, but they have also rejected the counter myth of Lincoln as a hopeless racist.[43] We are judging Lincoln by different standards now from those we used a decade ago. Our sense of presidential leadership has changed. We are no longer confident that strong leaders can solve our problems, and in the post-Vietnam, post-Watergate era, the idea of a president who moves far beyond the nation in implementing his ideas arouses our suspicions. We are far more ready now to recognize the conditions that limit the actions of strong leaders for good or for ill.

Within the limits of leadership, which are clearer to us now than they were a decade ago, Lincoln is still a relevant figure. He shows us how, despite fluctuations in the national will, a great president can use his office to support reform. His image is still available as comfort to those reformers who can use a prestigious American hero in their corner.

NOTES

1. Lerone Bennett Jr., "Was Abe Lincoln a White Supremacist?" *Ebony*, February 1968, 35–42.

2. Ibid., 35, 36, 37, 42.

3. The significance of a black person's attacking a symbol of black liberation was made by Arvarh Strickland in his perceptive comments at the Seventh Annual Abraham Lincoln Symposium, Springfield, Illinois, 12 February 1980 (copy in the Abraham Lincoln Association Papers, Illinois State Historical Library, Springfield). For the changing black views of Lincoln, see Mark E. Neely Jr., "Emancipation: 113 Years Later," *Lincoln Lore*, Number 1653 (November 1975): 1–3.

4. Herbert Mitgang, "Was Lincoln Just a Honkie?" *New York Times Magazine*, 11 February 1968, pp. 35, 100–107; Mark Krug, "What Lincoln Thought about the Negro," *Chicago Sun-Times*, Sunday, 10 March 1968, sec. 2, p. 2. The Mitgang and Krug articles are only two of the many outraged replies to Bennett; another example is Leo Kibby, "Lincoln Belongs to the Ages," *Journal of the West* 7 (1968): 456–60.

5. Richard Hofstadter, *The American Political Tradition and the Men Who Made It* (New York: Vintage Books, 1948), 93–136; Kenneth M. Stampp, *The Era of Reconstruction, 1865–1877* (New York: Knopf, 1965), 24–49.

6. The quotation is from Lincoln's House Divided Address, in Roy P. Basler, ed., Marion Dolores Pratt and Lloyd A. Dunlap, asst. eds., *The Collected Works of Abraham Lincoln*, 9 vols. (New Brunswick, N.J.: Rutgers University Press, 1953–55), 2:461 (hereafter, Basler, *Collected Works*).

7. Ibid., 3:145–46: see also the first debate at Ottawa, ibid., 12–30.

8. Mitgang, "Lincoln Just a Honkie?" 103. To demonstrate that Lincoln later came to support political rights for Negroes, Mitgang quotes extensively from Lincoln's letter to General James J. Wadsworth (106–7). For

reasons discussed below, I am convinced that the Wadsworth document is spurious. Fawn Brodie, taking a different tack, argues that in the debates with Douglas, Lincoln was not only debating his opponent but was also "conducting a kind of inner dialogue with himself, coming to terms with his own ambivalence to black men" ("The Political Hero in America," *Virginia Quarterly Review* 46 [1970]: 50–51).

9. George M. Fredrickson, "A Man but Not a Brother: Abraham Lincoln and Racial Equality," *Journal of Southern History* 41 (1975): 46–48; Basler, *Collected Works*, 3:16.

10. E. B. Smith, "Abraham Lincoln: Realist," *Wisconsin Magazine of History* 52 (1968–69): 163. Smith states that when Lincoln's remarks at Ottawa are viewed "against the background of its time, occasion, and purpose," they constitute "a rather advanced plea against racial discrimination."

11. Don E. Fehrenbacher, "Only His Stepchildren: Lincoln and the Negro," *Civil War History* 20 (1974): 303.

12. Christopher Breiseth argues that Lincoln's positions on slavery and Negro rights were "well in advance of the views of his neighbors in Sangamon County" ("Lincoln, Douglas, and Springfield in the 1858 Campaign," in *The Public and the Private Lincoln: Contemporary Perspectives*, ed. Cullom Davis et al. [Carbondale: Southern Illinois University Press, 1979], 101–20). See also Arvarh Strickland, "The Illinois Background of Lincoln's Attitude Toward Slavery and the Negro," *Journal of the Illinois State Historical Society* 56 (1963): 474–94; Eugene H. Berwanger, *The Frontier Against Slavery: Western Anti-Negro Prejudice and the Slavery Extension Controversy* (Urbana: University of Illinois Press, 1967), 44–59, 123–37; V. Jacque Voegeli, *Free but Not Equal: The Midwest and the Negro during the Civil War* (Chicago: University of Chicago Press, 1967), 1–9.

13. Basler, *Collected Works*, 3:16; Fredrickson, "A Man but Not a Brother," 46.

14. Stephen B. Oates, *With Malice Toward None: The Life of Abraham Lincoln* (New York: Harper, 1977), 37–39.

15. Stephen B. Oates, *Our Fiery Trial: Abraham Lincoln, John Brown, and the Civil War Era* (Amherst: University of Massachusetts Press, 1979), 73.

16. Herman Belz, *Emancipation and Equal Rights: Politics and Constitutionalism in the Civil War Era* (New York: W. W. Norton, 1978), 44–45. George Sinkler holds that "military necessity, humanitarianism, and public opinion each played its part in Lincoln's decision for liberation" (*The Racial Attitudes of American Presidents from Abraham Lincoln to Theodore Roosevelt* [Garden City, N.Y.: Anchor Books, 1972], 63).

17. Oates, *With Malice Toward None*, 313. Richard O. Curry makes the same point: "Far from establishing Lincoln's fundamental conservatism, this

statement [to Greeley] demonstrates beyond question his shrewdness as a politician" ("The Civil War and Reconstruction, 1861–1877: A Critical Overview of Recent Trends and Interpretations," *Civil War History* 20 [1974]: 222).

18. Basler, *Collected Works*, 5:388.

19. Oates, *With Malice Toward None*, 313.

20. Oates, *Our Fiery Trial*, 77–78, 80. Oates makes the same point in " 'The Man of Our Redemption': Abraham Lincoln and the Emancipation of the Slaves," *Presidential Studies Quarterly* 9 (1979): 20–21.

21. Ludwell Johnson, "Lincoln's Solution to the Problem of Peace Terms, 1864–1865," *Journal of Southern History* 34 (1968): 576–86. Johnson's article is frequently cited in discussions of Lincoln's plans for blacks after the war.

22. Mark E. Neely Jr, "The Lincoln Theme Since Randall's Call: The Promises and Perils of Professionalism," *Papers of the Abraham Lincoln Association* 1 (1979): 24–25.

23. Oates, *Our Fiery Trial*, 82.

24. Basler, *Collected Works*, 6:408.

25. Oates, *With Malice Toward None*, 404–6, and " 'The Man of our Redemption,' " 22.

26. For an excellent survey of changing attitudes toward Reconstruction, see Stampp, *Era of Reconstruction*, 3–23.

27. Paul David Nelson, "From Intolerance to Moderation: The Evolution of Abraham Lincoln's Racial Views," *Register of the Kentucky Historical Society* 72 (1974): 2–3.

28. Oates, *With Malice Toward None*, 312, 342. Gary R. Planck argues that in the early 1850s "Lincoln enthusiastically supported the program of black colonization" and came to reject it only in 1864, after the failure of the Chiriqui and A'Vache experiments ("Abraham Lincoln and Black Colonization: Theory and Practice," *Lincoln Herald* 72 [1970]: 63, 75).

29. G. S. Boritt, "The Voyage to the Colony of Lincolnia: The Sixteenth President, Black Colonization, and the Defense Mechanism of Avoidance," *Historian* 37 (1975): 620–21, 624, 627.

30. Fredrickson, "A Man but Not a Brother," 56–57.

31. Mark E. Neely Jr., "Abraham Lincoln and Black Colonization: Benjamin Butler's Spurious Testimony," *Civil War History* 25 (1979): 77–83. In his 1977 biography of Lincoln, Oates holds that even after the president had ceased to support colonization in public, he may have continued to view it, "maybe in the abstract," as "the only way to avoid racial conflict in America" (*With Malice Toward None*, 342). By 1979, however, Oates had changed his mind, and he chided Fredrickson for relying on Butler's testimony (*Our Fiery Trial*, 138n).

32. Hans L. Trefousse, *The Radical Republicans: Lincoln's Vanguard for Racial Justice* (New York: Knopf, 1969), 183, 211, 285–86. Trefousse concludes that Lincoln, in the last months of his administration, "was approaching the radicals' position on reconstruction" (304).

33. Oates refers to the Radical Republicans as "liberal Republicans" and as "so-called radicals." He sometimes uses the term radicals within quotation marks (*With Malice Toward None*, 252–53, 364).

34. Ibid., 273, 406–7, 371–72.

35. Oates, *Our Fiery Trial*, 84. Sinkler, on the other hand, supports Bennett's views; he maintains that Lincoln would have allowed Southerners to decide for themselves how to treat the freedmen, and he adds that "it is not too difficult to infer that the President's failure to include blacks in his plans for Reconstruction was due in part to his views on the race problem" (*Racial Attitudes*, 64, 65).

36. Basler, *Collected Works*, 7:101–2.

37. Mitgang, "Lincoln Just a Honkie?" 106–7; Krug, "What Lincoln Thought," 2. Robert Durden points out that both Bennett and Mitgang relied on spurious evidence: Bennett accepted Benjamin Butler's story that Lincoln continued to support colonization, while Mitgang accepted the authenticity of the letter to Wadsworth ("A. Lincoln: Honkie or Equalitarian," *South Atlantic Quarterly* 71 [1972]: 286–87).

38. Basler, *Collected Works*, 7:101–2, 102n. The newspaper claimed that it printed the letter because in it Lincoln supposedly endorsed "universal amnesty" and, the newspaper further claimed, that desire of the beloved president "is still withheld from the South, notwithstanding it is known that it was his intention to grant, without any exception, a general pardon." That contention is, of course, absurd. If Lincoln had been willing to grant a blanket pardon, most loyal Union supporters would have been outraged. The North had suffered too much to allow the leaders of the Confederate States to resume business as usual after the war. At a minimum, the top leaders of the Confederacy and those guilty of war crimes would not have been eligible for pardons.

39. Ludwell Johnson, "Lincoln and Equal Rights: The Authenticity of the Wadsworth Letter," *Journal of Southern History* 32 (1966): 83–87. Interestingly, Johnson does not argue that the paragraph on "universal amnesty" and "universal suffrage" is spurious.

40. Harold M. Hyman, "Lincoln and Equal Rights for Negroes: The Irrelevancy of the 'Wadsworth Letter,' " *Civil War History* 12 (1966): 259, 261, 262–63, 264. Johnson replied to Hyman, conceding to those who defend Lincoln's record on race that Lincoln did adapt to circumstances and might well have moved to support the radical position when that was necessary; as circumstances changed, however, Lincoln too would have changed.

Johnson concluded: "Can anyone doubt that he would have accepted the reactionary compromise of 1877, if he had been in Hayes's place?" ("Lincoln and Equal Rights: A Reply," *Civil War History* 13 [1967]: 66–73). Johnson's point is important. If we stress Lincoln's adaptability too much we concede one of the major points at issue—his moral stature.

41. Peyton McCrary, *Abraham Lincoln and Reconstruction: The Louisiana Experiment* (Princeton, N.J.: Princeton University Press, 1978), xi, xii. For a more critical judgment on Lincoln's role, see Peter C. Ripley, *Slaves and Freedmen in Civil War Louisiana* (Baton Rouge: Louisiana State University Press, 1976). Neely, in his review of McCrary's book, maintains that although McCrary "makes a great advance over the existing literature on the subject . . . he somewhat overstates his case" (*Lincoln Lore*, Number 1693 [March 1979]: 2).

42. McCrary, *Lincoln and Reconstruction*, 356, 9, 11, 210; Basler, *Collected Works*, 7:399–404. The argument that Lincoln was a revolutionary is developed by the DeKalb Socialist Historians Group (DeKalb, Illinois), who argue that "Abraham Lincoln and the broad coalition that made up the Republican Party were revolutionary because they overthrew a fully constitutional property system—because they used every means at their command, from legal electoral politics to extra-legal coercion and armed struggle, in effecting their purpose" ("Lincoln and the Second American Revolution," *In These Times* [Chicago], 9–15 February 1977, 12–14, 20). A similar argument is developed by Otto H. Olson, "Abraham Lincoln as Revolutionary," *Civil War History* 25 (1979): 213–24. In contrast to those who claim that Lincoln was a revolutionary, Louis S. Gerteis maintains that the federal government made sure that the changes produced by the war "would not be revolutionary"; moreover, Lincoln's influence was repeatedly exercised on the side of conservatism in dealing with black rights (*From Contraband to Freedom: Federal Policy Towards Southern Blacks, 1861–1865* [Westport, Conn.: Greenwood Press, 1973], 5, 30–31, 78, 148.

43. As Fehrenbacher has pointed out, the use of the word "racist" in describing someone who lived in a different age presents real complications. Moreover, the word itself has been defined in many ways. As I use it here, I mean what Fehrenbacher calls the "doctrine" of racism—"a rationalized theory of inherent Negro inferiority." As noted above, Lincoln did not hold that blacks were inherently inferior to whites ("Only His Stepchildren," 299).

2

Lincoln's Constitutional Dilemma: Emancipation and Black Suffrage

Eugene H. Berwanger

ABRAHAM LINCOLN has gotten bad press on the topics of emancipation and civil rights for blacks. Much revered as the Great Emancipator in the earlier part of this century, Lincoln in the post-World War II era became the Reluctant Emancipator. Among historians, it became fashionable in the 1950s and 1960s to dissociate Lincoln from his Radical Republican colleagues because of his seeming reluctance to interfere with slavery. According to these critics, the president took his time abolishing slavery; he appeared to like the idea of black suffrage even less. Describing Lincoln's moves to destroy the peculiar institution, one historian has characterized them as "tortoise-like." Another has declared: "If General McClellan had 'the slows' when it came to advancing against the Confederate army, [Lincoln] had the same affliction when it came to attacking slavery." Even in the most recently published text in United States history, a work entitled *A People and A Nation*, the authors stress Lincoln's deliberate caution in repudiating slavery; Lincoln, they argue, "would not let his personal feelings determine his political acts." Frederick Douglass, renowned black spokesman for equal rights, apparently concurred. In Douglass's estimation, Lincoln was "preeminently the white man's president."[1]

Historians have used Lincoln's own words to prove their assertion. They note, for example, his comment to a Cincinnati audience in 1859: "I now assure you, that I neither . . . had, nor have, nor ever had, any purpose in any way of interfering with the institution." Or they quote from Lincoln's statement to Horace Greeley, editor of the

New York Tribune: "My paramount object in this struggle *is* to save the Union, and is *not* either to save or destroy slavery."[2] And they emphasize the pressure upon Lincoln to move toward emancipation: international considerations and almost daily visits from Radical Republicans or humanitarian groups demanding abolition.[3] Thus by innuendo if not by direct statement, the Emancipation Proclamation was neither a humanitarian act nor a reflection of Lincoln's ideals. Lincoln's detractors suggest other motives. At best the Proclamation was an astute measure designed to keep Great Britain from recognizing the Confederacy; less charitably, Lincoln's signature may have represented a mere concession to radicals and other reformers lobbying tirelessly around the president.

This is a compromising picture of Lincoln the president, showing him sharply changed from Lincoln the aspiring politician of the 1850s. "I confess myself," he said in 1858, "as belonging to the class in the country who contemplate slavery as a moral, social, and political evil . . . and look hopefully to the time when as a wrong it may come to an end."[4] The view that Lincoln was reluctant on slavery implies a complete change of attitude once he took the presidential oath. Nothing could be further from the truth. Even as late as 1864 his ethical views were unqualified. "I am naturally anti-slavery," he wrote. "If slavery is not wrong, nothing is wrong. I can not remember when I did not so think, and feel."[5]

Inferring from Lincoln's words in the 1860s a reluctance toward abolition, historians have largely misjudged his position. At heart, Lincoln doubted any constitutional basis for emancipating the nation's slaves; he was not sure that federal authorities had such a mandate. Beyond that, Lincoln had always to measure his words. As president, he was in fact responsible to the diversity of public opinion on abolition, and he had, as a political reality, to please all factions whatever his personal view. Were he to speak forth in too liberal a tone, he might well alienate those Americans supporting the war but opposed to abolition; anything too conservative, in turn, could produce criticism from the radicals. Taken together, the president's words and efforts leave no reasonable doubt. Lincoln was committed to a free society and amenable to some limited form of black suffrage. And he moved with more conviction and even haste than he has been given credit for doing.

In the first year of the war, Lincoln feared chiefly that any move toward abolition might cause the border slave states, especially Missouri and Kentucky, to secede. In Missouri, Confederate and Union forces were battling for control in 1861; Kentucky had declared its neutrality, and Lincoln dared take no overt action lest the state be driven into the Confederacy. His judicious care in handling these states brought him into open conflict with General John C. Frémont in Missouri. Specifically, he countermanded Frémont's 1861 proclamation freeing the slaves of disloyal Missourians—a move some historians say is indicative of Lincoln's reluctance.[6] But the president had news, in fact, from western volunteers. They would stop fighting, they said, if Frémont's proclamation were not annulled. Coupled with an awareness that the pro-Union Kentucky legislature was demanding his intercession, the president hesitated no longer and rescinded the order. As Lincoln said: "I think to lose Kentucky is nearly the same as to lose the whole game. Kentucky gone, we can not hold Missouri, nor, as I think, Maryland."[7] Quite apart from these considerations, and even before the border states were firmly in Union hands, Lincoln was at work on the slavery issue. As early as 1861 he was formulating plans for emancipation, while doubts about the loyalty of Missouri and Kentucky lingered into early 1862. Only in that year did the battles of Pea Ridge and Mill Springs finally guarantee these states for the Union.[8]

A more important restraint on Lincoln was his conviction that the United States Constitution prohibited the federal government from abolishing slavery in states where it existed. Lincoln's high regard for the Constitution cannot be disputed. As early as 1837 he told a Young Men's Lyceum in Springfield, Illinois: "We must maintain a reverence for the Constitution and the laws." Later in the same year he presented resolutions in the state legislature, declaring: "Congress . . . has no power under the Constitution to interfere with . . . slavery in the different states." He echoed the same belief in 1859: "I believe we have not the power . . . to interfere with . . . slavery, or any other of the institutions of our sister states." And he carried the theme further in his First Inaugural Address: "I have no purpose, directly or indirectly, to interfere with the institution of slavery in the States where it exists. I believe I have no lawful right to do so."[9]

Despite his reservations, Lincoln did move forward on emancipation. Evidence indicates that he was beginning to devise emancipation schemes as early as November 1861—a mere eight months after his inauguration. On 18 November he informed George Bancroft, the historian, of his interest in emancipation—a problem to be handled with "all due caution, and with the best judgment I can bring it." Two weeks later in his annual message to Congress, the president requested a congressional law to bestow freedom on slaves who were fleeing to Union lines—a request Congress granted three months after.[10]

In ensuing weeks, Lincoln launched an effort to secure gradual, compensated emancipation in the border slave states. This approach he believed most viable, as it solved his constitutional dilemma. There could be no question about the constitutional legitimacy of state action. If the individual states were empowered to legalize slavery, they might just as legally abolish it. In Lincoln's own words, his gradual, compensated plan set up "no claim of a right, by federal authority, to interfere with slavery. . . . It is proposed as a matter of perfectly free choice with" the border slave states themselves.[11]

Gradual emancipation was the focus of Lincoln's plan; Delaware was his first target. Delaware as a choice was no surprise: pro-Union sentiment was stronger there than in the other border states. Slavery in the state was correspondingly weak: there were only 1,798 slaves in the entire state. At any rate, in December 1861 Lincoln worked out a legislative act with George P. Fisher, a Union-Republican representative from Delaware in Congress; it was Fisher who, according to plan, should get the bill introduced and passed by the state legislature. Under its terms, Delaware would abolish slavery over a period of years; in return, the federal government would grant the state $719,200 as compensation to slaveholders. Unfortunately, the plan died before it was born. Rumor of its inception evoked such strong opposition that its backers declined to bring it before Delaware's legislators at all.[12]

Undaunted, Lincoln continued his campaign for gradual, compensated emancipation. First, in March 1862—after he had been in office only one year—he asked for and secured from Congress a resolution favoring the idea. Next, he held conferences with representatives from the border slave states over a five-month period—from March to July 1862—and tried to persuade them to support his government-financed scheme: gradual emancipation over thirty years and federal compensation of $400 for each slave freed. Arguing that the Union could not be restored with slavery intact, Lincoln presented his plan as a means by which these states might abolish slavery at no cost to themselves. In a variety of appeals Lincoln continued his efforts until late summer. But the scheme pleased very few. Citizens in the border states and northern conservatives alike denied Congress's power to appropriate federal funds for compensated emancipation; radicals rejected the plan as "the most diluted, milk-and-water-gruel proposition that was ever given to the American nation."[13] Still, Lincoln would not be dissuaded. In his annual message of December 1862, he proposed a constitutional amendment authorizing Congress to compensate slaveowners in those states that passed legislation freeing their slaves.[14]

Even as he crusaded for emancipation in the border states, Lincoln was finalizing plans for military-decree emancipation in the Confederacy. Charles Sumner early took up the charge: ever since the firing on Fort Sumter in April 1861, he had been urging emancipation by military edict in the rebellious states. Lincoln at first seemed unimpressed by Sumner's argument. Either that, or he was unwilling to undertake emancipation by military decree while working to secure abolition in the border states. Once it became apparent, however, that the border states would reject gradual emancipation, Lincoln moved with resolution on his military edict. On 13 July 1862, the day after his final meeting with border state representatives, the president broached military emancipation with Gideon Welles and William Seward, trusted members of his cabinet. Gaining a favorable response, Lincoln then presented the terms of the Preliminary Emancipation Proclamation to his entire cabinet on 22 July and indicated his eagerness to issue the document immediately. Only Seward's suggestion that he wait for a Union military victory caused Lincoln to hesitate and reconsider the timing.[15]

Between the cabinet meeting in July and the issuance of the Preliminary Emancipation Proclamation on 22 September 1862, Lincoln sought to prepare the citizenry for its impact. Hence the letter to Horace Greeley on 22 August in which Lincoln offered ample justification of his views on slavery *vis à vis* the Union. "My paramount object in this struggle *is* to save the Union, and is *not* either to save or destroy slavery. If I could save the Union without freeing *any* slave I would do it, and if I could save it by freeing *all* the slaves I would do it; and if I could save it by freeing some and leaving others alone I would also do that. What I do about slavery, and the colored race, I do because I believe it helps to save the Union; and what I forbear, I forbear because I do *not* believe it would help save the Union."[16] Cited by itself and without reference to Lincoln's 22 July cabinet meeting, the passage indicates reluctance toward abolition on Lincoln's part. However, when the letter is given proper chronological context, showing that Lincoln had already formulated the Emancipation Proclamation and was merely awaiting the propitious moment for its announcement, the statement takes on a different tone. It was Lincoln's own way of softening for the conservative elements the blow of military emancipation. In a sense, he was preparing the public for what he knew was to come. By stressing the Union as his primary concern, Lincoln hoped to make emancipation more palatable for those opposing it. And, of course, the best way to reach as wide an audience as possible was through the *New York Tribune*, the largest newspaper in the nation. Even as he issued the final document to the nation in 1863, Lincoln continued to stress the theme of military necessity for emancipation.[17]

Civil War contemporaries and historians alike have criticized the Emancipation Proclamation. It did not free any slaves on the day it was promulgated; slavery was left undisturbed in the border states and in those portions of the Confederacy in Union hands; only the slaves in areas of rebellion were declared to be free. This semiabolition approach stemmed not from Lincoln's reluctance to terminate slavery, as some historians imply, but rather from his own doubts about the federal government's lack of authority to touch slavery in the loyal areas. The Emancipation Proclamation itself he regarded as a legitimate weapon of war—an act of confiscation "warranted by the Constitution upon military necessity," and an act that could apply only to areas still engaging in insurrection.[18]

Still other Lincoln detractors have criticized the Proclamation as superfluous. Congress, after all, in July 1862 had passed the Second Confiscation Act, a bill permitting military commanders to free slaves in the Confederacy. But the Confiscation Act was far more limiting than the Emancipation Proclamation. Loyal slaveholders were exempted from its provisions, and it did not set up legal procedures to be followed. As some constitutional historians have maintained, the act would have necessitated freeing slaves in case-by-case litigation in the federal courts. Lincoln's proclamation, to the contrary, was a sweeping measure that freed all slaves in unconquered portions of the Confederacy—of loyalists and rebels alike.[19]

Despite his defense of the Proclamation as a military measure, Lincoln retained lingering doubts about its constitutionality. Although he felt the courts would sustain it as a war measure, he questioned its force once peace were proclaimed. "A question might be raised," he conceded, "whether the proclamation is legally valid. It might be urged that it only aided those that came into our lines, and that it was inoperative as to those who did not give themselves up." Moreover, the courts might decide that the terms of the Proclamation did not extend to the children of slaves freed by it. Whether in jest or in sheer resignation, Lincoln suggested that the government encourage as many slaves as possible to flee to Union lines before the fighting stopped.[20]

During 1863, Lincoln must have mulled over the various piecemeal attempts at abolition. No clear program had been devised. The border states had refused to consider gradual emancipation. Even though the Proclamation was having its effect in the Confederacy, Lincoln feared that some blacks might remain in bondage after the war's end. He was looking for greater guarantees. Therefore, it was only natural that he support a constitutional amendment abolishing slavery throughout the nation when such a measure was introduced in Congress late in the year.

Despite the president's encouragement, the amendment failed to pass the House in the spring of 1864. Lincoln now became more aggressive. At his request, Republicans incorporated a call for an abolition amendment into their 1864 national platform. In his annual address in 1864, the president encouraged Congress to consider the amendment once again. And this time, after its second introduction in Congress, he used the full powers of his office to secure the amendment's passage. With both conservative Republicans and opposition Democrats, Lincoln argued the necessity for the amendment; to wavering Congressmen he made patronage promises. When passage seemed doubtful, he went so far as to release from military prison certain rebels who were related to Democratic members of Congress. Indeed, Lincoln's actions caused Thaddeus Stevens, one of the most ardent radicals in Congress, to remark: "The greatest measure in the nineteenth century was passed by corruption, aided and abetted by the purest man in America."[21]

If the Thirteenth Amendment passed Congress by less than honorable means, Lincoln felt no chagrin. It achieved total abolition, and
there could be no question about its constitutionality. "This amendment is a King's cure for all evils. It winds the whole thing up," he
told an audience shortly after its passage. Savoring his accomplishment further, Lincoln added: "If the people over the river had be-
haved themselves, I could not have done what I have."[22]

Lincoln's endeavors in behalf of black suffrage were even more
startling. Although he openly declared his opposition to equal suffrage in 1858, he became more receptive to the idea during the war.
On the eve of his assassination he publicly advocated voting rights
for some blacks. The road he took toward equal suffrage was similar
to that which led him to emancipation. When first convinced of the
reform's necessity, he tried to achieve action at the state level. Failing
that he alluded to the topic in private conversation and in one public
address. Finally, he indicated his willingness to secure the reform by
federal legislation.

Black suffrage was not an item in Lincoln's Reconstruction Proclamation of 1863. The topic was still too inflammatory, and the president doubted his authority to demand it because the states were
responsible for establishing their own voting requirements. But he
was certainly aware of equal suffrage as a burning issue. Salmon P.
Chase, secretary of the treasury, objected to Lincoln's reconstruction
plan during cabinet discussion because it did not enfranchise southern blacks. Shortly after Lincoln's reconstruction scheme was made
public, James Ashley, Ohio radical in the House of Representatives,
introduced his own version. Ashley called outright for black suffrage
in the seceded states. But the bill was superceded by the milder
Wade-Davis bill, which like Lincoln's plan did not mention suffrage.
Charles Sumner made the issue more compelling: almost daily he
appeared at the White House to argue the merits of equal suffrage.
"Slowly," reports David Donald, "both Senator and President came
to conclude that the only realistic guarantee [for the protection of
freedmen] was to give former slaves the ballot."[23]

A delegation who came before the president to plead the cause of
loyal, black Louisianans may have made the pivotal impression on
Lincoln. The group was headed by Jean Baptiste Roudanez and Ar-
nold Bertonneau, educated mulatto Creoles and New Orleans busi-
nessmen. In their presence, Lincoln remained noncommittal,

stressing the inability of the federal government to confer suffrage on private citizens. But the next day he wrote to loyalist Governor Michael Hahn of Louisiana, saying: "Now you are about to have a [constitutional] Convention which, among other things, will probably define the elective franchise. I barely suggest for your private consideration, whether some of the colored people might not be let in—as, for instance, the very intelligent and especially those who have fought gallantly in our ranks."[24] As the border states had reacted to Lincoln's suggestion of gradual emancipation, so Louisiana now responded to his suggestion of limited suffrage. Its constitutional convention failed to enfranchise any blacks but instead referred the question to the state legislature, meaning that suffrage never would be granted in Louisiana.

During the fall of 1864, Lincoln raised the black suffrage issue to various dignitaries visiting the White House. He also indicated his willingness to consider approval of a reconstruction measure then being discussed in Congress. In actuality a revision of the Wade-Davis bill which he vetoed the previous August, this new measure was more palatable. It omitted clauses Lincoln had opposed and gave specific recognition to his reconstructed government in Louisiana. Of greater significance, the bill extended the ballot to black servicemen and secured their right to participate in the reconstruction process. Still, the advance was unacceptable to certain radicals, and they amended the bill, granting suffrage to all black men. Accordingly the measure went down to defeat and never reached the president's desk.[25]

By the early months of 1865, Lincoln's more liberal stand on racial issues was strengthening. Even as he was promoting the Thirteenth Amendment, he was reaching the conclusion that Congress could impose limited black suffrage. Shortly, he would approve the Freedmen's Bureau Bill. Lincoln's less equivocal attitude did not go unnoticed. Hugh McCulloch, recently sworn in as secretary of the treasury, ventured that Lincoln might even favor a suffrage amendment. B. Gratz Brown informed the Missouri legislature, then debating a bill to abolish slavery, that it might also consider enfranchising some blacks because such action "was [being] prompted by the executive head of our nation himself." William Lloyd Garrison, Moncure D. Conway, Wendell Phillips, and Salmon P. Chase each in turn believed that Lincoln had come to accept black suffrage.[26]

Not only was Lincoln finding black suffrage more tolerable, but by 11 April he was willing to make his cause public, or undertake the "preparatory work," as he phrased it. Reviewing his efforts in Louisiana to a crowd gathered at the White House, Lincoln noted the convention's failure to enfranchise blacks. "I would myself prefer that [suffrage] were now conferred on the very intelligent, and those who served our cause as soldiers," he admitted. And this sentiment applied to other southern states as well, he assured his listeners; soon it might become necessary to make some new announcement to the people of the South, "when satisfied that action will be proper." Some historians attach capital importance to these particular remarks as an indication of change on Lincoln's part.[27] Actually they did not. The change had come earlier. If he had used his letter to Greeley to prepare conservatives for emancipation, he now seemed intent on readying the public for black suffrage. But the point will always remain debatable; whatever plans Lincoln may have had were cut short by the assassin's bullet.

During his presidency, Lincoln took a reasoned course which helped the federal government both destroy slavery and advance the cause of black suffrage. For a man who had denied both reforms four years earlier, Lincoln's change in attitude was rapid and decisive. He was both open-minded and perceptive to the needs of his nation in a postwar era. Once committed to a principle, Lincoln moved toward it with steady, determined progress. As Maria Lydia Child remarked: "I think we have reason to thank God for Abraham Lincoln. With all his deficiencies, it must be admitted that he has grown continually." Lincoln himself told Frederick Douglass: "I think it cannot be shown that when I have once taken a position, I have ever retreated from it."[28]

Despite his moves forward, Lincoln still received criticism from Radical Republicans for his so-called "reluctance." In their zealous quest to end slavery and secure civil equality for blacks, many radicals were prone to disdain all obstacles and disregard the feeling of the conservative element opposed to emancipation and black suffrage. As a president attempting to reunite angry factions in North and South, Lincoln had to move with greater caution. It was he who had to persuade conservatives that racial reform was in the best interest of the nation, and he who had to erode by legal means the constitutional barriers that impeded progress. His was far the more difficult task, and as a result he appeared less advanced on racial issues. Lincoln recognized this fact himself. As he told Charles Sumner, "the only difference between you and me on this subject is the difference of a month and six weeks in time."[29] Unlike the radicals, Lincoln did not rush into emancipation immediately. Instead he took steps that weakened slavery and made the Thirteenth Amendment more acceptable when it came. Unlike the radicals, Lincoln never advocated unlimited black suffrage. But in supporting the enfranchisement of educated blacks and those who had served in the military, he was driving a wedge, which in time would make unqualified black suffrage less repugnant to most white Americans. Lincoln and the radicals may have stood apart on the means of achieving racial reform, but in the end their goal was the same.

NOTES

1. William B. Hesseltine, *Lincoln's Plan of Reconstruction* (Chicago: Quadrangle Books, 1967), 133–35; T. Harry Williams, *Lincoln and the Radicals* (Madison: University of Wisconsin Press, 1941), 357–60; Benjamin Quarles, *The Negro in the Civil War* (Boston: Little, Brown, 1953), 132–63; Richard N. Current, *The Lincoln Nobody Knows* (New York: McGraw-Hill, 1958), 220–21; Mary Beth Norton et al., *A People and A Nation: A History of the United States*, 2 vols. (Boston: Houghton Mifflin, 1982), 1:380. Literature on Lincoln and racial issues arising out of the Civil War is too extensive to discuss here. Aside from books and articles cited in the following notes, recent studies include Don E. Fehrenbacher, "Only His Stepchildren: Lincoln and the Negro," *Civil War History*, 20 (1974): 293–310; George M. Fredrickson, "A Man but Not a Brother: Abraham Lincoln and Racial Equality," *Journal of Southern History*, 41 (1975): 39–58; Mark E. Neely Jr., "Abraham Lincoln and Black Colonization: Benjamin Butler's Spurious Testimony," *Civil War History*, 25 (1979): 77–83; Ludwell Johnson, "Lincoln and Equal Rights: The Authenticity of the Wadsworth Letter," *Journal of Southern History*, 32 (1966): 83–87; Johnson, "Lincoln and Equal Rights: A Reply," *Civil War History*, 13 (1967): 66–73; Harold M. Hyman, "Lincoln and Equal Rights for Negroes: The Irrelevancy of the 'Wadsworth Letter,'" *Civil War History*, 12 (1966): 258–66; Bruce Catton, *The Inescapable Challenge Lincoln Left Us* (Springfield, Ill.: Abraham Lincoln Association, 1970); Jason H. Silverman, "'In Isles Beyond the Main': Abraham Lincoln's Philosophy on Black Colonization," *Lincoln Herald*, 80 (1978): 115–21; Marvin R. Cain, "Lincoln's Views of Slavery and the Negro: A Suggestion," *The Histo-*

rian, 26 (1964): 502–20; Otto Olson, "Abraham Lincoln as Revolutionary," *Civil War History*, 24 (1978): 213–24; V. Jacque Voegeli, *Free but Not Equal: The Midwest and the Negro During the Civil War* (Chicago: University of Chicago Press, 1967); Benjamin Quarles, *Lincoln and the Negro* (New York: Oxford University Press, 1962); Kenneth M. Stampp, "Race, Slavery and the Republican Party," in *The Imperiled Union* (New York: Oxford University Press, 1980), 105–35.

2. John G. Nicolay and John Hay, eds. *Abraham Lincoln: Complete Works*, 2 vols. (New York: Century, 1894), 1:559 (hereafter, Nicolay and Hay, *Works*); Lincoln to Horace Greeley, 22 August 1862, in Roy P. Basler, ed., Marion Dolores Pratt and Lloyd A. Dunlap, asst. eds., *The Collected Works of Abraham Lincoln*, 9 vols. (New Brunswick, N.J.: Rutgers University Press, 1953–1955), 5:388 (hereafter, Basler, *Collected Works*).

3. See, for example, John Hope Franklin, *The Emancipation Proclamation* (Garden City, N.Y.: Doubleday, 1963), 1–30.

4. Speech in Galesburg, Illinois, 7 October 1858, Basler, *Collected Works*, 3:226.

5. Lincoln to Albert G. Hodges, 4 April 1864, ibid., 7:281.

6. See Quarles, *Negro in the Civil War*, 67–68.

7. Lincoln to Orville H. Browning, 22 September 1861, Basler, *Collected Works*, 4:531–33.

8. Clement Eaton, *A History of the Southern Confederacy* (New York: Macmillan, 1954), 156–57; James G. Randall and David Donald, *The Civil War and Reconstruction*, 2d ed. (Boston: D. C Heath, 1969), 200–203.

9. Nicolay and Hay, *Works*, 1:15, 559; Basler, *Collected Works*, 4:263; Allan Nevins, *The War for the Union*, 2 vols. (New York: Scribner's, 1959–71), 1:213; James G. Randall, *Lincoln the President*, 4 vols. (New York: Dodd, Mead, 1945–55), 2:126; James G. Randall, *Constitutional Problems under Lincoln*, rev. ed. (Urbana: University of Illinois Press, 1951), 350–351.

10. John G. Nicolay and John Hay, *Abraham Lincoln: A History*, 10 vols. (New York: Century, 1886–90), 5:202–3 (hereafter, Nicolay and Hay, *Lincoln*); Lincoln to George Bancroft, 18 November 1861, Basler, *Collected Works*, 5:25–26, and annual message, 48–49.

11. Basler, *Collected Works*, 5:145.

12. Nicolay and Hay, *Lincoln*, 5:204–217.

13. U.S. House. *Congressional Globe*, 37th Cong., 2d sess., 12 March 1862, pt. 2, 1154; Nevins, *War for the Union*, 2:31–34, 91–94, 114–18; Herman Belz, *Reconstructing the Union: Theory and Policy during the Civil War* (Ithaca, N.Y.: Cornell University Press, 1969), 74–75; Stephen B. Oates, *Our Fiery Trial: Abraham Lincoln, John Brown, and the Civil War Era* (Amherst: University of Massachusetts Press, 1979), 75–77; Nicolay and Hay, *Lincoln*, 5:209, 221–22; Randall, *Constitutional Problems*, 368–69.

14. Basler, *Collected Works*, 5:518–37; Randall, *Constitutional Problems*, 368–69.

15. Gideon Welles, *The Diary of Gideon Welles*, 3 vols. (Boston: Houghton Mifflin, 1911), 1:70–71; David Donald, *Charles Sumner and the Rights of Man* (New York: Knopf, 1970), 16–17, 54; Belz, *Reconstructing the Union*, 100–103; Franklin, *Emancipation Proclamation*, 31–38.

16. Lincoln to Horace Greeley, 22 August 1862, Basler, *Collected Works*, 5:388.

17. Ibid., 5:433–36; Richard O. Curry, "The Civil War and Reconstruction, 1861–1877: A Critical Overview of Recent Trends and Interpretations," *Civil War History*, 20 (1974): 222–23.

18. Franklin, *Emancipation Proclamation*, 131; James Ford Rhodes, *A History of the United States from the Compromise of 1850*, 7 vols. (New York: Harper, 1893–1906), 4:213n; Nicolay and Hay, *Works*, 2:397.

19. Oates, *Our Fiery Trial*, 77.

20. Randall, *Constitutional Problems*, 382–85; Randall, *Lincoln*, 2:192; Nicolay and Hay, *Lincoln*, 10:353–55; Basler, *Collected Works*, 8:254.

21. Hans L. Trefousse, *The Radical Republicans: Lincoln's Vanguard for Racial Justice* (New York: Knopf, 1969), 295–300; Basler, *Collected Works*, 6:172–73; Oates, *Our Fiery Trial*, 82–83; Randall, *Lincoln*, 2:192; Randall, *Constitutional Problems*, 315; Fawn Brodie, *Thaddeus Stevens: Scourge of the South* (New York: W.W. Norton, 1959), 204.

22. Basler, *Collected Works*, 8:254; Oates, *Our Fiery Trial*, 82.

23. Belz, *Reconstructing the Union*, 136–83, passim; Peyton McCrary, *Abraham Lincoln and Reconstruction: The Louisiana Experiment* (Princeton, N.J.: Princeton University Press, 1978), 7; Tyler Dennett. ed., *Lincoln and the Civil War in the Diaries and Letters of John Hay* (New York: Dodd, Mead, 1939), 132–34; *New York Tribune*, 23 December 1863; Donald, *Sumner*, 207–8.

24. Donald Edward Everett, "Free Persons of Color in New Orleans" (Ph. D. diss., Tulane University, 1952), 343; Lincoln to Michael Hahn, 13 March 1864, Basler, *Collected Works*, 8:243.

25. Belz, *Reconstructing the Union*, 240–63; Dennett, *Lincoln and the Civil War*, 245–46; James McPherson, *The Struggle for Equality: Abolitionists and the Negro in the Civil War and Reconstruction* (Princeton, N.J.: Princeton University Press, 1964), 308–9.

26. Belz, *Reconstructing the Union*, 307–8; Harold M. Hyman, *A More Perfect Union: The Impact of the Civil War and Reconstruction on the Constitution* (New York: Knopf, 1973), 266; McCrary, *Lincoln and Reconstruction*, 9; LaWanda Cox, *Lincoln and Black Freedom: A Study in Presidential Leadership* (Columbia: University of South Carolina Press, 1981), 128–29; David Donald, ed. *Inside Lincoln's Cabinet, The Civil War Diaries of Salmon P. Chase* (New York: Longmans, Green, 1954), 265–66.

27. Basler, *Collected Works*, 8:403; McCrary, *Lincoln and Reconstruction*, 4–13.

28. Lydia Maria Child to George W. Julian, 8 April 1865, in Belz, *Reconstructing the Union*, 28; Hyman, *A More Perfect Union*, 210–11; Frederick Douglass in *The Liberator* (Boston), 29 January 1864; David Lightner, "Abraham Lincoln and the Ideal of Equality," *Journal of the Illinois State Historical Society*, 75 (1982), 304–5.

29. Donald, *Sumner*, 48.

3

Abraham Lincoln and the Politics of Black Colonization

Michael Vorenberg

THE LAST DAY OF 1862 was a busy one for Abraham Lincoln. Aside from his daily trudge to the War Office, which in the wake of recent Union army defeats in the East at Fredericksburg and in the West at Vicksburg (the first assault) had become even ghastlier in its dependable gloom, the commander-in-chief also had to make final preparations for his boldest measure so far, the Final Emancipation Proclamation, which he was to sign the next day. Early in the day he presided over the final discussion of the Proclamation with his cabinet. That afternoon, with painstaking care, he began to write out the final document, working late into the night. Shortly after dawn, Lincoln finished the document, although perhaps still not to his satisfaction. He knew, as he told Senator Charles Sumner, "that the name connected with this document will never be forgotten."[1]

Also on 31 December 1862, Lincoln connected his name to a document that many of his adherents and later apologists would gladly forget: a contract with Bernard Kock, an ambitious and unscrupulous venturer, to use federal funds to remove some five thousand black men, women, and children from the United States to a small island off the coast of Haiti. It was Lincoln's last effort at colonizing blacks outside the United States, executed only one day before he was to sign a proclamation putting into effect his first official effort at permanently freeing slaves in the country.[2]

The juxtaposition of these two efforts—colonization, a remnant of a former generation's conservative approach to slaves and free blacks, and outright emancipation, a more progressive program with no provisions for sending freed slaves abroad or compensating their former owners—has long perplexed and frustrated historians, just as it did

Lincoln's contemporaries. Although most historians have conceded that Lincoln was motivated by politics as well as principle in his approach to emancipation and equal rights for blacks, there has been unending debate on his commitment to racial equality.[3] On the specific issue of colonization, scholars have focused far less on Lincoln's political calculations and far more on possible racial motivations.[4] Those who tend to see Lincoln as a racist usually assume that he never gave up the idea of deporting all free blacks, while those who believe in Lincoln as a racial egalitarian typically assert that his racial views matured as he realized that colonization could not work and came to believe that blacks had a legitimate claim to remaining in the United States.

An examination of Lincoln's efforts, and not just his rhetoric, in favor of colonizing blacks outside the United States suggests that Lincoln was as much motivated by political concerns as by his personal views toward blacks. His strategy was to propose colonization to sweeten the pill of emancipation for conservatives from the North and for the border states, the slave states that did not secede during the Civil War; at the same time, he used political manipulation to prevent radicals from thwarting the colonization program and thus jeopardizing his ultimate goal of making emancipation an acceptable war aim to the Union cause. Lincoln, always a careful politician, admitted nothing of political motives behind his advocacy of colonization, so we are left only with his actions and the opinions of his contemporaries to lend insight into his true intentions. Yet even with such limited evidence, a clear picture emerges of Lincoln using the prospect of black colonization to make emancipation more acceptable to conservatives and then abandoning all efforts at colonization once he made the determined step toward emancipation in the Final Emancipation Proclamation.

I

As a young politician in Illinois before the Civil War, Lincoln often voiced his belief that blacks and whites would live best if they lived separately. It was a belief he shared with the two American statesmen he revered most: Thomas Jefferson, an early advocate of gradual, voluntary emigration of blacks; and Henry Clay, a leader of the Whig

Party during the 1830s and 1840s and a founder of the American Colonization Society. The society, founded in 1816, sought to remove black Americans voluntarily to Africa. In 1821 the society purchased land in west Africa and set up the colony of Liberia, which remained a U.S. colony until it gained independence in 1846. The colonization movement foundered in the late 1840s but was resuscitated in the early 1850s as the American Colonization Society intensified its recruitment of black emigrants.[5]

Lincoln first proclaimed an interest in colonization during his eulogy for Henry Clay in 1852, when he admitted his allegiance to the esteemed Kentuckian's dual creed of gradual emancipation coupled with colonization. If slavery could be eliminated and the slaves returned to "their long-lost fatherland," claimed Lincoln, "it will indeed be a glorious consummation." Impressed by Lincoln's commitment to colonization, the members of the Illinois Colonization Society repeatedly asked him to speak at their meetings, and he obliged them in 1853 and again in 1855. Although by no means a leader of the colonization movement in Illinois, Lincoln still could use the issue to attach himself to the political tradition of Clay and, as inheritor of Clay's stately mantle, to become a leading politician of the West.[6]

Lincoln's belief in colonization also worked to his advantage in many debates with Illinois Senator Stephen A. Douglas. In 1854, while Douglas campaigned for reelection and Lincoln campaigned for the anti-Douglas coalition, the two met in a series of debates on the issue of the Kansas-Nebraska bill and its doctrine of popular sovereignty, which Douglas had helped formulate. Under Douglas's proposal, the people of any territory seeking admission to the Union would determine whether slavery could exist in the territory. Lincoln stood firmly against popular sovereignty and the extension of slavery that it would allow, but his stance left him politically vulnerable to Douglas's charge that he favored racial equality. Racism was prevalent in the Midwest in the 1850s. When Douglas tried to portray Lincoln as the friend of the blacks, Lincoln countered, as he did in a speech at Peoria, Illinois, by denying that he saw blacks as equals and by advocating the colonization of freed slaves in Liberia. Lincoln was aware, however, of the practical difficulties of such a program: "If they were all landed there [Liberia] in a day, they would all perish in the next ten days," he stated.[7]

Three years later in Springfield, Lincoln again debated Douglas. Now the issue was the Dred Scott case, and Douglas, the dominant force behind the Democratic Party in Illinois and throughout the nation, accused not only Lincoln but also the entire newly formed Republican Party of favoring black equality. Lincoln sidestepped Douglas's charge by discussing colonization instead: "I can say a very large proportion of its members are for it." Lincoln wanted the audience to believe that his advocacy of colonization was more than just a whimsical hope, that it was in fact a genuine party policy, albeit an unstated one. During the Senate race in 1858, Lincoln again invoked colonization, as well as an occasional statement of white superiority, to counter Douglas's charges that he favored racial equality. All through the debates Lincoln walked a narrow political path by refuting Douglas's support of slavery without claiming equal rights for blacks. Colonization, like no other issue, helped him stay the course.[8]

But Lincoln did not invoke colonization only when it was politically expedient to do so. In his first few months as president, at a time when there was no particular demand for a plan of colonization, Lincoln took important steps toward such a plan. In October 1861, he asked Caleb B. Smith, secretary of the interior, to look into a proposal for colonizing blacks on the isthmus of Chiriqui, a small area in the northwest of present-day Panama.[9]

In his annual message to Congress in December of that year, Lincoln made his first public statement as president in support of colonization. Former slaves seeking refuge across Union lines, who were regarded as contraband, had aroused the racist fears of northern whites and threatened to become an economic burden. To alleviate the problem, Lincoln suggested that Congress appropriate funds for colonizing slaves. He also advocated an additional step. "It might be well to consider," he submitted, "whether the free colored people already in the United States could not, so far as individuals may desire, be included in such colonization."[10] Thus he called for not just a relief plan for the freedmen, but for a full program of racial separation.

II

Congress answered Lincoln's call in the next few months. Although few legislators considered full separation of the races either desirable or practical, many of the Republicans, who held a majority in Congress, were willing to vote for small-scale colonization projects. During March and April 1862, as Congress debated whether to emancipate slaves in Washington, D.C., Senator James R. Doolittle of Wisconsin argued for appropriations for the voluntary emigration of the freed slaves from the District. His arguments incurred angry rebuttal from Senator Garrett Davis of Kentucky and many other border state Unionists who favored forced deportation of the former slaves. If the freedmen were not forced to leave, Davis said, "the negroes that are now liberated, and that remain in this city, will become a sore and a burden and a charge upon the white population." Doolittle rebutted such statements with impassioned pleas for the humanity of voluntary colonization. In addition, he argued against restrictions on how the president should use the $100,000 proposed for colonization. It was only after Doolittle received opposition on this point from a fellow northern Republican, John Hale of New Hampshire, that he suggested a generous maximum of $100 be spent on each emigrant.[11]

Meanwhile, Francis P. Blair Jr. of Missouri, a longtime advocate of colonization, defended Lincoln's policy in the House of Representatives. On 12 April 1862, the day after slavery was abolished in Washington, D.C., Blair admitted that Liberia had "failed to attract the freed negro population in any considerable numbers," but proclaimed his optimism about the possibility of Negro colonization in Central America. "There is a vast difference," he said, "between the idea of being colonized on our own continent, under our own flag, and being buried in Africa." Blair not only believed in colonization as a remedy to present and future racial hostilities, but also well understood how the promise of colonization could help undercut the political power of slaveholders in the Confederacy: "We can make emancipation acceptable to the whole mass of non-slaveholders at the South by coupling it with the policy of colonization. The very prejudice of race which now makes the non-slaveholders give their aid to hold the slave in bondage will induce them to unite in a policy which will rid them of the presence of the negroes."[12] The arguments of Blair in the House and Doolittle in the Senate helped lead to a congressional appropriation of $100,000 to be used by the president for colonizing the freedmen of the District.

Three months later, on 16 July 1862, Congress appropriated

$500,000 more for the colonization of any other freedmen under the Second Confiscation Act, which allowed military commanders to free slaves held by southern rebels. Thus, only six months after suggesting a colonization policy, Lincoln had received $600,000 in congressional appropriations.

Historians who have analyzed the colonization issue assert that Lincoln called for colonization and Congress answered. Thus, in the words of Benjamin Quarles, "Lincoln's support of colonization succeeded in breathing a little life into the long-ailing movement." Implicit in the scenario is an assumption about the relationship between Lincoln and the Congress that has received criticism from such scholars as Harold Hyman, who disputes the notion that Lincoln was the main force behind the government during the Civil War and calls for a more detailed analysis of the role of Congress in forming Lincoln's Civil War policy.[13]

Perhaps such an approach could allow more insight into the colonization issue. Rather than assuming that Congress was solely responding to Lincoln's agendas, historians might ask how congressmen with their own agenda influenced Lincoln's decisions. Even before Lincoln took office, Blair and Doolittle had argued for colonization, and Senator Benjamin F. Wade had supported a specific plan of colonization in Central America. This prior congressional action may have reinforced Lincoln's own inclination toward setting in motion a colonization plan. He could only be pleased that Congress, in its act to abolish slavery in the District of Columbia, joined emancipation to his own "two principles of compensation, and colonization . . . and practically applied [them] in the act."[14]

Furthermore, before Lincoln delivered his annual message of 1861, he had received key support for a plan of colonization in Chiriqui from Francis P. Blair Sr., the eternal sage of Silver Spring, Maryland, who had once served in President Andrew Jackson's "Kitchen Cabinet" and now occasionally advised Lincoln. Knowing that Blair's sentiments were shared by his sons, Francis P. Blair Jr. in the House, and Postmaster General Montgomery Blair in his cabinet, Lincoln could be confident of further support as he moved ahead in his plans for colonization.[15]

III

It is difficult to account for the lapse of time between the congressional appropriations for colonizing blacks in April 1862, and Lincoln's initiation of an actual plan of colonization four months later. He certainly had many options from which to choose. Caleb Smith, his secretary of the interior, had informed him on 9 May of private investors who owned available lands in Honduras, Costa Rica, and Chiriqui. Any of these plans of colonization might be suitable, Smith said, as long as the United States did not violate the terms of the Clayton-Bulwer treaty between the United States and Britain, which prohibited either country from exercising sovereignty over lands in Central America. Moreover, Smith wrote a week later, "Prompt action on the part of the Executive is required to meet the wishes of Congress and the growing sentiment of the country in favor of the experiment of colonization authorized by the law of April 16."[16]

Although Lincoln hesitated in approving any of Smith's plans, he was more than willing to use the prospect of colonization for political purposes. In an appeal to representatives from the border states on 12 July he reiterated his desire for gradual emancipation. He assured the delegation: "Room in South America for colonization can be obtained cheaply, and in abundance."[17] His reference to South America instead of Central America, the area most likely to be colonized, suggests that he cared less about the actual details of colonization than about offering it as a way of gaining border state acceptance of emancipation.

Perhaps Lincoln held all plans of colonization in abeyance at this time because he was more concerned about how to move on the larger issue of emancipation. During the ten days following his meeting with the border state representatives, he took definite steps toward freeing the slaves. On 13 July he told Secretary of State William H. Seward and Secretary of Navy Gideon Welles that he was considering emancipation, and on 21 July he proposed to his cabinet a military order to enlist blacks as troops, to employ them as laborers, and to colonize them in the tropics. This was the first time Lincoln introduced the colonization issue to the cabinet. According to Secretary of Treasury Salmon P. Chase, colonization was hardly discussed, and at the cabinet meeting the next day, it was dropped entirely, while the other two measures were accepted.[18] Because Lincoln had just signed an act approving $500,000 for colonization, he probably felt obliged to bring up the issue with his cabinet. Yet he was not so dedicated to it that he would force the issue at the expense of generating ill sentiment among cabinet members that might jeopardize the two remaining orders or the Emancipation Proclamation, the first draft of which Lincoln read to his cabinet at the 22 July meeting.

Lincoln was still committed, however, to the idea that emancipation had to be linked to colonization. From August to December 1862, as he came closer to a final Emancipation Proclamation, he simultaneously tried to effect a successful plan of colonization. First, he sought to colonize Chiriqui, setting that project in motion by appointing James Mitchell as commissioner of emigration on 4 August 1862. Mitchell's first assignment was to assemble a delegation of five black leaders to meet with the president at the White House on 14 August.[19]

At that meeting, the first and only time he would ever take the proposal of colonization directly to blacks, Lincoln assumed the unfortunate tone of a condescending father scolding ignorant children. "But for your race among us there could not be war," he observed, and he went on to prescribe their removal as the remedy. He had given up Liberia as an option for colonization because transportation there was too expensive and blacks preferred to remain on the American continent. Instead, he touted Central America, although not mentioning Chiriqui by name, as an area rich in coal where even a small band of colonists might succeed. When the prominent black abolitionist Frederick Douglass read about the meeting, he reacted with fury. "It expresses merely the desire to get rid of them," Douglass said of Lincoln's proposal for freed blacks, "and reminds one of the politeness with which a man might try to bow out of his house some troublesome creditor or the witness of some old guilt." Other blacks angry with Lincoln's words still supported his proposal. Henry Highland Garnet, a long-time advocate of voluntary emigration, praised the Chiriqui plan as "the most humane, and merciful movement which this or any other administration has proposed for the benefit of the enslaved."[20]

With seemingly no regard for black reaction to his plan, Lincoln pressed on. He was not even dissuaded upon receiving word on 5 September from the renowned scientist Joseph Henry that the coal deposits in Chiriqui were of the lowest grade. Lincoln went ahead and signed a contract with Ambrose Thompson, the land developer who owned the site, and he appointed Senator Samuel C. Pomeroy of Kansas as his agent of colonization. Pomeroy immediately began recruiting blacks for the new colony, now dubbed "Linconia" by the press.[21]

For a man who had decided to "advance slowly" on the issue of blacks, Lincoln seemed to be making some hasty and short-sighted decisions. Although he had told the black delegation to "take [their] full time" in making a decision about the Chiriqui venture, he himself forged ahead with the project before learning whether enough colonists would volunteer. He touted the rich coal deposits in Chiriqui, choosing to ignore Henry's dismal report. He signed a contract with Thompson despite the warnings of his secretary of the navy, who considered Thompson a scoundrel.

Perhaps Lincoln's most puzzling move was the appointment of Pomeroy as colonization agent. As a leading member of the New England Emigrant Aid Company in the 1850s, Pomeroy had experience in promoting an emigration program, and he had curried favor with Lincoln by supporting his candidacy at the 1860 Chicago convention. But the president certainly had heard the rumors that Pomeroy was a shady character, a man whom Welles suspected of having "a personal interest in the matter." No matter how sincere Pomeroy appeared in his desire to help execute the Chiriqui scheme, Lincoln should have been suspicious of a man who had opposed appropriations for colonization in April of that year and who in June had mocked the idea of colonization by proposing in its place a measure to colonize freed slaves together with their former masters.[22]

IV

Northern newspaper editors refused to be taken in by colonization schemers, and they ridiculed the proposals of the president. The Democratic press voiced nothing but scorn. The *New York Evening Express*, run by the ever-intemperate Congressman James Brooks, complained that the cost of such a program would "entail upon the White Labor of the North, the doom and debt of the tax-groaning serfs and labor-slaves of Europe."[23] The Republican press was equally critical. Henry Raymond's *New York Times* plainly gave its verdict: "No, Mr. Pomeroy. No, Mr. President. The enfranchised blacks must find homes, without circumnavigating the seas at the National expense." Joseph Medill of the *Chicago Tribune* agreed:

"The blacks can neither be colonized across the Gulf, or sent through our lines to the North. Their numbers utterly forbid and render futile these measures save on the most limited scale." Lincoln would have to look elsewhere for support of the Chiriqui project.[24]

Even members of the American Colonization Society expressed dismay over the Chiriqui venture, suggesting that it had been effected for the sake of expediency. "Are the leading minds of our time incapable of perceiving the necessary *temporary* character of all such expedients?" one member asked. William McLain, financial agent for the society, felt especially snubbed by Lincoln's proposal. On 14 August 1862, Lincoln had met with McLain and Joseph J. Roberts, president of Liberia, and told them that he thought Liberia a fine place where free blacks could flourish. Less than an hour later, he proposed the Chiriqui plan to the black delegation. Furious at Lincoln's apparent deceit in praising the Liberia effort, McLain ridiculed Mitchell, Pomeroy, and the entire Chiriqui plan: "Out upon all such men and such schemes!"[25]

Lincoln's decision to go forward with the Chiriqui plan in the face of such opposition may have been based on a purely political calculation. It was September of 1862, and Union armies were still faring poorly. Lincoln was ready to issue the Emancipation Proclamation as soon as there was a Union victory, but he knew how serious the effects of such a proclamation could be on the November elections.[26] Emancipation without colonization may have seemed to Lincoln so radical a policy that it could result only in the demise of the Republican Party in Congress and in the northern state legislatures.

Soon after Lincoln issued his Preliminary Emancipation Proclamation of 22 September 1862, he had to suspend the Chiriqui plan because ministers from Central American countries objected to any such scheme without a treaty. Yet the project had served its purpose by allowing Lincoln to claim publicly that he had done something for the colonization movement. "[T]he effort to colonize persons of African descent," he wrote in the Preliminary Emancipation Proclamation, "with their consent, upon this continent, or elsewhere, with the previously obtained consent of the Governments existing there, *will be continued* [author's emphasis]." In private, however, the president was not nearly so optimistic. He told Thompson that he was discouraged by rumors he had heard of the Chiriqui proprietor and some of his business associates using funds allocated to colonization to pay private debts. Finally, on 7 October 1862, Lincoln formally suspended the Chiriqui plan despite protest from Senator Pomeroy that 13,700 blacks had already applied for emigration.[27]

V

Two days after promising in his Preliminary Proclamation not to proceed with colonization without first entering into treaties with the Central American states, Lincoln assembled his cabinet to suggest that the United States make treaties with foreign governments in order to establish colonies. Welles remained against such treaties; Secretary of War Edwin M. Stanton was absent; and Seward, according to Welles's account, expressed some reservations. All others approved the proposal.[28]

That Lincoln waited so long to bring the Chiriqui plan to the attention of his full cabinet suggests another political dimension to colonization. He had dropped the colonization issue from cabinet discussions after 22 July 1862, when the issue threatened to distance his secretaries from him and from each other on the larger topic of emancipation; and, until the meeting of 24 September, he had acted on his own initiative in the Chiriqui venture. By late September, after he had written colonization into his preliminary proclamation and after the Chiriqui scheme had threatened to embroil the United States in a diplomatic conflict, Lincoln had to bring the issue to the cabinet. A cabinet that had rejected an order for colonization in July now lent its support to the idea.

The cabinet's reversal might be explained simply as a reaction to the steps Congress and Lincoln had taken toward colonization. With $600,000 in appropriations available to the president, and various proposals for him to choose from, it was now clear to all that colonization was more than mere rhetoric. Another possible explanation might lie in Lincoln's skill at political management. Blair, Smith, and Attorney General Edward Bates had supported colonization, while Welles and Stanton had opposed it. Seward and Chase held the balance. Lincoln met Seward's concerns by agreeing to seek treaties for colonization.[29]

He approached Chase more indirectly. In July 1862, the secretary had opposed colonization. But over the next two months, he came to support "simple arrangements, under the legislation of Congress, by which any persons who might choose to emigrate would be secured in such advantages as might be offered them by other States or Governments." The intervening impetus behind Chase's new opinion may have been the appointment of his ally, Senator Pomeroy. Possibly Chase was swayed by Pomeroy's conversion from staunch opponent of colonization to leading agent of the movement and further impressed by Lincoln's decision to employ Pomeroy in one of his schemes.[30]

The colonization issue may again have played a part in cabinet dynamics when Lincoln promoted John P. Usher to succeed Caleb Smith as secretary of the interior in December 1862. Smith had been a loyal supporter of colonization, and Usher, as assistant secretary of interior, had personally extolled its benefits to Lincoln: "It will, if adopted, relieve the free states of the apprehension now prevailing, and fostered by the disloyal, that they are to be overrun by negroes made free by the war, [and] it will alarm those in rebellion, for they will see that their cherished property is departing from them forever and incline them to peace." In Usher, Lincoln found yet another ally in the cause of colonization.[31]

VI

Supported by his cabinet in his commitment to find diplomatically feasible ways of colonizing the freedmen, Lincoln decided to initiate a colonization scheme at Vache Island, a small island off the coast of Haiti owned by land developer Bernard Kock. Kock claimed to have a diplomatic arrangement with Haiti that would permit the United States to colonize his island, although no one bothered to check the validity of his claim. Like Ambrose Thompson before him, Kock was a suspicious character. Even Bates, a consistent supporter of colonization, called Kock "an errant humbug." Despite these potential problems, Lincoln directed Usher to set up a contract with Kock; and on 31 December, one day before signing the Final Emancipation Proclamation, he approved a contract for the transportation of five thousand blacks to Vache Island.[32]

Once more Lincoln had entered into a bargain with a questionable man to colonize blacks in a questionable place. As to why Lincoln pursued the plan, the answer again seems to lie in the timing of the scheme. The political necessity of keeping emancipation tied to the colonization had become so fixed in Lincoln's mind that he may have believed any plan of emancipation that did not include colonization would be construed as a program of racial equality. No matter how much Lincoln's racial views had matured by 1863, he certainly was not ready to make such a statement. In his Preliminary Emancipation Proclamation, Lincoln had promised to continue colonizing blacks and had voiced his preference for gradual emancipation. He repeated these sentiments both privately in conversations with political conservatives and publicly in his annual message to Congress on 1 December 1862, which called for a constitutional amendment providing for the colonization of blacks outside the United States.[33] To follow through on his promise of colonization, he had to follow through on one of the proposals made to the government. Kock's plan seemed as good as any, if not better, because it seemed unlikely to infringe upon the territorial claims of foreign powers.

Yet, after Lincoln signed the Final Emancipation Proclamation, he took little interest in the Vache Island project. He made no public endorsement of colonization after delivering his annual message to Congress one month before the proclamation, and he suspended Kock's contract when Seward announced on 3 January that he wanted to investigate the venturer's reputation. When Seward verified that Kock was a swindler, the contract was cancelled. But the project continued. Paul Forbes and Charles Tuckerman, two New York financiers of Kock's project, offered to act as agents. On 6 April, Usher signed the contract, which Lincoln subsequently approved. One week later five hundred of the projected five thousand blacks departed for Vache Island.[34]

After the first shipload, no other blacks made the voyage to Vache Island, and in less than a year the venture failed dismally. By October 1863, the New York Daily Tribune could report: "The effort of the President to colonize 500 persons of color on the southwest coast of Haiti has proved a failure. Though unusual precaution was taken to contract with responsible parties to convey these people to their destination, many of them died of disease while others fled to more desirable localities." The Interior Department recalled the colonists in January 1864, and Usher, who had taken charge of overseeing the scheme, tried to play down the government's role in the fiasco.[35]

Stung by the Vache Island debacle, Congress decided to put an end to federally sponsored colonization. On 15 March 1864, Morton S. Wilkinson of Minnesota introduced a bill in the Senate withdrawing all funds for colonization. Congress passed the measure on 2 July, and Lincoln signed it. Of the $600,000 appropriated by Congress for colonization, the Lincoln administration had spent only about $38,000.[36]

Lincoln actually had given up on colonization long before Congress repealed funds for the program. Since the departure of the Vache Island colonists in April 1863, the president, while privately continuing to endorse efforts of independent agencies and foreign countries to recruit emigrants, had done nothing to promote colonization.[37] Even his appointed agent of colonization had come to suspect the president's halting commitment. In early 1863, Pomeroy, who recognized the Vache Island venture as a meager gesture, bitterly penned a letter to Lincoln, demanding to know whether he ever intended to honor his promise of colonizing blacks, fourteen thousand of whom had applied for emigration.[38]

In fact, there is no reason to believe that Lincoln ever espoused colonization after he issued the Final Emancipation Proclamation. Scholars who argue that Lincoln still hoped to colonize blacks after the proclamation rely on only two flimsy pieces of evidence. On 1 July 1864, the day before Congress voted to rescind its colonization appropriations, John Hay, Lincoln's personal secretary, recorded in his diary that "the president has sloughed off that idea of colonization."[39] Benjamin F. Butler, a leading Union general, claimed that early in 1865 Lincoln told him of the black soldiers, "I believe that it would be better to export them all to some fertile country with a good climate, which they could have to themselves." Yet Butler's account is at best dubious, and Hay's allows for the possibility that Lincoln had given up the idea before July 1864.[40]

VII

It is not difficult to understand why Lincoln gave up his idea of colonization. Union Party victories in 1863 in the border states and all the northern states but New Jersey lessened the pressure on Lincoln to accommodate racist sentiment against the Emancipation Proclamation. Even if Lincoln had continued to support colonization, blacks clearly never would. Opposition to Lincoln's colonization proposals from Frederick Douglass, among others, who ridiculed colonization as simply "a safety valve . . . for white racism" had never given way.[41] Also, blacks had taken a key role in the army, and the notion of sending abroad potential warriors against the Confederacy ran counter to common sense and military strategy. Moreover, alternatives to colonization outside the United States had proved more successful than any of Lincoln's schemes. Such efforts as Eli Thayer's military colonization in Florida and Lorenzo Thomas's refugee program in Mississippi may have given Lincoln a sense that blacks could have a future in this country.[42]

Advisors to Lincoln who had once flown the flag of colonization now showed different colors. Usher, whose counsel on colonization Lincoln had followed so far, wrote to the president in May 1863, just after Secretary Stanton formed the Bureau of Colored Troops, that the War Department's new policy toward blacks precluded further colonization; the office of the commissioner of emigration, wrote Usher, should be turned over to the Pension Bureau. One-time colonizationist Francis Blair Sr. now admitted that settling the freedmen within the nation's boundaries made far more sense than sending them abroad. Even Ambrose Thompson, the opportunistic schemer behind the Chiriqui plan, recognized that colonization was no longer practical or profitable. By June 1863, he had stopped offering Lincoln a plan of colonization and offered him instead a plan to employ thousands of blacks as well as white immigrants on a railroad running between Washington, D.C., and Pittsburgh.[43]

More troubling than the question of why Lincoln would give up the idea of colonization is the question of why he held on to the idea as long as he did. Lincoln's steadfast advocacy of colonization stemmed from more than just the common racist belief of the time that whites and blacks could not live in the same society. Lincoln seems also to have made a political calculation that he could not propose emancipation without at the same time proposing colonization. It was a calculation well understood by Horace Greeley, the editor of the *New York Tribune,* who recognized the "thriftless folly which gravely propose[s] the exportation of laborers by the millions," but who understood that colonization proposals might have to be entertained to make emancipation acceptable to conservatives:

"Gradualism, Compensation, Exportation—if these tubs amuse the whale, let him have them![44] Born from the political philosophy of Thomas Jefferson and Henry Clay and thrust into the hands of Lincoln the pragmatist, colonization became an effective tool in dealing with the politically charged issue of what would be done with slaves freed during the war. In using colonization as an expedient for emancipation during late 1862, Lincoln may have fused the two ideas even more tightly together in his mind, making it nearly impossible for him to believe that one could exist without the other.

On 21 March 1864, the ship *Marcia C. Day*, symbol of the dying dream of colonization, slowly steamed up the Potomac carrying what was left of the Vache Island expedition—about 350 malnourished and raggedly clad black men, women, and children. Seized upon by a multitude of military agents desperate to fill recently issued quotas, the black men again found themselves the recipients of an offer of government aid. But now the aid came not in the form of relocation outside the country of their birth, but instead in an offer of food, clothing, and even a small salary given in return for their enlisting in the Union army. Almost unanimously the colonists consented to the proposals of C. C. Gibbs, a Massachusetts military agent who boarded their ship just before it docked in Washington Harbor, to fight under the Massachusetts banner against the Confederacy.[45]

Here was a fitting end to Lincoln's final colonization effort: faced with the impracticalities of colonization and the tide of public opinion against it, and realizing that blacks could serve their country better within than without, Lincoln would now witness, and eventually lead, the transformation of a movement to separate blacks and whites into an effort to join the two races (in segregated regiments) in combat against a common enemy.

NOTES

1. Stephen B. Oates, *With Malice Toward None: The Life of Abraham Lincoln* (New York: Harper, 1977), 358–62; Carl Sandburg, *Abraham Lincoln: The War Years*, 4 vols. (New York: Harcourt Brace, 1939), 2:16.

2. Roy P. Basler, ed., Marion Dolores Pratt and Lloyd A. Dunlap, asst. eds., *The Collected Works of Abraham Lincoln*, 9 vols. (New Brunswick, N.J.: Rutgers University Press, 1953–55), 6:41n–42n (hereafter, Basler, *Col-*

lected Works). See Frederic Bancroft, "The Ile a Vache Experiment in Colonization," in *Frederic Bancroft: Historian,* ed. Jacob E. Cooke (Norman: University of Oklahoma Press, 1957).

3. Much of the recent debate was set off by Lerone Bennett Jr., "Was Abe Lincoln a White Supremacist?" *Ebony,* February 1968, 35–42. For a review of the literature over the next ten years, see Arthur Zilversmit, "Lincoln and the Problem of Race: A Decade of Interpretations," *Papers of the Abraham Lincoln Association* 2 (1980): 22–45.

4. There are few exceptions to this trend, perhaps most notably Don E. Fehrenbacher, "Only His Stepchildren: Lincoln and the Negro," *Civil War History* 20 (1974): 307–8, which recognizes political expediency as a possible motivation behind Lincoln's plan of colonization. The literature on Lincoln's philosophy of, and efforts at, colonization is extensive. See John G. Nicolay and John Hay, *Abraham Lincoln: A History,* 10 vols. (New York: Century, 1886–90), 6:354–67; James G. Randall, *Lincoln the President,* 4 vols. (New York: Dodd, Mead, 1945–55), 2:137–41; Charles H. Wesley, "Lincoln's Plan for Colonizing the Emancipated Negroes," *Journal of Negro History* 4 (1919): 7–21; Warren A. Beck, "Lincoln and Negro Colonization in Central America," *Abraham Lincoln Quarterly* 6 (1950): 162–83; Paul J. Scheips, "Lincoln and the Chiriqui Colonization Project," *Journal of Negro History* 37 (1952): 418–53; Willis D. Boyd, "Negro Colonization in the National Crisis, 1860–1870" (Ph.D. diss., University of California at Los Angeles, 1953); Robert H. Zoellner, "Negro Colonization: The Climate of Opinion Surrounding Lincoln, 1860–65," *Mid-America* 42 (1960): 131–50; Walter A. Payne, "Lincoln's Caribbean Colonization Plan," *Pacific Historian* 7 (1963): 65–72; Gary R. Planck, "Abraham Lincoln and Black Colonization: Theory and Practice," *Lincoln Herald* 72 (1970): 61–77; Gabor S. Boritt, "The Voyage to the Colony of Lincolnia: The Sixteenth President, Black Colonization, and the Defense Mechanism of Avoidance," *The Historian* 37 (1975): 619–32; Jason H. Silverman, " 'In Isles Beyond the Main': Abraham Lincoln's Philosophy on Black Colonization," *Lincoln Herald* 80 (1978): 115–22.

5. See P. J. Staudenraus, *The African Colonization Movement* (New York: Columbia University Press, 1961), 240–50.

6. Basler, *Collected Works,* 2:132; Planck, "Lincoln and Black Colonization," 61–63; Arvarh Strickland, "The Illinois Background of Lincoln's Attitude Toward Slavery and the Negro," *Journal of the Illinois State Historical Society* 56 (1963): 474–94. Marvin R. Cain points out that Lincoln's preference for voluntary emigration of blacks puts him more in the tradition of Jefferson than of Clay who advocated forced deportation of blacks ("Lincoln's Views on Slavery and the Negro: A Suggestion," *The Historian* 26 [1964]: 508). Why Lincoln waited until the 1850s to endorse the colonization

movement probably has as much to do with politics as with the resurgence of the colonization movement. His eulogy of Clay came in the midst of the renewed effort by the Free Soil Party to capture the presidency and the disaffection of many southern Whigs who feared the Whig Party was becoming overly committed to antislavery. By advocating colonization and claiming allegiance to the principles of a southern Whig such as Clay, Lincoln perhaps was hoping to present himself as a more moderate, less northern Whig.

7. Basler, *Collected Works*, 2:255. See V. Jacque Voegeli, *Free but Not Equal: The Midwest and the Negro during the Civil War* (Chicago: University of Chicago Press, 1967), 1–9.

8. Basler, *Collected Works*, 2:409; 3:15, 192, 233–34. At Charleston, Illinois, in 1858, Lincoln said about blacks and whites: "And inasmuch as they cannot so live, while they do remain together there must be the position of superior and inferior, and I as much as any other man am in favor of having the superior position assigned to the white race" (ibid., 3:145–46).

9. Ibid., 4:561.

10. Ibid., 5:48.

11. U.S. Senate. *Congressional Globe*, 37th Cong., 2d sess., 17 March 1862, 32, pt. 2, 1191, 1319.

12. Ibid., 11 April 1862, 32, pt. 2, 1633, 1634.

13. Benjamin Quarles, *Lincoln and the Negro* (New York: Oxford University Press, 1962), 109; Harold M. Hyman, "Lincoln and Congress: Why Not Congress and Lincoln?" *Journal of the Illinois State Historical Society* 68 (1975): 57–73. Since Hyman's query, much has been written on the relationship between Congress and Lincoln. See, for example, Allan G. Bogue, *The Congressman's Civil War* (New York: Cambridge University Press, 1989), especially ch. 2.

14. George M. Fredrickson, *The Black Image in the White Mind:The Debate on Afro-American Character and Destiny, 1817–1914* (New York: Harper, 1971; reprint, Middletown, Conn.: Wesleyan University Press, 1987), 148–49; Basler, *Collected Works,*5:192.

15. Francis P. Blair Sr., Silver Spring, to Lincoln, Washington, D.C., 16 November 1861 [with encls.], Robert Todd Lincoln Collection, Manuscript Division, Library of Congress (microfilm copy). See Scheips, "Lincoln and the Chiriqui Colonization Project," 421. Soon after the elder Blair wrote to Lincoln, Montgomery Blair reinforced his father's words with a letter to the president, pleading that colonization was "indispensable to prevent unspeakable horrors and will soon reconcile the non Slave holders to the union" (Blair to Lincoln, 21 November 1861, Robert Todd Lincoln Collection).

16. Caleb Smith to Lincoln, 16 May 1862, in 38th Cong., 1st sess., 1863,

S. Exec. Doc. 55, Serial 1238, 10 (hereafter, S. Exec. Doc. 55). For the proposed plans mentioned by Smith, see S. Exec. Doc. 55, 89.

17. Basler, *Collected Works,* 5:318.

18. Howard K. Beale, ed., *The Diary of Gideon Welles: Secretary of the Navy under Lincoln and Johnson,* 3 vols. (New York: W. W. Norton, 1960), 1:70–71; David Donald, ed., *Inside Lincoln's Cabinet: The Civil War Diaries of Salmon P. Chase* (New York: Longmans, Green, 1954), 95, 98.

19. For extensive details on the Chiriqui scheme, see Scheips, "Lincoln and the Chiriqui Colonization Project."

20. Basler, *Collected Works,* 5:370–75; Frederick Douglass, "The President and His Speeches," *Douglass Monthly,* September 1862; Henry Highland Garnet to Thomas Hamilton, in the *Pacific Appeal,* 11 October 1862; James M. McPherson, "Abolitionist and Negro Opposition to Colonization during the Civil War," *Phylon* 26 (1965): 394–96; David W. Blight, *Frederick Douglass' Civil War* (Baton Rouge; Louisiana State University Press, 1989), 134–47.

21. Basler, *Collected Works,* 5:370n–371n; Scheips, "Lincoln and the Chiriqui Colonization Project."

22. Beale, *Diary of Gideon Welles,* 1:123; U.S. Senate. *Congressional Globe,* 37th Cong., 2d sess., 28 June 1862, 32, pt. 4, 2997.

23. *New York Evening Express,* 23 September 1862, p. 2.

24. *New York Times,* 1 October 1862, p. 4; *Chicago Tribune,* 26 September 1862, p. 2. Perhaps the most common argument of white Northerners against colonization was that the postwar South could survive only if the labor force remained in place. See, for example, Robert Dale Owen, New York, to Edwin M. Stanton, 23 July 1862, Robert Dale Owen Collection, Manuscript Division, Library of Congress; the letter was reprinted in many newspapers during late 1862.

25. Franklin Butler, Windsor, N.H., to R. R. Gurley, Washington, D.C., 16 August 1862, W. W. McLain, Washington, D.C., to R. R. Gurley, Haddenfield, N.J., 26 August 1862, American Colonization Society MSS., Manuscript Division, Library of Congress (microfilm copy).

26. John Hope Franklin, *The Emancipation Proclamation* (Garden City, N.Y.: Doubleday, 1963), 42–44.

27. Basler, *Collected Works,* 5:434; Samuel C. Pomeroy, Washington, D.C., to James Rood Doolittle, Racine, Wis., 20 October 1862, James Rood Doolittle MSS., Manuscript Division, Library of Congress, reprinted in *Publications of the Southern Historical Association* 9 (1905): 401–2. Lincoln's frustration with financial misappropriation in the Chiriqui scheme is described in Ambrose Thompson, New York, to Richard Thompson, 6 October 1862, Papers of the Chiriqui Improvement Company, Illinois State Historical Library, Springfield (copy in Ambrose Thompson MSS., Manuscript Di-

vision, Library of Congress [hereafter, Thompson MSS.]). These collections—the personal papers of Ambrose Thompson at the Library of Congress and the papers of his company at the Illinois State Historical Library—provide numerous insights into Lincoln's action, or rather inaction, toward colonizing blacks and have remained almost untouched by historians.

28. Beale, *Diary of Gideon Welles*, 1:152–53; Donald, *Inside Lincoln's Cabinet*, 160.

29. That Lincoln and Seward, both astute politicians, should favor postponing all Central American colonization projects until treaties were secured reflected a lack of commitment to colonization, for both men must have at least suspected that no such treaty would be sustained by the Senate Foreign Relations Committee, whose chair, Charles Sumner, was well known as an ardent foe of black colonization. Pomeroy later believed that Lincoln and his secretary of state might be using this strategy to impede the Chiriqui project, and he was furious when Lincoln told him directly that he would take no further action until Congress met in December. See Pomeroy, Washington, D.C., to Orville Hickman Browning, 27 October 1862, Orville Hickman Browning MSS., Illinois State Historical Library; and C. S. Dyer, Washington, D.C., to Ambrose Thompson Jr., Philadelphia, 11 November 1862, Thompson MSS.

30. Donald, *Inside Lincoln's Cabinet*, 156. Although the reason for Pomeroy's conversion is unknown, there can be no doubt that he was sincere in his support for colonization. In his letter to Doolittle on 20 October 1862 (note 27), Pomeroy described how the issue had forced him "to separate and quarrel with my old and valued friends."

31. John P. Usher to Lincoln, 2 August 1862, Robert Todd Lincoln Collection. When word came to Charles Dyer, a clerk to Usher and an ally of the backers of the Chiriqui scheme, that Smith was soon to retire as secretary of interior and Usher was to take his place, he wrote to Ambrose Thompson that the change would assure the success of Thompson's plan; Dyer to Thompson, 1 November 1862, Thompson MSS.

32. Howard K. Beale, ed., *The Diary of Edward Bates, 1859–1866* (Washington, D.C.: United States Government Printing Office, 1933), 268; Basler, *Collected Works*, 6:41n–42n; Bancroft, "The Ile a Vache Experiment." Lincoln did not sign this contract with the confidence with which he signed the Emancipation Proclamation the next day. Distrusting Kock, Lincoln asked Secretary of State Seward not to countersign the contract or affix the seal of the United States to it, "but to retain the instrument under advisement." In this way, Lincoln never allowed the contract to become official.

33. Basler, *Collected Works*, 5:520–21, 530. Only a day or so before the annual message, Lincoln told T. J. Barnett, a minor Interior Department

official with powerful Democratic allies, that he still thought colonization plans could succeed; Barnett to Samuel L. M. Barlow, 30 November 1862, Samuel L. M. Barlow MSS., Henry E. Huntington Library, San Marino, Calif.

34. Basler, *Collected Works*, 6:41n–42n. Lincoln also ordered Seward to cancel his signature on the earlier contract with Kock (ibid., 6:178–79).

35. *New York Daily Tribune*, 17 October 1863, p. 4; Bancroft, "The Ile a Vache Experiment," 244–56.

36. Exactly $38,329.93 of the allocated funds was spent, and of this amount $25,000 was still unaccounted for in 1870; see S. Exec. Doc. 55, 3. For the bill, see U.S. Senate. *Congressional Globe*, 38th Cong., 1st sess., 15 March 1864, 33, pt. 2, 1108, and *U.S. Statutes at Large* 13 (1863–65), ch. 210.

37. On 13 June 1863, for example, Lincoln approved a plan proposed a year earlier that allowed British agents to recruit black emigrants for the colonies of Honduras and Guyana. See James Mitchell to Lincoln, 14 June 1862 (with Lincoln's endorsement of 13 June 1863), Records of the Secretary of the Interior Relating to the Suppression of the African Slave Trade and Negro Colonization, Library of Congress; reprinted in *Black Abolitionist Papers, 1830–1865*, ed. George E. Carter (New York: Microfilming Corporation of America, 1981).

38. Samuel C. Pomeroy to Lincoln, 16 April 1863, Papers of the Chiriqui Improvement Company. No copy of the letter exists in the Lincoln papers; perhaps Pomeroy did not send it.

39. Tyler Dennett, ed., *Lincoln and the Civil War in the Diaries and Letters of John Hay* (New York: Dodd, Mead, 1939), 203. Why Hay chose to make this statement on this date and not earlier is unclear. He may have been prompted by the action Congress was about to take on colonization or by a recent letter from the secretary of the interior to Lincoln, received on 29 June 1864, which stated that since the arrangements for the Vache Island expedition, "No further agreements have been entered into, and no further efforts made, looking to the colonization of persons of African descent beyond the limits of the United States." S. Exec. Doc. 55, 56–57.

40. Benjamin F. Butler, *Butler's Book* (Boston: A. M. Thayer, 1892), 903. Butler claimed that he persuaded Lincoln to consider a plan to send the armed blacks to dig a canal across the isthmus of Darien (in present-day Panama), a venture quite different from, and lacking the permanence of, the proposals for peaceful colonization Lincoln advocated in 1862. Mark E. Neely Jr., has shown that Butler fabricated his exchange with Lincoln and that the two men were not even in Washington at the same time when Butler remembered the conversation taking place ("Abraham Lincoln and Black Colonization: Benjamin Butler's Spurious Testimony," *Civil War History* 25 [1979]: 77–83).

41. As cited in Blight, *Frederick Douglass' Civil War*, 147; see also Mc-Pherson, "Abolitionist and Negro Opposition to Colonization," 397–99.

42. Randall, *Lincoln the President*, 4:26; Dudley T. Cornish, *The Sable Arm: Negro Troops in the Union Army, 1861–1865* (New York: Longmans, Green, 1956), 110–26.

43. S. Exec. Doc. 55, 33; Francis P. Blair Sr., Silver Spring, to Charles Sumner, 25 October 1863, and Francis P. Blair Sr., Silver Spring, to Francis P. Blair Jr., St. Louis, 23 December 1863, Blair Family MSS., Manuscript Division, Library of Congress; Thompson to Lincoln, 2 June 1863, Robert Todd Lincoln Collection.

44. *New York Tribune*, 2 December 1862, p. 4.

45. According to Thomas Drew, the primary military agent of Massachusetts, Gibbs claimed: "There [were] 206 able bodied men between 18 and 45 and about one hundred and twenty five women and children . . . the best looking lot of 'darks' he has ever seen together" (Gibbs, Washington, to John A. Andrew, Boston, 22 March 1864, and Thomas Drew, Washington, to John A. Andrew, Boston, 24 March 1863, John Andrew MSS., Massachusetts Historical Society, Boston).

4

Abraham Lincoln and the Recruitment of Black Soldiers

John T. Hubbell

For all the volumes written about Abraham Lincoln, for all the eloquent words spoken by Lincoln himself, for all the polls that mark him a great man, a national, even international, hero—the Civil War president remains something of an enigma.[1] Our continuation today of the "Lincoln and" tradition suggests our preoccupation with his views on great issues. Given a corollary interest in the topic of race in American history, it is not surprising that Lincoln's place in that central theme remains a subject of debate. The revolutionary developments of the post-World War II period in the area of what is broadly termed "civil rights" have led to a reevaluation of Lincoln—from the great emancipator to the reluctant emancipator to the white supremacist, or, in more vulgar terms, Lincoln as just another honkie.

Historians, ordinarily a judicious lot, are as much involved in the reevaluation as those with more obvious ideological interests. But historians should have a greater appreciation of context. Hence, to wrench Lincoln from context, from the backdrop of his times, from the exigencies of policy, from the fortunes of war, and from the historical record, is not a path calculated for arrival at something approximating historical truth. In our relativistic age, perhaps it is too much to expect fidelity to the record; perhaps Lincoln should remain more symbol than historical reality. Perhaps the record is discomfiting; it often is.

Abraham Lincoln was born into a political culture that was profoundly racist (to use a somewhat anachronistic term). For centuries, Europeans, whether living on the continent, in the United States, or elsewhere, had deemed the Africans a race apart, one that was in no guise the equal of the European. It was a combination of that racism with economic considerations that made the enslavement of the African fundamentally different from the slavery of other places and other times. Practically speaking, there was nothing in Lincoln's formative years that would lead us to expect him to be other than a man of his culture. The laws of Kentucky, Indiana, Illinois—in common with those of other political jurisdictions within the United States— held the African to be less than a citizen, less than a person.

Yet Lincoln imbibed other influences—the idea of political democracy (however limited), the idea of social mobility (however restricted), the idea of economic improvement (however problematic). Lincoln believed the words of the Declaration of Independence. He believed that a person should not be constrained by circumstances of birth; and he embraced the Whig notions of economic growth. As an individual he was, from all reports, singularly free from bigotry— against individuals and groups.[2]

As much as any public man of his day, he advocated the widest sharing in the American dream. His reentry into national politics in the wake of the exacerbated sectional conflict of the 1850s was predicated upon the ideas that slavery was an evil and that, in certain instances, racial bigotry was unworthy of a great nation. That his political fortunes, and those of his party, were tied to the geographical restriction of slavery, set him, and his party, apart from his political opponents. In the context of 1858 or 1860 (and 1948 or 1960), he could have been seen as something of a radical.

The threat to slavery perceived by Lincoln's election in 1860 precipitated a train of events that culminated in civil war. That war, whatever else it may have been, or whatever else we may wish it had been, was a titanic military struggle, frought with profound political and social consequences. Lincoln, as he remarked in his Second Inaugural Address, did not anticipate, nor did other Americans anticipate, those consequences any more than they anticipated the full horrors of that wretched conflict. Lincoln expected a relatively short war once the apparently overwhelming resources of the Union could be brought to bear against the Confederacy. Thus, the ancient prejudices of his country might have survived the war intact had the war indeed ended with Union victory in the first year or so. But that was not the case. Lincoln necessarily had to accept, and then defend, policies that arose from circumstances—circumstances that forced a reconsideration of the place of the African (more accurately, the African-American) in the United States.

The American political and military establishment decreed in 1861 that the war would be fought by white men. Lincoln concurred. The Congress decreed in July 1861 that the war would be fought for the Union—not for conquest or the abolition of slavery. Lincoln concurred. When his generals and cabinet officials moved beyond the president's plan, Lincoln overruled them. When black leaders asked that regiments of black soldiers be enrolled under the flag of freedom, Lincoln and his advisors refused.[3] Many Northerners, in stations high and low, seemed to fear a rebellion of slaves more than they feared a rebellion of slaveowners.[4] Had Northern arms prevailed in 1861 or even in early 1862, slavery might have remained *status quo ante bellum.*

The political attack on slavery was embodied in a series of laws termed the Confiscation Acts. Under the provisions of those laws, Lincoln could have enrolled black men as laborers and support elements for the armies in the field. Lincoln chose rather not to invoke these aspects of the statutes. A primary reason was his concern for the border states, especially Kentucky. Lincoln believed that wholesale emancipation or the enlistment of black soldiers would cause Kentucky, and probably Missouri and Maryland, to become even greater obstacles to the Union cause—to say nothing of antagonism elsewhere in the North. In the case of Kentucky he was correct. Holding that state in the Union necessitated either overwhelming military force or some deference to the wishes of its white population. Lincoln's policy reflected a combination of both. Eventually, more black men entered the army from Kentucky than from any other state except Louisiana. And the reaction of the white population in Kentucky was as negative as had been predicted. But by 1863, negative reaction in Kentucky was considerably less consequential than in 1861 or 1862.[5]

For practical political reasons, Lincoln did not openly lead the movement toward the enlistment of blacks. Prior to 1863, long before he expressed enthusiasm for the idea, he allowed others to take the first steps; he remained silent, overruled them, or caused them to be overruled. He was always sensitive to political considerations and to the prerequisites and powers of his office. Timing, the right moment, was critical—and Lincoln always deemed himself a better judge of the moment than those who advised him, formally or informally.

On 25 September 1861, Secretary of the Navy Gideon Welles allowed the recruitment of blacks into the navy, but only with the rank of "boy" and at a compensation of no more than $10.00 per month. The step caused little comment, perhaps because "boys" on ships were not expected to shoot rebels or to function as part of the military establishment.[6]

Simon Cameron, secretary of war, was less subtle. On 14 October 1861, he authorized Brigadier General Thomas W. Sherman to hire black fugitives for service in South Carolina, although he disclaimed any intent to arm them as soldiers. Lincoln seemed amenable to the idea of blacks as "auxiliaries," but the plan failed because General Sherman apparently wished neither to use blacks nor to offend unduly the sensibilities of white South Carolinians. In December, Cameron took a more direct step. In his annual report he openly advocated employment of slaves as soldiers. More important, he allowed the report to be copied and distributed before giving it to Lincoln. The president disavowed the offensive portions of the report and ordered them deleted from his own annual message to Congress. Because of that misstep, but also because he was a general embarrassment to the administration, Cameron was removed from the cabinet and named minister to Russia.[7]

During the first half of 1862, Congress moved toward bringing blacks into the army—March, surrender of slaves to military forbidden; April, abolition of slavery in D.C.; July, Second Confiscation Act and Militia Act. In April and May, the new secretary of war, Edwin Stanton, encouraged (at least implicitly) the arming of blacks in South Carolina. The situation there caused a great stir, because the general in command, David Hunter, proved to be politically inept and hence a political liability. He managed to offend many officers and men in the white regiments as well as two congressmen of a border state, Kentucky. When those congressmen demanded explanations of what was transpiring in South Carolina, Stanton retreated into his bureaucratic defenses but did ask General Hunter for a report, which was forwarded to Congress. Hunter's report was entertaining to some Republicans (referring to "fugitive rebels"), but to the border state congressmen—insulting.[8]

During the summer of 1862, Lincoln evinced no inclination to support Hunter, to implement the provisions of the Second Confiscation Act liberating the slaves of rebels, or to employ blacks other than as laborers. He stated his views to the cabinet in late July, and on 6 August he told a delegation of "Western gentlemen" that he would not arm blacks "unless some new and more pressing emergency arises." Such, he said, would turn "50,000 bayonets" in the border states against the Union. Steps short of actually arming blacks would be continued—upon this he and his critics did not differ. And in the same context, on 22 August he wrote his famous reply to Horace Greeley's "The Prayer of Twenty Millions": as president he would save the Union; all else would be subordinate to that goal.[9]

On 10 August the disheartened (if not chastened) General Hunter reported to Stanton that he was disbanding his regiment of South Carolina volunteers. But as the curtain fell on Hunter, Stanton on 25 August authorized Brigadier General Rufus Saxton at Beaufort, South Carolina, to "arm, uniform, equip, and receive into the service of the United States such number of volunteers of African descent as you may deem expedient, not exceeding 5,000." Why the reversal? Why had Stanton authorized Saxton to do what had been denied Hunter? A comment by Lieutenant Charles Francis Adams Jr. may be pertinent. Regarding Hunter: "Why could not fanatics be silent and let Providence work for awhile?"[10] (And if not Providence, at least the president.) In short, had Hunter managed to be more politic with respect to his fellow officers and the Congress, had he been able to restrain his rhetorical flourishes, he may not have run afoul of the critics of his policy, to say nothing of the president. The fact was, blacks were now to be brought into the service, not by a general acting more or less on his own authority but by order of the War Department—and the president.

In other corners of the conflict, namely Louisiana and Kansas, other generals proceeded to enlist blacks. In New Orleans, for example, Benjamin F. Butler earlier had negated enlisting efforts but now, encouraged by Secretary of the Treasury Chase (and by Mrs. Butler), called for free blacks to enter the service. By mid-fall three such regiments were formed in Louisiana. On 5 August 1862, the redoubtable abolitionist James H. Lane in Kansas wired Stanton that he was raising black as well as white regiments, and was there any objection? Stanton wrote Lane on 22 August and again on 23 September that such action was without the authority of the president. Lane never received authorization, but he continued enrolling black soldiers for the Union. Benjamin Quarles has termed such enrollments "trial balloons," which when no one of consequence tried to pop, Lincoln allowed to float.[11]

Of course, Lincoln was discussing another matter with his cabinet in the summer of 1862—namely, emancipation. In his "preliminary" proclamation of 22 September 1862, Lincoln did not mention black soldiers. In October, however, he presumably talked to one Daniel Ullmann of New York, who urged that very course. After hearing Ullmann's argument, Lincoln asked: "Would you be willing to command black soldiers?" Although stunned by the question, Ullmann replied in the affirmative.[12] Given the events of the late summer and early fall in South Carolina, Louisiana, and Kansas, Lincoln seemed to be evolving a plan—perhaps Ullmann would pilot another of those trial balloons.

The Emancipation Proclamation, issued on 1 January 1863, called for the enrollment of blacks in the Union army and navy. It was contained in an almost offhand passage—fully in keeping with Lincoln's tendency to hint, approach indirectly, and, finally, defend a stated policy. Yet the Proclamation was fundamental. It was a war message, a political document. The government of the United States, through the Office of the President, was now unequivocally on the side of emancipation and of bringing black men into the Army of the Republic.

Over the next several months the new policy was put into effect. Ullmann, appointed a brigadier general of volunteers, was specifically charged with raising four regiments of volunteers in Louisiana (where he found public opinion far from supportive). Colonel James Montgomery of Kansas was authorized to raise a black regiment in South Carolina, and the governors of Massachusetts and Rhode Island were given similar authorization.[13] Massachusetts Governor John A. Andrew, in fact, raised most of his black troops from the southern states.[14]

The major organizing effort was placed in the hands of Lorenzo Thomas, adjutant general of the army. His order of 25 March from Secretary Stanton was to proceed to the Mississippi Valley in order to enlist black troops and find white officers and enlisted men who would take commissions in black regiments. Thomas was an effective recruiter, stressing that he spoke with the full authority of the president, the secretary of war, and the general-in-chief. Henry W. Halleck (who was notorious for his General Order No. 3 in 1861) had fallen in line with administration policy and now was telling other officers in the Mississippi Valley to do the same. Of particular interest was the reaction of Ulysses S. Grant, who early in the war had no more sympathy for emancipation than did many other regulars. Yet Grant was certainly a man to follow orders from Washington. Indeed, he had already made provision for organizing "contrabands" into a work force. According to John Eaton Jr., in charge of the contrabands, Grant believed that if the occasion arose, the fugitives could carry rifles instead of hoes, rakes, and shovels.

Halleck's advice to Grant, in a friendly if somewhat patronizing letter, was an effective statement of administration policy. "From my position here, where I can survey the whole field, perhaps I may be better able to understand the tone of public opinion and the intentions of the Government." Grant then assured Halleck (and later the president) that he would support the policy even to the extent of ordering subordinate officers to be active in "removing prejudice" against blacks. Thomas's mission, after all, went beyond recruiting black men into the ranks. As Dudley Cornish has stated: "Rather was his task that of initiating Union policy on a grand scale, of breaking down white opposition to the use of Negro soldiers, of educating Union troops in the valley on this one subject, of starting the work of organization," and then leaving others to finish the work of recruiting and training. Lincoln approved of Thomas's work, telling Stanton that Thomas was "one of the best (if not the best) instruments for this service."[15] Perhaps Lincoln had been right after all. It was best to bring the general public along, then put the task in the hands of the professional soldiers who, while not without ideological biases, placed great stock in order, system, and hierarchy. The road to favor with the administration was not in embarrassing the president, but in efficiently following his policy, once that policy was clearly enunciated.

On Independence Day 1863, Vicksburg surrendered; the "Father of Waters" again flowed "unvexed to the sea." Thanks were given to not only the Great Northwest but also New England, and the "Sunny South, too, in more colors than one."[16]

In early August, Lincoln wrote to Grant congratulating him upon his magnificent military achievement, but also noting: "Gen. Thomas has gone again to the Mississippi Valley, with the view of raising colored troops. I have no reason to doubt that you are doing what you reasonably can upon the same subject. I believe it is a resource which, if vigorously applied now, will soon close this contest. It works doubly, weakening the enemy and strengthening us. We were not fully ripe for it until the river was opened."[17] On 26 August Lincoln wrote to a political friend in Illinois that some of his field commanders, "who have given us our most important successes, believe the emancipation policy, and the use of colored troops, constitute the heaviest blow yet dealt to the rebellion; and that, at least one of those important successes, could not have been achieved when it was, but for the aid of black soldiers." He could have recited the practical, some might say cynical, reasons given for bringing blacks into the army—saving the lives of white soldiers. Yet, said Lincoln, "Negroes, like other people, act upon motives. Why should they do any thing for us, if we will do nothing for them? If they stake their lives for us, they must be prompted by the strongest motive—even the promise of freedom. And the promise being made, must be kept." One day peace would come. "And then, there will be some black men who can remember that, with silent tongue, and clenched teeth, and steady eye, and well-poised bayonet, they have helped mankind on to this great consummation; while, I fear, there will be some white ones, unable to forget that, with malignant heart, and deceitful speech, they have strove to hinder it."[18]

The force of the effort for recruiting blacks lay in the deep South and in the Northeast. Lincoln still had no wish to press the issue in the border states. And his caution was well founded, although he did authorize (through Stanton) recruiting in Maryland, Kentucky, and Missouri.

Kentuckians were particularly resentful. When Ambrose Burnside suggested in June 1863 that the administration disavow any intention to conscript free blacks in Kentucky, Lincoln concurred that the effort would cost more than it would gain. In January 1864, however, the War Department established a recruiting post in Paducah. Kentucky Governor Thomas E. Bramlette traveled to Washington and protested directly to Lincoln. The president explained that he had come to his policy of emancipation and arming blacks after prudent delay—early in the war it was not an "indispensable necessity." He changed his mind when he knew that he had to choose between "surrendering the Union, and with it, the Constitution, or of laying strong hand upon the colored element." He had not been certain at that time that he had made the right decision, but after a year's experience, he was convinced of it. "We have the men [130,000]; and we could not have had them without the measure. And now let any Union man who complains of the measure, test himself by writing down in one line that he is for subduing the rebellion by force of arms; and in the next, that he is for taking these hundred and thirty thousand men from the Union side, and placing them where they would be but for the measure he condemns. If he can not face his case so stated, it is only because he can not face the truth." That letter contained Lincoln's memorable line, "I claim not to have controlled events, but confess plainly that events have controlled me."[19] Lincoln meant for the letter to be circulated among the white population of Kentucky. Although his correspondents expressed satisfaction with it, Kentuckians in general resented recruitment of blacks more intensely than did people of any other state. But Lincoln knew, and he made the point repeatedly from mid-1863 to the end of the war; without the black soldiers, there would be no Union.

Frederick Douglass said so well in 1876:

His great mission was to accomplish two things: first, to save his country from dismemberment and ruin; and second, to free his country from the great crime of slavery. To do one or the other, or both, he needed the earnest sympathy and the powerful cooperation of his loyal fellow-countrymen. Without those primary and essential conditions to success his efforts would have been utterly fruitless. Had he put the abolition of slavery before the salvation of the Union, he would have inevitably driven from him a powerful class of the American people and rendered resistance to rebellion impossible. From the genuine abolition ground, Mr. Lincoln seemed tardy, cold, dull, and indifferent; but measuring him by the sentiment of his country, a sentiment he was bound as a statesman to consult, he was swift, zealous, radical, and determined.[20]

The enlistment of blacks into the Union army was part of Lincoln's evolving policy on slavery and race, a policy charged with political, social, and psychological overtones. The black man as soldier—with rifle and bayonet—was a different figure from the slave. His presence, while a military necessity, was also a potent blow to the idea of the innate inferiority of the African, an idea not peculiar to the South.

Those who urged the enlistment of blacks realized its implications. Some political figures saw it as a necessity, calculated to outrage the South. Black leaders saw it from a different perspective. Not only would the enlistment of blacks serve a military purpose, but most assuredly it would also enhance the sense of manhood among black men, a sense deliberately blunted by public policy throughout the nation. Thus, while Douglass remarked on a "tardiness" of the president who "loved Rome more than he did Caesar," he insisted that emancipation and manhood, in the most profound sense, were indispensable steps toward participation in American society.

Lincoln acted as he did from necessity. His almost mystical devotion to the Union and his personal compassion for the dispossessed of the world combined into policy. Events moved him in the sense that events determined the time for action. During the Civil War a basic truth emerged: black people understood the meaning of the war and contributed to the great goal of freedom. Yet blacks were also objects; in order to defeat the white South, the white North needed black men. Lincoln was their emancipator, their savior, when he spoke as the cautious, prudent political leader and when he eloquently spoke of the magnificent contribution that black soldiers made to the Union. The war brought the time, and Lincoln— "preeminently the white man's President" —became the black man's hero.

NOTES

1. Cf. Frederick Douglass's perceptive comment: "Any man can say things that are true of Abraham Lincoln, but no man can say anything that is new of Abraham Lincoln. . . . He was a mystery to no man who saw him and heard him (*Life and Times of Frederick Douglass, Written By Himself* [Hartford, Conn.: Park Publishing , 1882], 541). The quoted words are from Douglass's magnificent oration "on the occasion of the unveiling of the Freedmen's Monument, in memory of Abraham Lincoln, in Lincoln Park, Washington, D.C., April 14, 1876."

2. When Douglass remarked that Lincoln "shared the prejudices common to his countrymen towards the colored race," he was speaking in the context of public policy. Note also his moving description of Lincoln's Second Inaugural and subsequent conversation with the president (ibid., 364–66, 402–7, 488). In a letter to Joshua Speed, 24 August 1855, Lincoln wrote:

"As a nation, we begin by declaring that '*all men are created equal.*' We now practically read it 'all men are created equal, *except negroes.*' When the Know-Nothings get control, it will read "all men are created equal, except negroes, *and foreigners, and catholics.*' When it comes to this I should prefer emigrating to some country where they make no pretence of loving liberty—to Russia for instance, where depotism can be taken pure, and without the base alloy of hypocracy." Roy P. Basler, ed., Marion Dolores Pratt and Lloyd A. Dunlap, asst. eds., *The Collected Works of Abraham Lincoln,* 9 vols. (New Brunswick, N.J.: Rutgers University Press, 1953–55), 2:323 (hereafter, Basler, *Collected Works*).

3. Dudley T. Cornish, *The Sable Arm: Negro Troops in the Union Army, 1861–1865* (New York: Longmans, Green, 1956), 1–12.

4. See, for example, Ulysses S. Grant to his father, Jesse Root Grant, 6 May 1861, in John Y. Simon, ed., *The Papers of Ulysses S. Grant,* 22 vols. to date (Carbondale: southern Illinois University Press, 1967–), 2:20–22: "A Northern army may be required in the next ninety days to go south to suppress a negro insurrection."

5. Allan Nevins, *The War For the Union,* 4 vols. (New York: Scribner's, 1959–71), 513; Benjamin Quarles, *Lincoln and the Negro* (New York: Oxford University Press, 1962), 163–66; James G. Randall, *Lincoln the President,* 4 vols. (New York: Dodd, Mead, 1945–55), 2:1–16.

6. Cornish, *The Sable Arm,* 17–18.

7. Ibid., 18–24; Randall, *Lincoln the President,* 4:54–61; Benjamin P. Thomas and Harold M. Hyman, *Stanton: The Life and Times of Lincoln's Secretary of War* (New York: Knopf, 1962), 131–37.

8. Ibid., 234–37; Cornish, *The Sable Arm,* 43–46.

9. Ibid., 50–52; Nevins, *War for the Union,* 2:231–33.

10. Cornish, *The Sable Arm,* 52–55, 80 (Adams's remark is on p. 55).

11. Ibid., 56–78; Quarles, *Lincoln and the Negro,* 155–56.

12. Cornish, *The Sable Arm,* 100.

13. Ibid., 101–6.

14. Richard H. Abbott, "Massachusetts and the Recruitment of Negro Soldiers, 1863–1865," *Civil War History,* 14 (1968): 197–210.

15. Cornish, *The Sable Arm,* 111–31, contains an excellent account of Thomas's recruiting efforts. The reference to Eaton is in John Eaton, *Grant, Lincoln and the Freedmen* (New York: Longmans, Green, 1907), 9–15. Grant's exchanges with Hallack are in Simon, *Papers of Ulysses S. Grant,* 8:90–94.

16. Lincoln to James C. Conkling, 26 August 1863, Basler, *Collected Works,* 6:409.

17. Lincoln to Grant, 9 August 1863, ibid., 374.

18. Lincoln to Conkling, 26 August 1863, ibid., 408–10. This letter was

intended to be a campaign document for the fall elections in Illinois and a public statement on his policy regarding blacks.

19. Quarles, *Lincoln and the Negro*, 163–65; Lincoln to Albert G. Hodges, 4 April 1864, Basler, *Collected Works*, 7:281–82.

20. Douglass, *Life and Times of Frederick Douglass*, 541–42.

5

Lincoln and Frederick Douglass: Another Debate

Christopher N. Breiseth

THE CIVIL WAR, whatever else it may have been, was America's struggle over slavery. The relationship between Frederick Douglass, born
a slave in Maryland, and Abraham Lincoln, born in Kentucky to a
poor white family, reveals much about the debate over race during
the Civil War. The relationship between the two men was punctuated
by profound disagreement but culminated in expressions of deep mutual regard. The evolution of their relationship closely paralleled the
evolution of Lincoln's thoughts on race. As politician and president,
Lincoln was masterful in conveying his earnest consideration of
voices pressing in on him from every side. He heard the conflicting
arguments of a nation at war with itself and sought to blunt the differences and establish a common ground for preserving the Union.
Frederick Douglass, representing an almost powerless people, re-
lentlessly bore in upon Lincoln the irresistible logic that the war
could be won and the Union preserved only if slavery were abolished. Proving the influence of one individual upon another is difficult and inconclusive. But one can say that by 1865 Lincoln and
Douglass had a fundamental similarity of vision about the profound
causes and consequences of the Civil War.

In the volatile politics of the prewar decade, both Lincoln and
Douglass displayed a combination of calm practicality and moral
vigor. Lincoln helped build the Republican Party by drawing together a coalition of widely differing groups and individuals who,
though disagreeing on specific policies, understood the threat to the
Union posed by the slavery issue. The groups Lincoln sought to mobilize included those at one extreme who opposed the extension of
slavery into the territories, in part because they hated blacks and

wished them confined to the South, and those abolitionists at the other extreme who regarded the enslavement of blacks as America's prime offense against mankind. If Lincoln was cautious in trying to build a Republican coalition, he was unequivocal in his judgment that slavery was morally wrong and that the nation could not continue to live half slave and half free. Helped by his rivalry with the defiant white supremacist Stephen A. Douglas, Lincoln acquired the political skills that conveyed to a troubled electorate a mixture of political common sense, honesty, and personal independence.

A remarkable personal independence also characterized Frederick Douglass. Brought into the abolitionist movement in the early 1840s by William Lloyd Garrison, Douglass was regarded as a prize exhibit of Negro manhood, but he gradually broke with the antipolitical policies of Garrison and other white abolitionists. Douglass rejected the Garrisonian position that the Constitution was a proslavery document and that the free states should advocate secession from the morally reprehensible slave states. Douglass, through his own monthly journal, insisted upon the need to use the ballot and political parties to abolish slavery. Twenty years a slave, he could not separate abolitionist theories from the possible consequences of those theories for blacks still in slavery. His ideological caution extended to his own personal situation. In 1846 he had agreed to accept the help of English friends to buy his freedom from his old master, a concession to the slave system that many white abolitionists deplored. (Douglass reminded white critics that *they* did not have to worry that the Fugitive Slave Law might be enforced against them.) Douglass's practicality also led him to refuse to join John Brown's armed rebellion of slaves at Harpers Ferry. The decision was difficult because Douglass admired Brown above all others. But Douglass also understood that his best weapons in the cause of liberation were his tongue, his pen, and his disciplined intellect. Douglass, a self-made man like Lincoln, was not prepared to weaken his hard-won position of leadership by actions that were out of harmony with his own character, temperament, and understanding of events.[1]

As he studied the situation in June 1860, Douglass departed from many abolitionist colleagues and publicly applauded the nomination of Lincoln, whom he labeled a "radical republican . . . fully committed to the doctrine of the irrepressible conflict." During the campaign, however, as Lincoln opposed only the extension of slavery and did not advocate outright abolition, Douglass grew troubled.[2] But, faced with the political realities of the election, he concluded that friends of abolition should not waste their votes on the Liberty Party candidate.[3] Douglass thought that Lincoln's election in November was a hopeful sign; but he feared that while Lincoln's guarantees to slaveowners during the campaign would preserve the Union, they would actually prolong slavery. The situation looked so bleak that Douglass declared that the dissolution of the Union might be necessary for the cause of liberty. His own course, he told his readers in December, was clear: "We shall join in no cry, and unite in no demand less than the complete and universal *abolition* of the whole slave system. Slavery shall be destroyed."[4]

The single objective of Lincoln's Inaugural Address, in the face of secession by several slave states, was to preserve the Union. Acknowledging that slavery was the only real source of disunion, Lincoln sought to reassure the Southern states that he had no desire to interfere with their peculiar institution. He indicated support for the rights of free Negroes but guaranteed enforcement of the Fugitive Slave Law, and went so far as to state that he would not oppose a constitutional amendment permanently guaranteeing noninterference with the institution of slavery.[5] Douglass was outraged. To grant the slaveholders the constitutional right of owning their slaves, he charged, was to give up the whole argument. He found some solace in Lincoln's cautious interest in protecting the rights of free Negroes but was disgusted by the president's heartless attitude toward those still in slavery. "Mr. Lincoln has avowed himself ready to catch them if they run away, to shoot them down if they rise against their oppressors, and to prohibit the Federal Government *irrevocably* from interfering for their deliverance."[6]

The Rebel's attack on Fort Sumter in April 1861, precipitating the outbreak of the Civil War, transformed Douglass's despair to hope. He thought that the attack would unite the efforts of the North to put down the rebellion and would inevitably strengthen the antislavery cause. "The slaveholders themselves have saved our cause from ruin!" Douglass exclaimed.[7] Lincoln could end the war quickly, counseled Douglass, by calling blacks, slave and free, into a liberating army that would raise the banner of emancipation among slaves.[8] In July, Douglass insisted that there should be no escaping the central fact of the war: "The very stomach of this rebellion is the Negro in the condition of the slave."[9]

Lincoln did not take Douglass's advice. He refused to enlist free blacks as soldiers. He did not at first countermand the orders of generals who refused to give protection to slaves escaping into Union lines. He delayed authorizing General Benjamin Butler's practice of considering escaped slaves as contraband. In his special message to Congress on 4 July 1861, Lincoln made no direct reference to slavery.[10] Finally, in August, he countermanded the emancipation proclamation of General John C. Frémont. By October, Douglass concluded that Lincoln's unfolding strategy had been determined by his desire to keep the border slave states in the Union; those slave states, Douglass held, were a millstone about the neck of the government and served as a shield for the treason of the cotton states.[11]

Toward the end of 1861, Lincoln seemed to Douglass to be moving in a more hopeful direction. By November, Lincoln had approved the confiscation of Rebel property, tacitly allowed protection for fugitive slaves behind Union lines, and authorized use by Union forces of black labor.[12] But when Lincoln, in his annual message in December, proposed colonization of freedmen, Douglass privately confessed to his bewilderment at "the spectacle of moral blindness, infatuation and helpless imbecility which the Government of Lincoln presents."[13]

In March 1862, Lincoln asked for a joint resolution of Congress for compensated emancipation. Sounding more like Douglass and other abolitionists, Lincoln told Congress that to deprive the slave states of their hope to secure slavery permanently would substantially end the rebellion.[14] In April, Lincoln signed the bill to emancipate slaves in the District of Columbia, a move that Douglass happily described as "the first great step toward the righteousness which exalts a nation."[15] In August, Lincoln summoned a five-man Negro delegation to the White House, the first formal meeting between a president and a group of blacks.[16] Describing the sharp physical difference between the two races and the consequent suffering for both black and white, Lincoln insisted that "without the institution of Slavery and the colored race as a basis, the war could not have an existence." He asked for the support of such free Negroes as those before him, men "capable of thinking as white men," to give leadership to his colonization plans. "If you could give a start to white people," he said, "you would open a wide door for many to be made free."[17]

Douglass had only contempt for this speech of "our garrulous and joking President." In the September issue of *Douglass' Monthly* he charged Lincoln with being "a genuine representative of American prejudice and Negro hatred and far more concerned for the preservation of slavery, and the favor of the Border Slave States, than for any sentiment of magnanimity or principle of justice and humanity." By suggesting that the differences between the races were so great that separation was the only remedy, Lincoln had furnished "a weapon to all the ignorant and base, who need only the countenance of men in authority to commit all kinds of violence and outrage upon the colored people of the country." The logic that blamed blacks as the first cause of the war was the same that blamed the horse for the horse thief and the money in the traveler's pocket for the robbery. Douglass said that the very prejudice against Negroes was the result of slavery, "that root of all crimes and evils."[18] It was Douglass's most unsparing attack upon the president.

Despite Lincoln's apparent ambivalence about emancipation, as revealed by the August interview with the black delegation and his statement a week later that his "paramount object in this struggle *is* to save the Union, and is *not* either to save or to destroy slavery," Lincoln, on 22 September 1862, issued his Preliminary Emancipation Proclamation, forever freeing, as of 1 January 1863, all slaves residing within a state or part of a state in rebellion.[19] He had been carefully preparing the ground of public opinion for that controversial act.[20]

The two great objectives, preservation of the Union and abolition of slavery, had now begun to come together. Douglass was jubilant. "Common sense, the necessities of war, to say nothing of the dictation of justice and humanity have at last prevailed," he wrote. "We shout for joy that we live to record this righteous decree." Douglass had no fear that the president would turn back: "If he has taught us to confide in nothing else, he has taught us to confide in his word."[21] Despite some last-minute maneuvering to induce the slave states to lay down their arms and avoid outright emancipation,[22] Lincoln was true to his word. The Emancipation Proclamation, issued on 1 January 1863, made no mention of compensation or colonization. Moreover, blacks were at last allowed to put on the Union Army uniform.[23]

Many abolitionists charged that the proclamation only ended slavery where the Union had no power and left it untouched among loyal Union slaveholders, but Douglass responded with a 2,000-mile speechmaking tour in behalf of Lincoln's righteous act. "Assuming that our Government and people will sustain the President and his Proclamation," Douglass told a New York audience in February, "we can scarcely conceive of a more complete revolution in the position of a nation." It was time to stop fighting the Rebels with only the North's soft white hand, Douglass said, and to unleash its iron black hand. The problem of anti-Negro prejudice in the North had to be conquered, he warned, or the Proclamation would be worthless. Douglass castigated those who said Negroes would not fight.

> In one breath the Copperheads tell you that the slaves won't fight, and in the next they tell you that the only effect of the Proclamation is to make the slaves cut their masters' throats [laughter] and stir up insurrections all over the South.—The same men tell you that the Negroes are lazy and good for nothing, and in the next breath they tell you that they will come North and take the labor away from the laboring white men here. [Laughter and cheers.] In one breath they tell you that the Negro can never learn the military art, and in the next they tell you that there is danger that white men may be outranked by colored men. [Continued laughter.][24]

In a broadside titled "Men of Color, To Arms!" printed in papers throughout the North, Douglass declared to his black brethren that he could at last counsel them to take up arms.[25] But the hideous draft riots in New York City in July 1863, in which blacks were beaten to death, and their homes, orphanages, and churches burned, provided ominous evidence of the depth of Northern white prejudice. Black regiments (in which Douglass's own sons served) went into bloody battle amidst threats by Jefferson Davis to enslave or butcher black prisoners. Meanwhile, in almost every way the black troops were given inferior treatment by the Union Army. After six months of effort, Douglass surveyed the situation and in August told Major George L. Stearns, who was in charge of black recruitment, that he could no longer urge black men to fight unless Lincoln promised them the same protection given white soldiers.[26] Douglass called on every man with a sense of right, decency, and gratitude "to speak out trumpet-tongued in the ears of Mr. Lincoln and his Government and demand from him a declaration of purpose, to hold the rebels to a strict account for every black federal soldier taken as a prisoner."[27]

Stearns persuaded Douglass to travel to Washington and lay his grievances before Lincoln. Douglass expected to wait half a day in the crowded White House anterooms on 10 August 1863. But within moments after announcing himself, he was summoned to see the president. Douglass later recalled, "I could hear, in the eager multitude outside, as they saw me pressing and elbowing my way through, the remark, 'Yes, damn it, I knew they would let the n——r through,' in a kind of despairing voice—a Peace Democrat, I suppose." The president received the former slave as a gentleman. Douglass urged Lincoln to pay black soldiers wages equal to those paid white soldiers, to protect black prisoners like any other soldiers, to retaliate in kind for any black prisoners killed in cold blood by the Confederates, and, finally, to reward black soldiers by distinction and promotion precisely as whites were rewarded. Lincoln responded to Douglass's remarks by saying that prejudice against blacks could be overcome only gradually. Black soldiers, Lincoln said, should be willing to serve under any conditions because they had stronger motives for fighting than did the white troops. As for protection of black prisoners, the president declared that the recent bloody losses of blacks at Milliken's Bend, Port Hudson, and Fort Wagner were necessary to prepare the way for his "Order of Retaliation" of 30 July. In time, Lincoln promised, black troops would receive equal treatment.[28] He also promised to sign any commission for black soldiers recommended by the Secretary of War. For his part, Lincoln protested against a public charge by Douglass that Lincoln was slow and vacillating. Lincoln admitted that he might seem slow; but to the charge of being vacillating, he objected. "Mr. Douglass," Lincoln said, "I do not think that charge can be sustained; I think it cannot be shown that when I have once taken a position, I have ever retreated from it." In relating that remark to the annual meeting of the American Anti-Slavery Society in December 1863, Douglass described it as the most significant point in their conversation. Although not in total agreement with Lincoln's views, Douglass "was so well satisfied with the man and the educating tendency of the conflict" that he determined to continue recruiting black men for the Union cause.[29]

After his interview with Lincoln, Douglass proceeded directly to Secretary of War Edwin M. Stanton and came away with what he regarded as the pledge of a commission and orders to join General Lorenzo Thomas as assistant adjutant in recruiting black troops in the Mississippi Valley. Douglass hurried home to Rochester, New York, and wrote his valedictory for *Douglass' Monthly*, ending a journal that, under various names, had been his mouthpiece for nearly sixteen years.[30] But the commission never came, and Douglass refused the request to join Thomas. Douglass privately ascribed Stanton's reversal to timidity to face a step that suggested a policy of racial equality. He complained to Stearns that he considered himself "trifled with and deceived."[31]

Douglass made nothing of the rebuke in public. In articles and speeches, he carried on his efforts to convert the Union cause into an unsparing war for the total abolition of slavery. In the aftermath of Lincoln's annual message in December 1863, in which the president said he wished he could have put down the rebellion without abolishing slavery, Douglass was scornful of the absence of moral consideration in Lincoln's utterances. He compared Lincoln's everlasting talk about the Union with Stephen Douglas's talk about popular sovereignty, each trying to escape a moral judgment on slavery. Douglass insisted that not union but abolition must be the grand objective of the war. "Events are mightier than our rulers," Douglass told a New York audience in February 1864. "These Divine forces, with overpowering logic, have fixed upon this war, against the wishes of our Government, the comprehensive character and mission I have ascribed to it."[32]

As he looked toward the 1864 presidential election, Douglass regarded the key issue to be the enfranchisement of blacks in the South to assure a just peace.[33] He attacked Lincoln bitterly for his silence on the issue.[34] Unknown to Douglass, Lincoln had taken a modest step toward black suffrage. In March 1864 he had suggested in a letter to Michael Hahn, governor of the Louisiana government set up under the amnesty proclamation of December 1863, that the franchise be given to blacks who were very intelligent and who had fought gallantly for the Union. "They would probably help, in some trying time to come, to keep the jewel of liberty within the family of freedom," he said. Lincoln stressed that the proposal was only a suggestion, however, and added that the contents of the letter were confidential.[35] John Eaton, a key figure in government efforts for the freedmen, was aware of Douglass's dissatisfaction and reported it to

Lincoln in August. The president asked Eaton to arrange another interview and wondered if Douglass knew of the contents of the letter to Hahn. Lincoln had assured Eaton "that considering the conditions from which Douglass rose, and the position to which he had attained, he was, in his judgment, one of the most meritorious men in America."[36]

The interview was arranged, and Douglass found Lincoln on 19 August in a melancholy mood. The Union forces seemed unable to turn back the Rebels, and cries for peace were heard everywhere. Lincoln feared that his own reelection was in doubt. His "To Whom It May Concern" letter, making abolition one of the conditions for peace, had caused a furor among some of his supporters. Lincoln brought out the draft of a letter that had been written to reassure his friends. In that letter Lincoln said that he could not carry on a war for abolition without the support of the country and the Congress. Douglass objected strongly to the letter. "It would be given a broader meaning than you intend to convey," Douglass explained. "It would be taken as a complete surrender of your anti-slavery policy, and do you serious damage. In answer to your Copperhead accusers, your friends can make the argument of your want of power, but you cannot wisely say a word on that point." Lincoln did not send the letter. Lincoln then asked Douglass to plan a kind of underground railroad to help slaves escape to the North before war's end.[37] That plan was prompted by Lincoln's fear for the fate of slaves in Rebel states should he lose the election or be forced to conclude the war on terms short of complete abolition.

Douglass returned home and began making plans for the new underground railroad.[38] Douglass told Eaton that he was satisfied that Lincoln was doing all that circumstances permitted. From that date, Douglass's enthusiastic regard and support for Lincoln were apparent. Eaton wrote later that the encounter was an illustration of how Lincoln handled his critics, drawing them in to wrestle with problems as they looked from the presidential desk.[39] The letter Lincoln showed Douglass and the proposal for an underground railroad may have been devices for enlisting Douglass's involvement in the fate of the Lincoln administration; the encounter also indicates that Lincoln treated Douglass with respect. Less than one month later the outlook for the Union cause had improved. Sherman's capture of Atlanta turned the tide of the war and assured Lincoln's reelection.

Later in September, a letter written by Douglass the previous June was published in William Lloyd Garrison's *The Liberator*. In that letter Douglass had lashed out at the "*swindle* by which our Government claims the respect of mankind for abolishing slavery."[40] Douglass was disturbed that the letter had been printed. In a response to the editor, he pointed out, without retracting his criticism of Lincoln, that political circumstances had changed since June because of McClellan's nomination by the Democrats. "With this alternative clearly before us," Douglass wrote, "all hesitation ought to cease, and every man who wishes well to the slave and to the country should at once rally with all the warmth and earnestness of his nature to the support of Abraham Lincoln and Andrew Johnson, and to the utter defeat and political annihilation of George B. McClellan and Pendleton."[41]

Douglass did not campaign actively for Lincoln because, he said, the Republicans "did not wish to expose themselves to the charge of being the 'N—r' party."[42] He did express his views to the Colored National Convention, which met in Syracuse, New York, in the first week of October. In his "Address to the People of the United States," he sought to underscore the identity of interest between the freed black man and a unified, healthy United States. The address acknowledged Lincoln's antislavery sentiment but expressed alarm at the devious efforts of the Republican Party to hide that sentiment.[43]

Douglass attended the inaugural ceremony on 4 March 1865, and heard Lincoln make an unequivocal commitment to abolition. While the most often quoted portion of the speech is its last sentence, beginning, "With malice toward none; with charity for all," the section that most moved Douglass spelled out Lincoln's belief that Divine Providence intended slavery to be abolished. Transcending the cold, legalistic language of so many of his wartime utterances, including the Emancipation Proclamation, Lincoln declared:

> Fondly do we hope—fervently do we pray—that this mighty scourge of war may speedily pass away. Yet, if God wills that it continue, until all the wealth piled by the bond-man's two hundred and fifty years of unrequited toil shall be sunk, and until every drop of blood drawn with the lash, shall be paid by another drawn with the sword, as was said three thousand years ago, so still it must be said, "the judgments of the Lord, are true and righteous altogether."[44]

After the address, Douglass availed himself of the citizen's right to shake hands with the president at a White House reception in the

East Room. In the receiving line Lincoln told Douglass he had seen
him during the speech and asked how he liked it. Douglass hesitated,
not wishing to detain the president. "No, no," Lincoln said, "you
must stop a little, Douglass; there is no man in the country whose
opinion I value more than yours. I want to know what you think of
it." "Mr. Lincoln," Douglass replied, "that was a sacred effort." "I
am glad you liked it!" Lincoln said. Douglass passed on, "feeling that
any man, however distinguished, might well regard himself honored
by such expressions from such a man."[45] Douglass was perhaps
uniquely qualified among all the people in Lincoln's acquaintance to
comprehend and acknowledge the moral and political significance of
Lincoln's ascribing to Divine intent the Civil War as the instrument
for abolishing slavery.

As military victory approached and a committed abolitionist president stood at the beginning of a second four-year term, Douglass at
last regarded the black man's prospects with optimism. Two days
after the fall of Richmond, Douglass addressed a tumultuous victory
celebration in the abolitionist capital of Boston. He announced that
the Negro, the old Lazarus of the South, was rising. The slaveholder,
formerly the rich Dives of the South, seemed stunned at his change
of circumstance. Douglass told the audience:

> That rich man is lifting up his eyes in torments *down there* (tremen-
> dous applause), and seeing Lazarus afar off, in Abraham's bosom [tu-
> multuous laughter and applause], is all the time calling on Father
> Abraham to send Lazarus back. But Father Abraham say, "If they hear
> not Grant nor Sherman, neither will they be persuaded though I send
> Lazarus unto them." [prolonged and vociferous applause] I say we are
> way up yonder now, no mistake. [This was said with an expressive
> gesture, that called forth another outburst of applause.][46]

The previous day, 4 April, Abraham Lincoln had arrived unannounced in a rowboat at the fallen Rebel capital of Richmond and
was quickly surrounded by a crowd of black men, women, and children who hailed their emancipator. There was pandemonium as Lincoln walked up the hill to Jefferson Davis's mansion. There are
contradictory reports about what Lincoln said to the freedmen, but
the symbolism of the occasion was rich without words.[47] The sponta-
neous, Palm-Sunday-like processional in Richmond was followed by
assassination on Good Friday in Washington little more than a week

later. The *Atlantic Monthly* of June 1865, suggested that the resentment of Confederates toward Lincoln's reception may have been a motive for the assassination. When Lincoln removed his hat and bowed to the joyous blacks, "It was a bow which upset the forms, laws, customs, and ceremonies of centuries. It was a death-shock to chivalry, and a mortal wound to caste."[48]

When news of the assassination reached Rochester, Frederick Douglass warned his fellow townspeople not to be in too much haste to restore the Union of North and South. "Let us not be in a hurry to clasp to our bosom the spirit that gave birth to Booth. . . . When we take . . . as brethren, our Southern foes, let us see to it that we take also our Southern friends. Let us not forget that justice to the Negro is safety to the nation."[49]

Eleven years later, on 14 April 1876, Douglass delivered an address at the unveiling of the Freedmen's Memorial Monument to Lincoln. The speech was the black liberator's testament to the white emancipator, before an audience of common people and the nation's leaders, including President Grant. Lincoln was "preeminently the white man's President," Douglass explained, "ready and willing at any time during the first years of his administration to deny, postpone, and sacrifice the rights of humanity in the colored people to promote the welfare of the white people of this county." Black Americans, on the other hand, were his "step-children by adoption." For whites, Douglass declared, "Abraham Lincoln saved . . . a country, [but] he delivered us from a bondage, according to Jefferson, one hour of which was worse than ages of the oppression your fathers rose in rebellion to oppose." The black man's faith in Lincoln was often taxed and strained to the uttermost, but never failed. "When he tarried long in the mountain; when he strangely told us that we were to leave the land in which we were born; when he refused to employ our arms in defence of the union; when, after accepting our services as colored soldiers, he refused to retaliate our murder and torture as colored prisoners; when he told us he would save the Union if he could with slavery; when he revoked the Proclamation of Emancipation of General Fremont; . . . when we saw all this, and more, we were at times grieved, stunned, and greatly bewildered; but our hearts believed while they ached and bled." Black men measured him "by a broad survey, in the light of the stern logic of great events" and concluded that the "hour and the man of our redemption had somehow met in the person of Abraham Lincoln." Even Lincoln's white prejudice increased his ability to organize the loyal American people for two great objectives, to save the country from dismemberment and to save the country from the crime of slavery. Had Lincoln put the abolition of slavery before the salvation of the Union, Douglass admitted, he would not have been able to collect the powerful forces necessary to suppress the rebellion. "Viewed from the genuine abolition ground," Douglass said, "Mr. Lincoln seemed tardy, cold, dull, and indifferent; but measuring him by the sentiment of his country, a sentiment he was bound as a statesman to consult, he was swift, zealous, radical, and determined."[50]

Abraham Lincoln fought for the Union. Douglass fought for the abolition of slavery. Each viewed the other's issue in light of his own. The men and the issues came together at the climax of a Civil War that saved the Union and abolished slavery. Douglass was the spokesman for nearly 180,000 black men whose fighting Lincoln regarded as decisive in saving the Union.[51] Lincoln came to understand their struggle for freedom and his role as an instrument of their emancipation. From Douglass's perspective, Lincoln at last grasped the enormity of African chattel slavery, seeing it as destructive of the founding principles of the Republic as well as of the humanity of black Americans. Lincoln's teachers, we may surmise, included hard, irrepressible circumstances and men like Frederick Douglass who insisted that the equalitarian assumptions of the Declaration of Independence and the Constitution were at the heart of the struggle against the slaveholders. The figure of Frederick Douglass personified the insistent voice of black Americans.

We can never know whether Lincoln as President during Reconstruction would have moved to secure the political rights of the freedmen. But we are left with the distinct impression that the exchange between Lincoln and Douglass in the East Room, five weeks before the assassination, was a careful mutual attempt by two men, drawn inexorably together by great events, to grasp the majesty in their common cause and in their common humanity. How different Reconstruction might have been with a seasoned, politically skillful president who understood that the heart of the challenge facing the reunited nation was the black man in the condition of a citizen.

NOTES

1. Frederick Douglass was born Frederick Augustus Washington Bailey sometime in February 1817, in Talbot County, Maryland. He escaped from slavery in 1838, traveling in disguise by train from Baltimore to Philadelphia. As a laborer in New Bedford, Mass., he came in contact with William Lloyd Garrison and the abolitionist movement. From 1841 to 1847 Douglass was an active Garrisonian, lecturing to antislavery audiences throughout the North and in Britain. In 1847 he broke with Garrison and in Rochester, N.Y., began publishing his own abolitionist journal, *The North Star*. The name of the journal was changed to *Frederick Douglass' Paper* and then to *Frederick Douglass' Monthly*; it continued publication until August 1863. Douglass wrote three autobiographies, *Narrative of the Life of Frederick Douglass, an American Slave* (Boston: Anti-Slavery Office, 1845), *My Bondage and My Freedom* (New York: Miller, Orton & Mulligan, 1855), and *Life and Times of Frederick Douglass, Written by Himself* (first issued in 1881 by Park Publishing Co., Hartford, Conn., and revised in 1882, 1892, and 1893; the edition hereafter cited is the 1962 edition by Collier Books, N.Y., a reprint of the 1892 edition).

2. Philip S. Foner, ed., *Life and Writings of Frederick Douglass*, 4 vols. (New York: International Pub., 1950–55), 2:483–86, 520–25.

3. Douglass recalled throwing himself into the contest "with firmer faith and more ardent hope than ever before, and what I could do by pen or voice was done with a will" (Douglass, *Life and Times*, 327). That overstates Douglass's commitment to Lincoln in October 1860. For the ambiguity of Douglass's position in 1860, see Philip S. Foner, *Frederick Douglass: A Biography* (New York: Citadel Press, 1964), 184–86.

4. Foner, *Life and Writings*, 2:526–30.

5. Roy P. Basler, ed., Marion Dolores Pratt and Lloyd A. Dunlap, asst. eds., *The Collected Works of Abraham Lincoln*, 9 vols. (New Brunswick, N.J.: Rutgers University Press, 1953–55), 4:262–71 (hereafter, Basler, *Collected Works*).

6. Foner, *Life and Writings*, 3:71–80.

7. Ibid., 89–91.

8. Ibid., 94–96.

9. Ibid., 114–17.

10. Basler, *Collected Works*, 4:421–41.

11. Foner, *Life and Writings*, 3:159–62.

12. For Douglass's assessment of the reluctant progress of the government by the end of 1861, see ibid, 176–79.

13. Basler, *Collected Works*, 5:35–53. See Douglass's letter to Gerrit Smith, 22 December 1861, Foner, *Life and Writings*, 3:184.

14. Basler, *Collected Works*, 5:144–46. Lincoln anticipated this message in conversations with Carl Schurz in February; see Carl Schurz, *The Reminiscences of Carl Schurz*, 3 vols. (New York: McClure, 1907–08), 2:310–22.

15. Basler, *Collected Works*, 5:192; *Douglass' Monthly*, May 1862, quoted in Benjamin Quarles, *Frederick Douglass* (Washington, D.C.: Associated Pub., 1948), 194. According to Orville Hickman Browning, Lincoln waited until 16 April to sign the act, which had been passed on 11 April, because "Gov [sic] Wickliffe had two family servants with him who were sickly, and who would not be benefitted by freedom, and wanted time to remove them, but could not get them out of the City until Wednesday" (Theodore Calvin Pease and James G. Randall, eds., *Diary of Orville Hickman Browning, 1850–1864*, Collections of the Illinois State Historical Library, Vol. 20 [Springfield: Illinois State Historical Library, 1925], 541).

16. Foner, *Frederick Douglass*, 204.

17. Basler, *Collected Works*, 5:372–73.

18. Foner, *Life and Writings*, 3:266–70.

19. Lincoln made the remark in a letter to Horace Greeley, 22 August 1862 (Basler, *Collected Works*, 5:388–89; for text of Proclamation: 433–36).

20. For an analysis of the evolution of Lincoln's decision to issue the Emancipation Proclamation, see John Hope Franklin, *The Emancipation Proclamation* (Garden City, N.Y.: Doubleday, 1963), ch. 2.

21. Foner, *Life and Writings*, 3:273–77.

22. Basler, *Collected Works*, 5:518–37.

23. Ibid., 6:28–31.

24. Foner, *Life and Writings*, 3:321–37.

25. The broadside was issued at Rochester on 21 March 1863.

26. Foner, *Life and Writings*, 3:367–69.

27. Ibid., 369–72.

28. Basler, *Collected Works*, 6:357.

29. That account of their first visit is drawn from Douglass's recollections on two occasions; see Foner, *Life and Writings*, 3:378–86, and Douglass, *Life and Times*, 346–49.

30. Foner, *Life and Writings*, 3:374–77.

31. Frederic May Holland, *Frederick Douglass: The Colored Orator* (New York: Funk & Wagnalls, 1891), 302–3. For other analyses of the commission incident, see Douglass, *Life and Times*, 349–50; Foner, *Frederick Douglass*, 217–19; and Benjamin Quarles, *Lincoln and the Negro* (New York: Oxford University Press, 1962), 212.

32. Foner, *Life and Writings*, 3:386–403.

33. Ibid.

34. Foner, *Frederick Douglass*, 224–25.

35. Basler, *Collected Works*, 7:243.

36. John Eaton, *Grant, Lincoln and the Freedmen: Reminiscences of the Civil War, with Special Reference to the Work for the Contrabands and Freedmen of the Mississippi Valley* (New York: Longmans, Green, 1907), 173–76. Shortly after Douglass died, Eaton eulogized him and relayed Lincoln's assessment of Douglass with a slightly different and more flattering twist: "Considering the conditions from which he had arisen and the obstacles that he had overcome, and the position to which he had attained . . . [Lincoln regarded Douglass as] one of the most meritorious men, if not the most meritorious man in the United States" (Eaton, *In Memoriam: Frederick Douglass* [Philadelphia: n.p., 1897], 70–71, quoted in Foner, *Frederick Douglass*, 224–25).

37. Basler, *Collected Works*, 7:451. The account of the visit is from Douglass's letter to Theodore Tilton, 15 October 1864, in Foner, *Life and Writings*, 3:422–24.

38. Douglass's liberation plans were sent in a letter to Lincoln, dated 29 August 1864, quoted in Foner, *Life and Writings*, 3:405–6.

39. Eaton, *Grant, Lincoln and the Freedmen*, 175.

40. Foner, *Life and Writings*, 3:404.

41. Ibid., 406–7.

42. Ibid., 422–24.

43. Ibid., 408–22.

44. Basler, *Collected Works*, 8:333.

45. The account is from Douglass, *Life and Times*, 365–66. Elizabeth Keckley, the black modiste to Mary Todd Lincoln, reported seeing Douglass at a friend's house after the meeting with Lincoln. She recalled the following account by a pleased and happy Douglass: "Mr. Douglass stood face to face with the President. Mr. Lincoln pressed his hand warmly, saying: 'Mr. Douglass, I am glad to meet you. I have long admired your course, and I value your opinions highly'" (Keckley, *Behind the Scenes: Or Thirty Years a Slave, and Four Years in the White House* [New York: Carleton, 1868], 159–60).

46. *Boston Daily Journal*, 5 April 1865.

47. There are several accounts of the Richmond visit, some indicating that Lincoln made no public remarks, others quoting him directly. Certainly the most remarkable report of a speech comes from Isaac J. Hill, *A Sketch of the 29th Regiment of Connecticut Colored Troops* (New York: Daugherty, Maguire, 1867), 27. Lincoln is alleged by Hill to have said: "In reference to you, colored people, let me say God has made you free. Although you have been deprived of your God-given rights by your so-called masters, you are now as free as I am, and if those that claim to be your superiors do not know that you are free, take the sword and bayonet and teach them that you are—for God created all men free, giving to each the same rights of life,

liberty and the pursuit of happiness." Some doubt must be cast upon that source because the entire preceding account by Hill of his supposed observations of Lincoln's landing and being surrounded, up to the alleged speech, is a verbatim repetition of 'Carleton's' article for the *Boston Daily Journal* of 8 April, except for alteration of black dialect to standard English. 'Carleton' was Charles Carleton Coffin, a correspondent for the *Boston Daily Journal*, who included the event in his memoir, *The Boys of '61* . . . (Boston: Estes and Lauriat, 1881), 510–14. He makes no reference to any speech by Lincoln. Admiral David D. Porter, who accompanied Lincoln and apparently was at his side during the processional, reported in his memoir, *Incidents and Anecdotes of the Civil War* (New York: Appleton, 1885), 297–98: "At length [Lincoln] spoke. He could not move for the mass of people—he had to do something. 'My poor friends,' he said, 'You are free—free as air. You can cast off the name of slave and trample upon it; it will come to you no more. Liberty is your birthright. God gave it to you as he gave it to others, and it is a sin that you have been deprived of it for so many years. But you must try to deserve this priceless boon. Let the world see that you merit it, and are able to maintain it by your good works. Don't let your joy carry you into excesses. Learn the laws and obey them; obey God's commandments and thank him for giving you liberty, for to him you owe all things. There, now, let me pass on; I have but little time to spare. I want to see the capital, and must return at once to Washington to secure to you that liberty which you seem to prize so highly.' " Porter also was convinced that John Wilkes Booth was the man who unsuccessfully tried to deliver a message to Lincoln on board the *Malvern*, the night after the Richmond visit. (303) The problem merits further pursuit to discover Lincoln's attitudes toward the future position of blacks in the South and any unusual verbal provocation he might have given the white South in their fallen capital.

48. "Late Scenes in Richmond . . . Visit of President Lincoln," *Atlantic Monthly*, June 1865, 753–55.

49. Amy Hammer-Croughton, *Anti-Slavery Days in Rochester*, Rochester Historical Society Publications, Vol. 14 (Rochester: Rochester Historical Society, 1936), 151–52, quoted in Foner, *Frederick Douglass*, 233 and 415n. 53.

50. Foner, *Life and Writings*, 4:309–19.

51. Looking back on Lincoln's attentions to him, Douglass said, "While I have no doubt that Messrs. Seward and Chase had spoken well of me to him, and the fact of my having been a slave, and gained my freedom, and of having picked up some sort of an education, and being in some sense a 'self-made man,' and having made myself useful as an advocate of the claims of my people, gave me favor in his eyes; yet I am quite sure that the main thing which gave me consideration with him was my well known relation to

the colored people of the Republic, and especially the help which that relation enabled me to give to the work of suppressing the rebellion and of
placing the Union on a firmer basis than it ever had or could have sustained
in the days of slavery" (Douglass, *Life and Times*, 360). On another occasion,
Douglass accounted for Lincoln's kindness to him "because of the similarity
with which I had fought my way up, we both starting at the lowest round of
the ladder" (Douglass, "Lincoln and the Colored Troops," in *Reminiscences
of Abraham Lincoln by Distinguished Men of His Time*, ed. Allen Thorndike
Rice, rev. ed. [New York: Harper, 1909], 315–25).

2
LINCOLN AND PRESIDENTIAL POLITICS

6

Lincoln's Wartime Leadership: The First Hundred Days

Don E. Fehrenbacher

A LETTER FROM INDIANA, arriving at the White House in late June 1861, must have pleased and amused Abraham Lincoln. For one thing, its spelling was worse than his own:

> To His honor the president of this United States of America Mr Abraham Lincoln. you Will pleas pardon Me for taking the Liberty of Addressing you Apon this ocasion. Honorable Sir, having had the plesur of Casting my Ballot for you the second father of My Country, I hav seen fitt to Name My youngest Son, Abraham Lincoln Tudor. he was Born february the 8th 1861 and Was Duly Crisond on the fourth of March of the same. Sir you May think it strange of Me taking this liberty but sir lett me asure you, that the Love for My Country and the presant choise of its Cheafe Executiv has Induced Me to Take the Corse I have. As a Mechanic and An American I feel that All i can bequeath to him is his good Name and fitt him for his Country to the best of My Ability. I have An other Son George Washington. With those glorious Names Recorded in My Bible I feel Confident of There success in life hoping dear sir you Will Take No Offence of the liberty I have taken or of my remarks hear I have Made and With your Best Wishes for my little Linky, I Remain your humble Servent.
>
> Jacob L. Tudor[1]

Mr. Tudor may well have been the first person to place Lincoln beside Washington in the national pantheon. Today they remain the two greatest heroes of the Republic, honored for what they did, what they said, what they were, and what they have become in American memory and imagination. But this preeminence, however much it reflects personal character, is obviously related also to the historical setting of their respective careers. Coming to prominence in times of crisis and unusual opportunity, they were to exercise supreme leadership at the two greatest turning points of American history. And how much of a *difference* did each of these men make? Was Washington indeed the "indispensable man," as his biographer James Thomas Flexner has labeled him? To what extent did Lincoln determine, or at least strongly affect, the course of events? The net influence of the individual in history is a problem so complex that it defies satisfactory solution and yet so important that it demands earnest attention.

Presumably, every human life exerts some measure of causal force in history. Any person who exerts a significant amount of such force and does so principally by influencing other persons is commonly called a leader. Leadership, to be sure, does not fall easily within the confines of a single definition. In some contexts, for instance, the word means a quality of personal character; in others, a pattern of individual behavior. As a social phenomenon, however, leadership is essentially a special kind of power—one marked less by command and obedience than by interaction.

Power, pure and simple, is control over the behavior of other people. It is a relation in which influence flows largely in one direction, and the purposes or goals of the behavior induced are primarily those of the power-wielder. *Leadership* is a more complex relation because influence flows reciprocally between leaders and followers, and there is an assimilation or sharing of purposes. True leaders do not dictate, says James MacGregor Burns. Instead, they engage and activate "the fundamental needs, wants, aspirations, and expectations" of their followers. Leadership is thus a mobilizing rather than a coercive force, uniquely capable of exploiting mass social energies and therefore more likely than naked power to have "lasting causal influence as measured by real change."[2]

The measure of leadership, according to Burns, is the "degree of production of intended effects."[3] And successful leadership proceeds through more or less distinct stages: selection of purpose or goal, mobilization of collective effort, and achievement of purpose. Motive and capacity blend into accomplishment.

Of course it is not all that simple or rational. Leadership may proceed not directly but obliquely or circuitously toward its goal. It may even be exercised not in purposive action but rather in deliberate inaction. Crucial leadership decisions are often expressions of individual personality rather than being objective, rational choices from carefully surveyed alternatives. And leaders can seldom escape for long the necessity of resolving conflicts or assigning priorities among multiple purposes. There are times when leaders play only contributory or passive roles in actions initiated or decisions worked out by subordinates. Important decisions, moreover, are not always made in one piece at one time. They may instead develop in increments as trains of lesser decisions, with responsibility dispersed and leadership consequently hard to identify. Finally, there is the problem of discerning the causal limits of leadership in any particular situation—that is, the problem of discriminating between events within the control and events beyond the control of identifiable persons associated with those events.

Even outstanding leadership is often unsuccessful. The best laid plans and mightiest efforts may fail to produce the intended effects. But it is also true (and perhaps more important to historians) that leadership, like all human actions, often has unintended consequences. And even intended consequences may in turn produce unintended but important secondary effects. Also, the means adopted to achieve a certain purpose sometimes have effects that overshadow the original purpose. So the total historical influence of a leader is not necessarily proportionate to his or her intended achievements, even if such achievements are the proper measure of leadership. For sound assessment of a person's role in history, one needs to consider all the significant consequences—fully intended, partly intended, and unintended—of that person's presence on earth. In the case of leaders of the first rank, the consequences are likely to reach large numbers of people and extend over long periods.

Lincoln's positive achievements are commonly summed up in the assertion that he "saved the Union and freed the slaves." To those two historical consequences, flowing from his leadership, one might want to add that Lincoln profoundly influenced the character of the presidency and, in doing so, significantly modified the American constitutional system. But notice the differing degrees of intent in each of the three historical effects.

Lincoln's prime commitment to restoration of the Union, his mobilization of the war effort, his eloquence in rationalizing the national purpose, and the total triumph achieved at Appomattox—all together, these constitute an almost perfect model of purposive, effective leadership.

Emancipation was a different and more complex matter, however. Formally renounced as part of the national purpose at the beginning of the war,[4] it became only gradually a secondary objective, ostensibly justified as a means to the always primary end of victory and reunion. Many historians believe that Lincoln came to emancipation under pressure, as a matter of necessity rather than choice. And he himself disclaimed leadership in the freeing and arming of slaves. "I claim not to have controlled events," he said, "but confess plainly that events have controlled me."[5] There are other scholars, to be sure, who regard the disclaimer as part of a subtle strategy whereby Lincoln led the way while seeming to follow the lead of others. Nevertheless, emancipation must be regarded as an achievement at first intended only vaguely and tentatively, if at all.

As for Lincoln's extraordinary expansion of presidential power, which he defended with a constitutional argument that gave startling new meaning to the commander-in-chief clause, there is no deliberate intent, no purposive leadership visible at all. Lincoln had taken the professions of law and politics as he found them, and he never evinced any desire to remodel the presidency. His bold exercise of unprecedented executive authority was strictly a wartime means to a wartime end. Yet, as a political and constitutional precedent, it had consequences no less momentous than if remodeling the presidency had been his primary goal in life.

Lincoln's presidential career was bounded at one end by the secession crisis and at the other end by the cluster of problems associated with reconstruction. It was also complicated by the increasing entanglement of slavery and emancipation with the conduct of the war. Thus great moral issues of war and peace, of racial oppression and human rights, intrude upon any effort at a comprehensive evaluation of his leadership. The question of how capably he handled the Fort Sumter crisis, for instance, is overshadowed by the intrinsically unanswerable question of whether he was morally right in forcing the issue there at the high risk of war.

There may be some advantage, then, in examining Lincoln's presidential leadership over the limited period of one hundred days between the firing on Fort Sumter and the first battle of Bull Run—a time when the issue of war and peace had already been decided, and when the issues of emancipation, reconstruction, and the racial future of the nation had not yet become matters of urgent public concern.

During his first six weeks in office, Lincoln was more or less a prisoner of the circumstances inherited from his predecessor. To be sure, in his inaugural he emphatically rejected secession and declared that it would mean civil war, but he had no means of bringing any significant force to bear against the seceders. There was neither sufficient military power nor sufficient public support for an effort to disperse the new Confederate government and coerce the seceded states back into the Union.

The United States in early 1861 had a widely scattered, poorly equipped army of sixteen thousand men, with an officers corps shot through with sympathy for the Confederacy. The militia system had been allowed to become dilapidated; in many states it was little more than a public joke.

Congress had done nothing to prepare for possible civil war, not even in the secession winter of 1860–61, when it was preoccupied with futile schemes for sectional compromise. On 11 December, incredibly, with South Carolina already preparing to secede, the Senate passed a resolution asking the War Department whether military expenses could not be further reduced. In the House of Representatives, a bill authorizing the president to employ the militia and accept volunteers to suppress insurrection was not acted upon.[6]

Lincoln's options in those first six weeks were therefore few, especially since he had chosen, in a significant act of negative leadership, *not* to call Congress immediately into special session. He did draft, on 18 March, an order to the secretary of war for appointment of an "Inspector General of Militia" and the creation of a separate military bureau that would be responsible for "promoting a uniform system of organization, drill, equipment, &c. of the U.S. Militia." But he abandoned the plan when Attorney General Edward Bates advised him that he had no power to establish such an office.[7]

Lincoln's only opportunity for significant decision was in respect of the Southern forts still in federal hands, especially Fort Sumter. There, as of 4 March, he had three options: an effort at forcible resupply and reinforcement, peaceable evacuation, and postponement of action. By early April, the third option was running out. It is not accurate to say categorically that Lincoln at this point chose war in preference to withdrawal. He did reject peaceable evacuation, but he would have settled for further postponement. So, trying to thread the needle, he offered the Confederates another alternative to war: peaceable resupply without reinforcement.

In retrospect, it appears that the Confederates would have been wise to accept the option, for the effect would have been to continue the Lincoln administration in its condition of relative helplessness. But, in the setting of feverish excitement and bitter suspicion, perhaps acceptance would have been impossible, even if Jefferson Davis and his cabinet had resolved upon it.

At any rate, the firing on Fort Sumter, which brought to an end the antebellum period of American history, radically altered Lincoln's responsibilities and the nature of his leadership: first, because of its energizing effect on northern public opinion; second, because, as an act of war, it provided a constitutional basis for vigorous executive action that had hitherto been lacking; and third, because, coming as it did when Congress was not in session, the Fort Sumter episode gave Lincoln the opportunity to seize the initiative from the legislative branch—an initiative that he never relinquished.

Historians have given much attention to the role of presidential leadership in bringing the nation to each of its wars: James K. Polk's ordering Zachary Taylor to the banks of the Rio Grande, for instance; Lincoln and Fort Sumter; Woodrow Wilson and German submarine warfare; Franklin D. Roosevelt and Pearl Harbor; Lyndon Johnson and the Gulf of Tonkin resolution. But historians have given less systematic and comparative attention to presidential leadership in determining, once war has come, precisely what kind of war it should be.

Thus, whatever may be said about the causes of the war with Mexico, it was the Polk administration that promptly sent Stephen Watts Kearney marching westward to New Mexico and California, converting a boundary conflict into a war of conquest. And when Congress declared war on Spain in April 1898, the McKinley administration was ready with its imperialistic decision to carry the fight for Cuban freedom into the waters of Manila Bay.

But those were foreign wars and relatively simple matters compared with the tangled web of circumstances that Lincoln faced in the period of precisely one hundred days between the firing on Fort Sumter and the first Battle of Bull Run. For one thing, secession resumed, swallowing up Virginia, North Carolina, Tennessee, and Arkansas, and threatening to gain the upper hand in Maryland, Kentucky, and Missouri. The boundary between the old United States and the new Confederate States thus shifted northward, but it continued to be blurred. For several weeks after the fall of Fort Sumter, Washington itself seemed to be in danger of capture. The air was filled with rumors of an impending Confederate attack, to be aided by an uprising of Southern sympathizers within the city.[8] According to one report, Mrs. Jefferson Davis was sending out invitations to a reception to be held in the White House on 1 May.[9] By that date, in fact, enough troops had arrived from the North to make the capital reasonably secure.

Civil war always entails the difficult, painful necessity of sorting out loyalties, and there were few guidelines for governmental procedure in such a crisis. The very nature of the war was unclear, and the legal status of the Confederates was consequently in doubt. Sooner or later, the Lincoln administration would have to decide whether to treat them as foreign enemies or as domestic traitors.

Furthermore, although the attack on Fort Sumter aroused the North, it did not unite *all* Northerners for defense of the Union. Many Democrats agreed with a Maine editor who denounced "this unholy and unjustifiable war" launched for the purpose of "subjugation and tyranny."[10] One New York newspaper advised Lincoln that the way to restore peace was to issue a proclamation saying that he accepted and would enforce the Dred Scott decision.[11] Another insisted that Southerners were simply claiming the same right exercised by the thirteen colonies in the Revolution. "Let us learn from the Confederate States what they demand," it proposed, "and if consistent with national honor, grant it and let them go in peace."[12] Even some members of Lincoln's own party had begun to draw back at the thought of armed conflict. On the day after the surrender of Fort Sumter, for instance, a Massachusetts Republican wrote to Secretary of State William H. Seward, declaring that the administration must "avoid all use of force" because war would surely mean "death to the Union."[13]

More numerous and troublesome than the peace advocates were the war enthusiasts, who demanded virtually an immediate military offensive and swift punishment of the Rebels. "Carry the War South," trumpeted the *New York Times*. "Action! action! is the watchword." An army of twenty-five thousand, it said, should advance directly on Richmond and end the war in sixty days.[14] Horace Greeley's *New*

York Tribune called for the capture of Richmond before the Confederate Congress met there, as it was scheduled to, on 20 July.[15] The *New York Herald* estimated that total victory might take as much as six months,[16] and the *Chicago Tribune* more or less agreed. In late May, under the headline "Forward March," the *Tribune* declared: "The 4th of July should and can be celebrated by the two patriotic armies in Richmond and Memphis. The fall and winter campaign will then close the war and crush the serpent's head."[17]

Lincoln's original call for seventy-five thousand troops was widely viewed as far too modest. That would not be enough, said a Seward correspondent, to "bring every traitor to the rope's end."[18] The president of the University of Michigan wrote to Lincoln advising that five grand armies, each one hundred thousand strong, should be sent marching toward the strategic centers of the Confederacy to finish the work quickly.[19] The figure five hundred thousand was frequently specified as the total number of men needed. The public at large seemed to have little understanding of the enormous effort that would be required just to raise, equip, train, and feed such a military force, let alone move it into decisive battle.

There were also angry demands that the administration deal more severely with the agents of rebellion, that it root disloyalty out of the Army and Navy and out of the Washington bureaucracy, and that captured Rebels be summarily punished instead of being released after taking a worthless oath. "By no government in the wide world other than ours," said the *New York Times*, "is treason treated so kindly or rebellion sprinkled with so much rosewater."[20] From Detroit, a local Republican politician wrote to Lincoln: "The People of Michigan think the time has come to commence hanging & so think I."[21] In most of this outpouring, the obvious difficulty of imposing such a draconian program within the limits of the Constitution was conveniently ignored.

Thus, in what remained of the United States, the weeks after the firing on Fort Sumter were a time of incredibly unrealistic expectations in the presence of problems unprecedented in their magnitude and urgency—all confronting a new president fresh from a provincial capital in the hinterland and with his shirttail barely tucked in; a chief executive who had never held any kind of administrative position; a commander-in-chief with military experience only as an Indian fighter who self-admittedly never saw a live, fighting Indian, although he did claim to have had a good many bloody battles with mosquitoes.[22]

It is not surprising that many observers at home and abroad should have regarded Lincoln as a man patently out of his depth in a crisis of such magnitude. To the *London Times*, for instance, he seemed weak, dilatory, and destined to be more of a follower than a leader in the conduct of the government.[23] Yet the very confusion of circumstances, the very uniqueness and urgency of the problems confronting him, amounted to a slate wiped clean, offering an extraordinary opportunity for the exercise of leadership. How did Lincoln respond? *Decisively*, beyond question. Within the first three weeks following the attack on Fort Sumter:

- He issued proclamations of a blockade, dated 19 and 27 April, that were tantamount to declaring the existence of a state of civil war.[24]
- He initiated preparations for waging war, calling for seventy-five thousand ninety-day militia under an act of 1795, calling for forty-two thousand three-year volunteers, and ordering the enrollment of an additional forty thousand men in the regular Army and Navy.[25]
- He ordered the charter or purchase of about twenty steamships by the Navy, to be armed for coastal-waters defense.[26]
- He directed the secretary of the treasury to advance, without security, $2 million to three private citizens of New York, to be used for expenditures in connection with military recruiting and the arming and transporting of troops.[27]
- He authorized General Winfield Scott to suspend the writ of habeas corpus along the line of military transportation from Philadelphia to Washington, via Annapolis. Later (2 July), the suspension was extended to New York City.[28]
- He called Congress into special session, but at the late date of 4 July, thereby retaining a free hand for an additional two and one-half months.[29]

No other president had ever claimed and exercised so much new power within so short a span of time. But of course decisiveness is not the same thing as effectiveness. How *effective* was Lincoln's leadership in the hundred days between Fort Sumter and Bull Run?

With war virtually declared, his primary task had obviously become a military one: to oversee the raising and equipping of a sufficient military force, design a strategy for suppression of the rebellion, and put both into action as quickly as possible.

The military enterprise was also in many respects a political and economic, even a diplomatic, enterprise. For instance, the raising of more than a half-million troops during the first year of the war involved the administration in some complicated relationships with the state governors. The equiping of troops involved the administration in an even more complex network of relationships with a host of suppliers and purchasing agents. And in distributing the military patronage, Lincoln felt constrained to gratify all of the constituencies upon which he was depending for support of the war effort—including, for example, loyal Democrats and various ethnic groups. (Lincoln's political generals were not, on the whole, a very successful lot, but then the same can be said of a good many professional generals as well. For every Ben Butler there was a Burnside, and it took time for the emergence to full view of Grant, Sherman, Sheridan, and Thomas. In any case, given the system of raising troops, it would have been impossible to avoid appointing a good many civilian leaders to command positions.)

In raising an army, Lincoln had to rely heavily upon the state governors and upon his secretary of war, Simon Cameron, who proved unequal to his responsibilities. Cameron's appointment, an unwise concession to political expediency, is strong evidence that Lincoln did not come to the presidency expecting a real civil war. The president corrected his mistake as soon as he could decently do so—in mid-January 1862—sending Cameron about as far away as possible, to the American ministry in St. Petersburg.

In the disposition of military forces, Lincoln relied heavily upon his military commanders, especially the head of the Army, seventy-five-year-old Winfield Scott. Yet, he did not accept Scott's grand strategy for winning the war as painlessly as possible: the "anaconda plan." Or, to be more accurate, Lincoln embraced the positive aspects of the plan (blockade of Southern ports and a drive for control of the Mississippi all the way to New Orleans), but he eventually rejected its negative aspects, which would have entailed adopting a defensive posture on the Virginia front and sitting tight until Unionist sentiment got the upper hand in the South.[30] It seems unlikely that the anaconda plan could have succeeded; it seems *certain* that Northern public opinion in its aroused state would not have permitted a sustained implementation of the plan.

The Lincoln administration's formulation of a policy in response to secession well exemplifies decision making as an incremental process and leadership as a concentrated expression of popular will. There can be little doubt that Lincoln was committed from the beginning of the secession crisis to preservation of the Union by force if necessary. But only gradually did the amount and kind of force to be applied become clear. In his inaugural, he asserted only a very limited purpose: "The power confided to me, will be used to hold, occupy, and possess the property, and places belonging to the government, and to collect the duties and imposts; but beyond what may be necessary for these objects, there will be no invasion—no using of force against, or among the people anywhere."[31] After the attack on Fort Sumter, he went further, declaring an intent to reclaim it and other federal forts seized by the Confederates. That, he announced in his proclamation of 15 April, would be the first task assigned to the seventy-five thousand militia he was calling to active duty.[32] Yet at the same time he continued to assure various Southerners that his intentions were purely defensive. "I have no objection to declare a thousand times," he wrote to Reverdy Johnson of Maryland ten days after the fall of Sumter, "that I have no purpose to *invade* Virginia or any other State, but I do not mean to let them invade us without striking back."[33]

Seventy-five thousand ninety-day militia certainly did not constitute a strong enough force with which to launch a general offensive against the Confederacy. And when Lincoln, on 3 May, issued another proclamation calling for additional volunteers and enlistments, that too might have been regarded as essentially defensive in nature, although he did specify that the additional troops were needed to suppress "insurrectionary combinations now existing in several States."[34] Even the first military actions, such as the seizing of Alexandria and the clearing of West Virginia, could be justified as efforts to safeguard Washington and the Baltimore and Ohio Railroad, respectively. And all of these things certainly would have fitted in with the anaconda concept of limited warfare. By the time of his message to Congress on 4 July, however, Lincoln had moved on to the point of projecting an all-out war. "It is now recommended," he said, "that you give the legal means for making this contest a short, and a decisive one; that you place at the control of the government, for the work, at least four hundred thousand men, and four hundred millions of dollars."[35]

In viewing Lincoln's progress from a strategy of defense to a strategy of total war, one can see him as the mere echo of public opinion, or, at the other extreme, as a Machiavellian schemer resolved all along to mount a full-scale war. From the evidence, however, I get the impression of a man feeling his way uncertainly to a plan of action, guided in some degree by his advisers and by public feeling, but influenced most by his own reading of the situation.

The formal decision to undertake a military offensive in the summer of 1861 was essentially Lincoln's, overriding the reluctance of his top generals. The reports from the battlefront were favorable at first. The New York Times of 22 July carried the headline: "Victory at Bull's Run—Sumter Avenged." Then, on the next day, the headline became: "Disaster to the National Army." The Times brazenly laid the blame on "popular clamor, promoted by certain reckless journals" with their "senseless and incessant cry of 'Onward to Richmond.'" But the ultimate responsibility for the humiliating defeat obviously lay with Lincoln. "The impression here is very general," wrote Charles Francis Adams Jr. to his father in England, "that Scott's policy was interfered with by the President in obedience to what he calls the popular will."[36] There was also some feeling that Lincoln had risked God's displeasure by allowing a major battle to be fought on a Sunday.[37]

Yet the decision to launch an attack, however much it may have been influenced by the public clamor for action, was probably sound. The Union forces had a numerical superiority, and General Irvin McDowell's plan of battle was well conceived. With a little luck, the outcome might have been a victory. The widespread belief that the war could be ended swiftly with a few bold strokes *had* to be tested. This was the first opportunity to do so, and here, as in the case of Fort Sumter, there was probably more to be lost by inaction (a decline of public morale, for instance, and perhaps European recognition of the Confederacy) than by action, whatever its result.

The defeat, although bitterly unwelcome, proved salutary in some ways. It defined the war in realistic terms for the North and dissolved the fantasies of quick victory. A grimmer resoluteness set in, and preparation for the real war began. "If this is to be a war of years instead of months, let it be so," declared the Chicago Tribune.[38] Indeed, the Northern response to this shocking setback was full of portent; for, given the great superiority of the North in manpower and material, the outcome of the war may have depended less on Union victories than on the Northern capacity to sustain defeat.

In the first weeks after the firing on Fort Sumter, however, the primary task of raising a great army and sending it into battle seemed less urgent than a problem that required both military and political action, delicately combined. That was the necessity of holding the loyalty of the Great Border, especially Maryland, Kentucky, and Missouri. In this difficult enterprise, Lincoln's guiding hand was always visible, and his political skill was put to one of its severest tests.

Different circumstances dictated the adoption of different policies in each state. Maryland, where pro-Confederate violence temporarily isolated Washington, was held in the Union primarily by force, seasoned with political persuasion. The loss of Kentucky was prevented, in contrast, by a policy of patience and lenience in which Lincoln's role was especially prominent. In Missouri, the administration had less control over its own agents and less success. The state became a battleground and had to be subdued by military conquest that might have been avoided if more prudent policies had prevailed.

Still another urgent problem at the beginning of the hundred days was the danger of foreign intervention in a manner favorable to the Confederacy. The magnitude of that danger is difficult to estimate, but high British officials had certainly threatened serious action if the cotton trade were interrupted. It seems likely that the emphatic, even bellicose, response of the Lincoln administration to the talk about intervention discouraged the British from going beyond their recognition of Confederate belligerency in May. By late June, Charles Francis Adams, American minister to England, could report that such aggressiveness had produced a healthy change in the attitudes of British officialdom.[39]

This, to be sure, was largely the work of William H. Seward rather than Abraham Lincoln, but not entirely so. The two men discussed foreign policy frequently, and Lincoln more than once exercised a restraining influence upon his adventurous secretary of state. For one thing, right at the beginning he had thrown a blanket of quiet rejection over Seward's plan for reuniting the Republic by precipitating a foreign war.[40] For another, he intervened to soften the impact of Seward's famous Dispatch Number 10 to Adams (21 May), not only by moderating its language, but also by altering the means of its presentation.[41]

Thus, under Lincoln's leadership during the period from Fort Sumter to Bull Run, there was a mixture of general success with some specific failures in the raising and fielding of an army, in the struggle for the Great Border, and in resistance to foreign intervention. Furthermore, one notes considerable variation in his active input from one category to another. He took fullest charge of the border state policy, which called for so much political sensitivity and skill. He shared with General Scott and other experts the responsibility of directing military policy, for in that realm he was still very much of a learner. And, except at rare moments, he played a passive, consultative role in the conduct of foreign policy. But these variations illustrate the varieties of leadership and its essentially *interactive* quality, including the capacity to delegate authority without utterly relinquishing it. The members of the cabinet knew who was in charge, whatever amount of departmental autonomy they were allowed. "Executive skill and vigor are rare qualities," Seward wrote in early June. "The President is the best of us."[42]

In venturing that estimate, Seward was speaking for a small minority, however. Far more Americans of 1861, in Washington and elsewhere, believed that they had a good-natured, well-intentioned mediocrity in the White House. That impression persisted to the very end of Lincoln's life, even among many persons who knew him well. But there were others among his contemporaries who came, quickly or gradually, to perceive the peculiarly appropriate quality of his leadership in the nation's most critical hour. Who came to appreciate, for instance, Lincoln's capacity for eloquence and for plain talk when either was needed. Who came to realize how effectively he combined tenacity of purpose with flexibility of method. Who came to understand that without arrogance he had confidence in his own powers, and without sentimentality he had faith in the people.

Faith in the people—the common people. The best leadership is creative interaction, and perhaps Lincoln was thinking just a little about Jacob Tudor and George Washington Tudor and Abraham Lincoln Tudor when, in his message to Congress of 4 July 1861, he made his first public effort to define the meaning of the war: "This," he said, "is essentially a People's contest. On the side of the Union, it is a struggle for maintaining in the world, that form, and substance of government, whose leading object is, to elevate the condition of men—to lift artificial weights from all shoulders—to clear the paths of laudable pursuit for all—to afford all, an unfettered start, and a fair chance, in the race of life."[43]

NOTES

1. In a postscript, Tudor indicated that he was giving the letter to his congressman, William S. Holman (a Democrat) for delivery by hand. Jacob L. Tudor to Lincoln, 23 June 1861, Robert Todd Lincoln Collection, Manuscript Division, Library of Congress. The letter is published in David C. Mearns, ed., *The Lincoln Papers: The Story of the Collection with Selections to July 4, 1861*, 2 vols. (Garden City, N.Y.: Doubleday, 1948), 2: 638.

2. "Political Leadership in America: A Discussion with James MacGregor Burns," *The Center Magazine* 13 (July–August 1980): 10; James MacGregor Burns, *Leadership* (New York: Harper, 1978), 439. See also Burns, "Wellsprings of Political Leadership," *American Political Science Review* 71 (1977): 273–75; Andrew S. McFarland, *Power and Leadership in Pluralist Systems* (Stanford, Calif.: Stanford University Press, 1969), 153–76.

3. Burns, *Leadership*, 22.

4. Most notably by implication in the Crittenden and Johnson resolutions passed by the House of Representatives and the Senate on 22 and 25 July 1861. But for the limited significance of the resolutions, see Herman Belz, *Reconstructing the Union: Theory and Policy during the Civil War* (Ithaca, N.Y.: Cornell University Press, 1969), 24–28.

5. Roy P. Basler, ed., Marion Dolores Pratt and Lloyd A. Dunlap, asst. eds., *The Collected Works of Abraham Lincoln*, 9 vols. (New Brunswick, N.J.: Rutgers University Press, 1953–55), 7:282 (hereafter, Basler, *Collected Works*). It is important to note, however, that Lincoln made this statement in a letter to a Kentucky editor.

6. U.S. House of Representatives. *Congressional Globe*, 36th Cong., 2d sess., 1860, 46, 1001, 1225–32.

7. Basler, *Collected Works*, 4:291–92.

8. *New York Herald*, 25, 30 April 1861; Charles Keating Tuckerman to William H. Seward, 13 April; James H. Bostwick to Seward, 14 April; J. E. Hadnett to Seward, 15 April; P. H. Cooney to Thomas C. Theaker, 20 April 1861, William H. Seward Papers, University of Rochester; James Henderson to Lincoln, 16 April; Neal Dow to Lincoln, 22 April 1861, Robert Todd Lincoln Collection.

9. William Holdredge to Seward, 17 April 1861, Seward Papers.

10. *Bangor Democrat*, 18 April 1861, quoted in Herbert Mitgang, ed., *Lincoln, as They Saw Him* (New York: Rinehart, 1956), 256–57.

11. *New York Evening Day Book*, 18 April 1861.

12. *New York Journal of Commerce*, quoted in *New York Times*, 16 April 1861.

13. J. M. Churchill to Seward, April 15, 1861, Seward Papers.

14. *New York Times*, 18, 20, 21, 22 April 1861.

15. *New York Tribune*, 1 June 1861. On 19 June, a *Tribune* editorial declared: "The war should be closed in triumph within one year from the time it commenced."

16. *New York Herald*, 24 April 24 1861.

17. *Chicago Tribune*, 23 May 1861.

18. George W. Patterson to Seward, 18 April 1861, Seward Papers.

19. Henry P. Tappan to Lincoln, 19 April 1861, Robert Todd Lincoln Collection.

20. *New York Times*, 30 June 1861.

21. B. Chandler to Lincoln, 15 June 1861, Robert Todd Lincoln Collection.

22. Basler, *Collected Works*, 1:510.

23. *London Times*, 20 May 1861.

24. Basler, *Collected Works*, 4:388–39, 346–47.

25. Ibid., 331–32, 353–54.

26. Ibid., 5:241.

27. Ibid., 242.

28. Ibid., 4:347, 419.

29. Ibid., 332.

30. *The War of the Rebellion: A Compilation of the Official Records of the Union and Confederate Armies*, 128 vols. (Washington, D. C.: Government Printing Office, 1880–1901), series 1, vol. 51, part 1, 369–70; Charles Winslow Elliott, *Winfield Scott: The Soldier and the Man* (New York: Macmillan, 1937), 721–24. Lincoln's attorney general proposed a similar strategy on the day after the fall of Fort Sumter. It would be, he maintained, "the cheapest and most humane method" of destroying the Confederacy. See Howard K. Beale, ed., *The Diary of Edward Bates,1859–1866* (Washington, D.C.: U.S. Government Printing Office, 1933), 182–85.

31. Basler, *Collected Works*, 4:266.

32. Ibid., 332.

33. Ibid., 343.

34. Ibid., 353.

35. Ibid., 431–32.

36. Worthington Chauncey Ford, ed., *A Cycle of Adams Letters, 1861–1865*, 2 vols. (Boston: Houghton Mifflin, 1920), 1: 22.

37. S. D. Pardee to Gideon Welles, 30 July 1861, Gideon Welles Papers, Manuscript Division, Library of Congress.

38. *Chicago Tribune*, 23 July 1861.

39. Adams to Seward, 21 June 1861, in 37th Cong., 2d sess., H. Exec. Doc. 1, serial 1117, 109–11; Martin B. Duberman, *Charles Francis Adams, 1807–1886* (Boston: Houghton Mifflin, 1961), 268–69.

40. Basler, *Collected Works*, 4: 316–18. The *New York Herald* offered a similar grandiose plan on 27 June 1861, proposing that the two great armies facing each other join together in conquering Canada, Mexico, Central America, and the West Indies.

41. Basler, *Collected Works*, 4:376–80; Glyndon G. Van Deusen, *William Henry Seward* (New York: Oxford University Press, 1967), 297–98.

42. Frederick W. Seward, *Seward at Washington, as Senator and Secretary of State: A Memoir of His Life with Selections from His Letters, 1846–1861* (New York: Derby and Miller, 1891), 590.

43. Basler, *Collected Works*, 4:438.

7

The Hedgehog and the Foxes

James M. McPherson

TO MANY READERS the title of this article may seem whimsical if not
obscure. "Lincoln a hedgehog?!" remarked the baffled president of
the Abraham Lincoln Association when he first heard the proposed
title. Lincoln himself might have appreciated the analogy—given his
penchant for animal metaphors and his fondness for *Aesop's Fables*.
This particular analogy might at first glance appear to be unflattering,
though; the *Encyclopaedia Britannica* says of the hedgehog that "the
brain is remarkable for its low development." Like its larger American cousin the porcupine, the hedgehog's distinguishing characteris-
tic is self-defense by its sharp spines, or quills.

But the notion of comparing Lincoln to a hedgehog was suggested
by a line from the Greek poet Archilochus: "The fox knows many
things, but the hedgehog knows one big thing." Classical scholars
have disagreed about the purport of this adage. It may mean nothing
more than that the fox, despite his cleverness, cannot overcome the
hedgehog's one defense. But in a famous essay on Leo Tolstoy with
the similar title of "The Hedgehog and the Fox," the British philosopher Isaiah Berlin has provided a more profound rendering of Archilochus's words. The hedgehog is a thinker or leader who "relate[s]
everything to a single central vision . . . a single, universal, organizing
principle," writes Berlin, while the fox "pursue[s] many ends, often
unrelated and even contradictory."[1]

In this sense, Abraham Lincoln can be considered one of the foremost hedgehogs in American history. More than any of his Civil War
contemporaries, he pursued policies that were governed by a central
vision, expressed in the Gettysburg Address, that this "nation, conceived in Liberty, and dedicated to the proposition that all men are
created equal . . . shall not perish from the earth." Lincoln was surrounded by foxes who considered themselves smarter than he but

who lacked his depth of vision and therefore sometimes pursued un-related and contradictory ends. Two of the most prominent foxes were William H. Seward and Horace Greeley. Both were cleverer than Lincoln, more nimble-witted and brilliant in conversation. They shared Lincoln's nationalism and his abhorrence of slavery. But while Lincoln navigated by the lodestar that never moved, Seward and Greeley steered by stars that constantly changed position. If they had been at the helm instead of Lincoln, it is quite likely that the United States would have foundered on the rocks of disunion.

Several of Lincoln's associates testified to the slow but tenacious qualities of his mind. Greeley himself noted that Lincoln's intellect worked "not quickly nor brilliantly, but exhaustively." A fellow law-yer in antebellum years said that in analyzing a case, writing a letter, preparing a speech, or making a decision Lincoln was "slow, calculat-ing, methodical, and accurate."[2] The volatile William Herndon some-times showed impatience with his partner's deliberate manner of researching or arguing a case, but conceded that while Lincoln "thought slowly and acted slowly," he "not only went to the root of the question, but dug up the root, and separated and analyzed every fibre of it." In a legal case or a political debate, recalled Leonard Swett, Lincoln would concede nonessential points to his opponent, lulling him into a false sense of complacency. "But giving away six points and carrying the seventh he carried his case . . . the whole case hanging on the seventh. . . . Any man who took Lincoln for a simple-minded man would wind up with his back in a ditch."[3]

During the war, Lincoln expressed this hedgehog philosophy of concentrating on the one big thing, to the exclusion of nonessentials, in a speech to an Ohio regiment: "No small matter should divert us from our great purpose. . . . [Do not] let your minds be carried off from the great work we have before us."[4] Herndon told a story that illustrated Lincoln's remarkable capacity to focus on what he consid-ered the essentials of any matter. Herndon visited Niagara Falls some time after Lincoln had seen the falls in 1849. Telling Lincoln his impressions of this wonder of nature, Herndon waxed eloquent in typical nineteenth-century romantic fashion, declaiming of rush and roar and brilliant rainbows. Exhausting his adjectives, he asked Lin-coln what had made the deepest impression on him when he saw the falls. "The thing that struck me most forcibly," Lincoln replied, "was, where in the world did all that water come from?" After nearly forty years, Herndon recalled this remark as an example of how Lincoln "looked at everything. . . . His mind, heedless of beauty or awe, followed irresistibly back to the first cause. . . . If there was any secret in his power this surely was it."[5]

The "first cause," the central vision that guided Lincoln the hedgehog, was preservation of the United States and its constitutional government, which he was convinced would be destroyed if the Confederate States established their independence. Lincoln's nationalism was profound. It was not merely chauvinism, not the spread-eagle jingoism typical of American oratory in the nineteenth century. It was rooted in the Declaration of Independence and the ideals of liberty and equal opportunity that the Declaration had implanted as a revolutionary new idea on which the United States was founded. One of the first books he had read as a boy, Lincoln told the New Jersey senate in Trenton on 21 February 1861, was Parson Weem's *Life of Washington*. Nothing in that book fixed itself more vividly in his mind than the story of the Revolutionary army crossing the ice-choked Delaware River in a driving sleet storm on Christmas night 1776, at a low point in the American cause, to attack the British garrison at Trenton. "I recollect thinking then, boy even though I was, that there must have been something more than common that those men struggled for . . . something even more than National Independence . . . something that held out a great promise to all the people of the world for all time to come." This it was, said Lincoln next day at Independence Hall in Philadelphia, "which gave promise that in due time the weights should be lifted from the shoulders of all men, and that *all* should have an equal chance."[6]

On the eve of taking the oath as president of a nation that seemed to be breaking apart, Lincoln was "exceedingly anxious that this Union, the Constitution, and the liberties of the people shall be perpetuated in accordance with the original idea for which that struggle was made." Three weeks after calling out the militia to suppress the insurrection that began at Fort Sumter, Lincoln told his private secretary John Hay that "the central idea pervading this struggle" was the necessity "of proving that popular government is not an absurdity." If in a free government "the minority have the right to break up the government whenever they choose," it would "go far to prove the incapability of the people to govern themselves."[7] On 4 July 1861 Lincoln said that "our popular government has often been called an experiment." Confederate success would destroy that experiment, warned Lincoln on this and other occasions, would seal the doom of that "last best, hope" for maintaining in the world "government of the people, by the people, for the people."[8]

This was the fixed and unmoving North Star by which Lincoln charted his course through the Civil War when foxes seemed to navigate by the revolving planets. During the secession winter of 1860–61, several Republican spokesmen, fearing another proslavery compromise to keep slave states in the Union, expressed a preference for letting them go in peace. "If the Cotton States shall become satisfied that they can do better out of the Union than in it, we insist on letting them go," wrote Horace Greeley in his powerful *New York Tribune*. "We hope never to live in a republic whereof one section is pinned to the residue by bayonets."[9] Whether Greeley really meant this, or hedged it around with so many qualifications and reservations as to make it meaningless, has been the subject of debate among historians. Whatever the mercurial Greeley meant, many of his contemporaries including Lincoln seem to have read his Go-in-Peace editorials literally. Lincoln complained of the *Tribune*'s "damaging vagaries about peaceable secession." Greeley wrote to the president-elect in December 1860 that what he most feared was "another disgraceful back-down of the Free States. Let the Union slide—it may be reconstructed. . . . But another nasty compromise, whereby everything is conceded and nothing secured, will so thoroughly disgrace and humiliate us that we can never raise our heads."[10]

"Let the Union slide—it may be reconstructed" is the language of the fox. Lincoln the hedgehog knew better. Once the principle of secession was recognized, the Union could never be restored. The United States would cease to exist. The next time a disaffected minority lost a presidential election, it would invoke the precedent of 1860 and go out of the Union. Monarchists and reactionaries throughout the world would rejoice in the fulfillment of their prediction that this upstart democracy in North America could not last. Lincoln's refusal to sanction disunion *or* compromise eventually brought Greeley around to the same position. In the process, though, Lincoln the hedgehog had to bristle his spines against an even wilier fox than Greeley.

William H. Seward had not fully accepted his eclipse as leader of the Republican Party by Lincoln's nomination and election as president. Seward not only aspired to be the "premier" of the Lincoln administration, but he also emerged as the foremost Republican advocate of conciliation toward the South during the secession winter. Seward's "Higher Law" and "Irrepressible Conflict" speeches had made him the South's *bête noire* during the 1850s. But in January 1861 he wrote to Lincoln that "every thought that we think ought to be conciliatory, forbearing and patient" toward the South.[11] Lincoln was willing to go along part way with this advice. But Seward flirted with the idea of supporting the Crittenden Compromise, whose centerpiece was an extension of the Missouri Compromise line of 36° 30′ between slavery and freedom to all present and future territories. This would have been a repudiation of the platform on which the Republicans had stood from the beginning, and on which they had just won the election.

Lincoln could not contenance this. "Entertain no proposition for a compromise in regard to the *extension* of slavery," he wrote to key Republican leaders including Seward. Crittenden's compromise "would lose us everything we gained by the election. . . . Filibustering for all South of us, and making slave states would follow . . . to put us again on the high-road to a slave empire." The proposal for Republican territorial concessions, Lincoln pointed out, "acknowledges that slavery has equal rights with liberty, and surrenders all we have contended for. . . . We have just carried an election on principles fairly stated to the people. Now we are told in advance, the government shall be broken up, unless we surrender to those we have beaten. . . . If we surrender, it is the end of us. They will repeat the experiment upon us *ad libitum*. A year will not pass, till we shall have to take Cuba as a condition upon which they will stay in the Union."[12]

Lincoln's firmness stiffened Seward's backbone, but it did not end his desire to dominate the administration. The next contest between this fox and the hedgehog occurred over the issue of Fort Sumter. As Seward's biographer Glyndon Van Deusen puts it, during the Sumter crisis "Seward's mind moved restlessly from one possibility to another."[13] He emerged as leader of a faction that wanted to withdraw Union troops from the fort and yield it to the Confederacy. He hoped that this would reassure Southern Unionists of the government's peaceful intent, thereby keeping the upper South in the Union and cooling passions in the lower South.

Most of the cabinet and General-in-Chief Winfield Scott seemed

at first to concur with this policy. Only Postmaster General Montgomery Blair shared Lincoln's conviction that to give up Sumter
would constitute a recognition of Confederate legitimacy and thus
concede the principles of Unionism and national sovereignty. With
the help of Blair's brother-in-law Gustavus Fox, Lincoln devised a
plan to resupply the garrison at Sumter to put the onus of starting a
war on the Confederacy if Southern artillery tried to stop the supply
ships.

When Seward learned of this, he panicked. On his own authority
he had clandestinely assured Confederate commissioners that Sumter would be evacuated. Now all his foxy maneuvers would be ex-
posed as deceitful if not worse. In apparent desperation he sent to
Lincoln his April Fool's Day memorandum. But Seward meant it
seriously. It was a perfect illustration of Isaiah Berlin's definition of
the fox as one whose thought is "scattered or diffused, moving on
many levels." Contending that the administration lacked a "policy"
to deal with secession, Seward suggested one and offered to carry it
out in his self-assumed role as premier of the administration. He
would give up Fort Sumter but reinforce the other principal southern
fort in Union possession, Fort Pickens guarding Pensacola Harbor.
This, said Seward mysteriously, would *"change the question before
the Public from one upon Slavery, or about Slavery . . . for a question
upon Union or Disunion."* (Seward had convinced himself that only
antislavery Republicans wanted to hold Sumter, while all factions
in the North wanted to hold the less controversial and more easily
reinforced Pickens as a symbol of national sovereignty.) Seward then
proposed to provoke a war with Spain or France by demanding explanations from them for their interventionist policies in Santo Domingo
and Mexico. This presumably would reunite North and South in a
mutual crusade to enforce the Monroe Doctrine.[14]

What Lincoln thought privately of this bizarre memorandum from
his secretary of state is unknown. The president's formal reply to
Seward was temperate but resolute, as befit a hedgehog. He dismissed the suggestion of a foreign war by ignoring it. As for the critical matter of the forts, Lincoln could "not perceive how the reinforcement of Fort Sumpter [sic] would be done on a slavery, or
party issue, while that of Fort Pickens would be on a more national,
and patriotic one." He reminded Seward that the government did
have a "policy" on the forts, announced a month earlier in Lincoln's

inaugural address: "to hold, occupy and possess the property and places belonging to the government." That was still the policy; Lincoln was determined to carry it out even at the risk of war over Sumter. And "if this must be done," he concluded pointedly, "*I* must do it."[15]

Like Lincoln's courtroom adversary described by Leonard Swett, Seward had landed on his back in a ditch. And he knew it. He no longer had any illusions about who was to be the premier of this administration. Seward became one of Lincoln's most loyal and trusted subordinates. Lincoln repaid that loyalty by protecting Seward against an attempt by Republican senators to force him from the cabinet in December 1862—another notable occasion when the hedgehog outwitted several foxes.

After April 1861, Horace Greeley became one of the most prominent men who played fox to Lincoln's hedgehog. An early wartime instance of this occurred in the days after the Union defeat at Bull Run on 21 July 1861. In the weeks before this battle, the banner headlines "FORWARD TO RICHMOND" in Greeley's *New York Tribune* had contributed to the pressure that prodded the Army into what turned out to be a premature offensive. From a feeling of remorse, or panic, Greeley suffered something of a nervous breakdown after the battle. "This is my seventh sleepless night," he began a letter to Lincoln on 29 July. "On every brow sits sullen, black despair. . . . If the Union is irrevocably gone, an armistice for thirty, sixty, ninety, one hundred and twenty days—better still for a year—ought at once to be proposed, with a view to a peaceful adjustment. . . . If it is better for the country and for mankind that we make peace with the rebels at once, and on their own terms, do not shrink even from that."[16]

Lincoln too endured some sleepless nights after Bull Run, but he did not deviate a hair's breadth from his central vision of preserving the Union by winning the war. Lincoln's secretary John Nicolay wrote two days after the battle that "the fat is in the fire now. . . . Preparations for the war will be continued with increased vigor by the government." While Greeley was writing in despair to Lincoln, the president was outlining military strategy in a pair of memoranda that called for intensifying the blockade, increasing the Army, and pushing forward offensives in Virginia and Tennessee.[17] In essence, this remained Lincoln's determined policy until Appomattox, through victory and defeat and frustration with incompetent or irresolute military commanders. It was a policy sustained by the spirit manifested in a letter Lincoln wrote during the Seven Days battles in 1862, another Union defeat that plunged many Northerners into a despondency that matched Greeley's a year earlier. "I expect to maintain this contest," declared Lincoln, "until successful, or till I die, or am conquered, or my term expires, or Congress or the country foresakes me."[18]

By 1864 this meant prosecuting the war until Confederate forces surrendered unconditionally. But by midsummer of that year the prospects of accomplishing this goal seemed bleak. The two principal Union armies had suffered nearly a hundred thousand casualties without fulfilling the high hopes of spring that Richmond and Atlanta would fall and the war end by the Fourth of July. War-weariness and a desire for peace—perhaps even peace at any price—crept over the North. "Who shall revive the withered hopes that bloomed at the opening of Grant's campaign?" asked the *New York World* in July. "Patriotism is played out," declared another Democratic newspaper. "All are tired of this damnable tragedy."[19] In the middle of his campaign for reelection, it appeared that Lincoln would lose to a Democrat running on a peace platform. In August, Lincoln himself fully expected to lose. Other Republicans were equally pessimistic. "Lincoln's reelection is an impossibility" unless he can bring peace or victory, wrote Seward's alter ego Thurlow Weed. "The people are wild for peace."[20]

During this grave crisis—perhaps the gravest of Lincoln's presidency—Horace Greeley set in motion a peace overture that once more contrasted Lincoln's steady focus on the one big thing with Greeley's mercurial wavering. Learning of the presence of Confederate agents at Niagara Falls, Canada, Greeley wrote Lincoln urging him to explore with them the possibility of peace negotiations. "Our bleeding, bankrupt, almost dying country also longs for peace—shudders at the prospect of fresh conscriptions, of further wholesale devastations, and of new rivers of human blood." Seeing an opportunity to use Greeley to expose the impossibility of securing peace by negotiations except on Confederate terms, Lincoln immediately authorized him to bring to Washington under safe conduct "any person anywhere professing to have any proposition of Jefferson Davis in writing, for peace, embracing the restoration of the Union and abandonment of slavery."[21]

Of course no such person existed, and Lincoln knew it. There followed a comic-opera scenario in which Greeley tried to wriggle out of responsibility for carrying through the initiative he had set in motion while Lincoln pressed him to go forward. Reluctantly Greeley did so, eliciting just what Lincoln expected and wanted—public statements from Confederate leaders that they would negotiate no peace that did not include independence. An embarrassed Greeley squirmed and twisted, trying to shift the blame to Lincoln in a private letter that condemned the president's strategy of unconditional surrender as a "fatuity." "No truce! No armistice! No negotiation! No mediation! Nothing but surrender at discretion!" Greeley exclaimed. "There is nothing like it in history. It must result in disaster, or all experience is delusive." Never mind that this had been pretty much the policy advocated by the *Tribune* during the three years between Greeley's crises of confidence in July 1861 and July 1864. Greeley now believed that "no Government fighting a rebellion should ever close its ears to any proposition the rebels may make."[22]

But Lincoln had a firmer grip on reality. He pointed out in his annual message to Congress on 6 December 1864 that Jefferson Davis had repeatedly made it clear that his terms for peace were independence and nothing less. "He does not attempt to deceive us," said Lincoln. "He affords us no excuse to deceive ourselves. He cannot voluntarily reaccept the Union; we cannot voluntarily yield it. Between him and us the issue is distinct, simple, and inflexible. It is an issue that can only be tried by war, and decided by victory."[23] When Lincoln said this, military fortunes had turned decisively in favor of Union victory. But that only vindicated the steadfast sagacity of Lincoln's refusal to give in to despair and defeatism during the dark days of the previous summer.

The peace-negotiations exchange between Lincoln and Greeley involved the issue of slavery as well as of Union. Clever disinformation tactics by Confederate agents and northern Peace Democrats had spread the notion that only Lincoln's insistence on emancipation as a prior condition of negotiations prevented peace. Greeley seems to have bought this line, at least temporarily. "We do not contend," he wrote in the *Tribune* on 25 July, "the reunion is possible or endurable only on the basis of Universal Freedom. . . . War has its exigencies which cannot be foreseen . . . and Peace is often desirable on other terms than those of our choice." If this meant anything, it meant that Greeley was willing to drop emancipation as a condition. Although the pressure on Lincoln from even staunch Republicans to do the same became so intense that the president almost caved in, he ultimately stood fast. He denied that he was "now carrying on this war for the sole purpose of abolition. It is & will be carried on so long as I am President for the sole purpose of restoring the Union. But no human power can subdue this rebellion without using the Emancipation lever as I have done." The Emancipation Proclamation was a solemn promise. To break it in a chimerical quest for peace would be "a cruel and astounding breach of faith" for which "I should be damned in time & eternity. . . . The world shall know that I will keep my faith to friends & enemies, come what will."[24]

Greeley and Lincoln appeared to have switched sides since their exchange of public letters on emancipation two years earlier. On that occasion Greeley had castigated the president for his reluctance to adopt emancipation as a war policy. Lincoln had replied with the famous words: "My paramount object in this struggle *is* to save the Union, and is *not* either to save or to destroy slavery. If I could save the Union without freeing *any* slave I would do it, and if I could save it by freeing *all* the slaves I would do it; and if I could save it by freeing some and leaving others alone I would also do that."[25] In 1864 Lincoln's critics were asking him to revert to the first or third of these alternatives—to free none or only some of the slaves—while he was now committed to the second one of freeing all, since he supported the Thirteenth Amendment, passed by the Senate and endorsed by the Republican platform on which he was running for reelection. There was no inconsistency between the Lincoln of 1862 and the Lincoln of 1864; on both occasions his paramount object *was* to save the Union, with emancipation as a potential "lever" to help do the job. In 1864 he was convinced that the lever was essential; in August 1862 he had also been convinced of this, although he was then waiting for a propitious time to announce it. It was Greeley, not Lincoln, who zig-zagged on slavery between 1862 and 1864.

Yet there was an apparent contradiction in Lincoln's position on slavery. To resolve that contradiction will go to the heart of the theme of Lincoln as hedgehog. Lincoln had always considered slavery "an unqualified evil to the negro, the white man, and the State," a "monstrous injustice" that "deprives our republican example of its just influence in the world—enables the enemies of free institutions, with plausibility, to taunt us as hypocrites."[26] If anything had been the "single central vision" of his political career before 1861, it had been this. A study of Lincoln as a public speaker maintains that the 175 speeches he gave from 1854 to 1860 showed him to be a "one-issue man" whose "central message" was the necessity of excluding slavery from the territories as the first step toward putting the institution on the path to ultimate extinction.[27]

The Declaration of Independence was the foundation of Lincoln's political philosophy. "I have never had a feeling politically that did not spring from the sentiments embodied in the Declaration," he said in 1861. Lincoln insisted that the phrase "all men are created equal" applied to black people as well as to whites. This powered his conviction that the Founders had looked toward the ultimate extinction of slavery. That is why they did not mention the words *slave* or *slavery* in the Constitution. "Thus the thing is hid away, in the constitution," said Lincoln in 1854, "just as an afflicted man hides away a wen or cancer, which he dares not cut out at once, lest he bleed to death; with the promise, nevertheless, that the cutting may begin at the end of a given time."[28]

These were the principles that for Lincoln made America stand for something unique and important in the world; they were the principles that the heroes of the Revolution whom Lincoln revered had fought and died for; without these principles the United States would become just another oppressive autocracy. That is why the Kansas-Nebraska Act propelled Lincoln back into politics in 1854; that is what fueled the 175 speeches he gave during the next six years. The repeal of the Missouri Compromise restriction on slavery's expansion seemed to legitimize the permanence of the institution; Stephen A. Douglas's statement that he cared not whether slavery was voted down or up represented a despicable moral indifference; Douglas's denial that blacks were included in the phrase "all men are created equal" was a lamentable declension from the faith of the Founders. "Near eighty years ago we began by declaring that all men are created equal," said Lincoln at Peoria in 1854, "but now from that beginning we have run down to the other declaration, that for SOME men to enslave OTHERS is a 'sacred right of self-government.' . . . Our republican robe is soiled, and trailed in the dust. Let us repurify it.

. . . Let us re-adopt the Declaration of Independence, and with it, the practices, and policy, which harmonize with it. . . . If we do this, we shall not only have saved the Union; but we shall have so saved it, as to make, and keep it, forever worthy of the saving."[29]

In his famous "lost speech" at Bloomington, Illinois, in 1856, Lincoln said, according to the only contemporary summary of the speech, that "the *Union must be preserved in the purity of its principles as well as in the integrity of its territorial parts.* It must be 'Liberty and Union, now and forever, one and inseparable.'" Note that Lincoln here placed liberty first and Union second; the Union was a *means* to promote the greater *end* of liberty; it was the promise of liberty that made the Union meaningful. In his speech at Independence Hall on Washington's birthday, 1861, Lincoln made the same point more dramatically. The principle of universal liberty in the Declaration of Independence, he told a cheering crowd, was what had kept the United States together for eighty-five years. "But, if this country cannot be saved without giving up that principle—I was about to say I would rather be assassinated on this spot than to surrender it."[30]

Yet when Lincoln became president, he assured Southerners that he had no intention of interfering with slavery in their states. When the war broke out, he reassured loyal slaveholders on this score, and revoked orders by Union generals emancipating the slaves of Confederates in Missouri and in the South Atlantic states. This was a war for Union, not liberty, said Lincoln over and over again—to Greeley in August 1862, for example: "If I could save the Union without freeing *any* slave I would do it." In a letter to his old friend Senator Orville Browning of Illinois on 22 September 1861—ironically, exactly one year before issuing the Preliminary Emancipation Proclamation—Lincoln rebuked Browning for his support of General John C. Frémont's order purporting to free the slaves of Confederates in Missouri. "You speak of it as being the only means of *saving* the government. On the contrary it is itself the surrender of the government." If left standing, it would drive the border slave states into the Confederacy. "These all against us, and the job on our hands is too large for us. We would as well consent to separation at once, including the surrender of this capitol."[31] To keep the border states—as well as northern Democrats—in the coalition fighting to suppress the rebellion, Lincoln continued well into the second year of the war to resist antislavery pressures for an emancipation policy.

The Union—with or without slavery—had become the one big thing, the "single central vision" of Lincoln the hedgehog. What accounted for this apparent reversal of priorities from liberty first to Union first? —from Union as a means to promote liberty to Union as an end in itself? Primarily it was the responsibility of power, and Lincoln's conception of constitutional limitations on that power. As president, Lincoln had taken an oath to preserve, protect, and defend the Constitution. This duty constrained his options. "I am naturally anti-slavery," he said in an 1864 letter explaining these constraints. "If slavery is not wrong, nothing is wrong. . . . Yet I have never understood that the Presidency conferred upon me an unrestricted right to act officially upon this judgment and feeling." His oath of office "forbade me to practically indulge my primary abstract judgment on the moral question of slavery." The Constitution protected slavery; Lincoln was sworn to protect the Constitution.[32]

But wars generate a radical momentum of their own. As Lincoln expressed it in the same letter: "I claim not to have controlled events, but confess plainly that events have controlled me." By 1862 the limited conflict to suppress an insurrection had become a total war in which both sides were trying to mobilize all of their resources. It was becoming clear that the necessity of deferring to border state and Democratic opinion on slavery was outweighed by the necessity to strike at one of the Confederacy's principal resources—its labor force—and to avoid alienating antislavery Northerners, who provided the driving energy and commitment crucial to winning the war. Lincoln's conception of the constitutional relationship between slavery and Union shifted during 1862. "My oath to preserve the constitution," he explained two years later, "imposed upon me the duty of preserving, by every indispensable means, that government—that nation—of which that constitution was the organic law." Lincoln decided in the summer of 1862 to use his war powers as commander in chief to seize enemy property employed to wage war against the United States; he proclaimed the emancipation of the principal form of that property as a "military necessity" to help win the war.

Lincoln used one of his favorite metaphors to illustrate the point. "By general law life *and* limb must be protected; yet often a limb must be amputated to save a life. . . . I felt that measures, otherwise unconstitutional, might become lawful, by becoming indispensable to the preservation of the constitution, through the preservation of the nation." When he revoked Frémont's emancipation order in September 1861, he did not think the indispensable necessity to amputate that diseased limb of slavery had come. Nor had it come by May 1862, when Lincoln revoked a similar order by General David Hunter for the South Atlantic states. But in the dark days of defeat during the summer of 1862, the time came. "Driven to the alternative of either surrendering the Union, and with it, the Constitution, or of laying strong hand upon the colored element[,] I chose the latter."[33]

The Emancipation Proclamation and its corollary, the enlistment of black troops, did help to win the war and preserve the nation. They were also, of course, crucial steps in the abolition of slavery. All of this is well known. Less often noted is another important fact about the Emancipation Proclamation: it also liberated Abraham Lincoln from the agonizing contradiction between his "oft-expressed *personal* wish that all men everywhere could be free" and his oath of office as president of a slaveholding republic.[34] It fused the "organizing principle" of liberty that guided Lincoln before 1861 with the "single central vision" of Union that became his lodestar during the war. Liberty and Union became "the one big thing" instead of two big things, enabling Lincoln to become a true hedgehog. The "new birth of freedom" that he invoked at Gettysburg restored the Union to the role envisaged for it by the Founders: a means to achieve the end of liberty. And in hedgehog fashion, Lincoln expressed in his second inaugural address a steadfast determination to stick with his policy of total war to total victory even "if God wills that it continue, until all the wealth piled by the bond-man's two hundred and fifty years of unrequited toil shall be sunk, and until every drop of blood drawn with the lash, shall be paid by another drawn with the sword."[35]

Notes

1. Isaiah Berlin, *The Hedgehog and the Fox: An Essay on Tolstoy's View of History* (New York: Simon and Schuster, 1966), 1.

2. Harlan Hoyt Horner, *Lincoln and Greeley* (Urbana: University of Illinois Press, 1953), 251–52; Henry Clay Whitney quoted in Waldo W. Braden, *Abraham Lincoln: Public Speaker* (Baton Rouge: Louisiana State University Press, 1988), 65.

3. Paul M. Angle, ed., *Herndon's Life of Lincoln* (Cleveland: World, 1942), 272–73, 270.

4. Roy P. Basler, ed., Marion Dolores Pratt and Lloyd A. Dunlap, asst. eds., *The Collected Works of Abraham Lincoln*, 9 vols. (New Brunswick,N.J.: Rutgers University Press, 1953–55), 7:505 (hereafter, Basler, *Collected Works*).

5. Angle, *Herndon's Lincoln*, 238–39.

6. Basler, *Collected Works*, 4:235–36, 240.

7. Ibid., 236; Tyler Dennett, ed., *Lincoln and the Civil War in the Diaries and Letters of John Hay* (New York: Dodd, Mead, 1939), 19–20.

8. Basler, *Collected Works*, 4:438–39; 5:537; 7:23.

9. *New York Tribune*, 9 November 1860.

10. Horner, *Lincoln and Greeley*, 192–93; Greeley to Lincoln, 22 December 1860, Abraham Lincoln Papers, Library of Congress. For the debate over what Greeley really meant, see David M. Potter, "Horace Greeley and Peaceable Secession" and "Postscript," in *The South and the Sectional Conflict* (Baton Rouge: Louisiana State University Press, 1968), 219–42; and Thomas N. Bonner, "Horace Greeley and the Secession Movement," *Mississippi Valley Historical Review* 38 (1951): 425–44.

11. Seward to Lincoln, 27 January 1861, Abraham Lincoln Papers.

12. Basler, *Collected Works*, 4:150–51, 154, 183, 155, 172.

13. Glyndon G. Van Deusen, *William Henry Seward* (New York: Oxford University Press, 1967), 280.

14. Basler, *Collected Works*, 4:317n–318n.

15. Ibid., 316, 317.

16. Greeley to Lincoln, 29 July 1861, Abraham Lincoln Papers.

17. Basler, *Collected Works*, 4:457–58.

18. Ibid., 5:292.

19. *New York World*, 12 July 1864; Frank L. Klement, *The Copperheads in the Middle West* (Chicago: University of Chicago Press, 1960), 233.

20. Edward Chase Kirkland, *The Peacemakers of 1864* (New York: Macmillan, 1927), 108.

21. Greeley to Lincoln, 7 July 1864, and Lincoln to Greeley, 9 July 1864, Basler, *Collected Works*, 7:435 and n.

22. Greeley to Lincoln, 8 August 1864, Abraham Lincoln Papers. For a discussion of this episode, see Horner, *Lincoln and Greeley*, 296–323.

23. Basler, *Collected Works*, 8:151.

24. Ibid., 7:51, 507.

25. Ibid., 5:388.

26. Ibid., 3:92; 2:255.

27. Braden, *Abraham Lincoln: Public Speaker*, 35–36.

28. Basler, *Collected Works*, 4:240; 2:274.

29. Ibid., 2:275–76.

30. Ibid., 2:341; 4:240. When Lincoln made this extemporaneous speech at Independence Hall, he had already been warned of the plot in Baltimore to assassinate him as he passed through; this matter was obviously on this mind.

31. Ibid., 4:532.

32. Ibid., 7:281.

33. Ibid., 7:281–82.

34. Ibid., 5:389; Stephen B. Oates makes a similar point (*Abraham Lincoln: The Man Behind the Myths* [New York: Harper, 1984], 112.

35. Basler, *Collected Works*, 8:333.

8

Abraham Lincoln and the Border States*

William E. Gienapp

"I HOPE to have God on my side," Abraham Lincoln is reported to
have said early in the war, "but I must have Kentucky." Unlike most
of his contemporaries, Lincoln hesitated to invoke divine sanction of
human causes, but his wry comment unerringly acknowledged the
critical importance of the border states to the Union cause. Following
the attack on Fort Sumter and Lincoln's call for troops in April 1861,
public opinion in Maryland, Kentucky, and Missouri was sharply divided and these states' ultimate allegiance uncertain. The residents
of the border were torn between their close cultural ties with the
South, on the one hand, and their long tradition of Unionism and
political moderation on the other. At the same time, the expansion of
the railroad network in the 1850s had disrupted these states' traditional trade patterns with the South by directing a growing amount
of commerce, including farmstuffs, northward, so economically they
looked in both directions. With popular emotions running high, there
was a very real possibility that they would follow the Upper South
out of the Union and join the Confederacy.

Together Delaware, Maryland, Kentucky, and Missouri had a
white population of almost 2.6 million, nearly half that of the population of the eleven states of the Confederacy.[1] In none of the border
states did slavery approach the importance it had in the Deep South,
but only in Delaware, with fewer than 2,000 slaves out of a total
population of about 112,000, was it insignificant (Table 1). Delaware
stood alone among the border states in not containing a serious movement for secession.[2]

*I wish to thank Mark E. Neely Jr., who commented on an earlier version of this
article, for a number of helpful suggestions.

TABLE 1. NUMBER OF SLAVES AND TOTAL POPULATION IN 1860

Region	Slaves	Population	Proportion (%)
Border States[1]			
Delaware	1,798	112,212	1.6
Maryland	87,189	687,049	12.7
Kentucky	225,483	1,155,651	19.5
Missouri	114,931	1,181,912	9.7
Upper South[2]	1,208,758	4,168,723	29.0
Deep South[3]	2,312,352	4,868,449	47.5

Source: James M. McPherson, *The Negro's Civil War* (New York: Pantheon Books, 1965), Appendix A.

[1] In addition, the District of Columbia contained 3,185 slaves out of a total population of 75,079.
[2] Virginia, North Carolina, Tennessee, and Arkansas.
[3] South Carolina, Georgia, Florida, Alabama, Mississippi, Louisiana, and Texas.

Smaller and less heavily populated than either Kentucky or Missouri, Maryland nevertheless occupied a key strategic position, for it bordered the District of Columbia on three sides. In addition, Washington's telegraph and rail links to the north and west traversed its territory. Loss of Maryland would force the federal government to abandon Washington, a humiliating development that would entail a potentially fatal loss of prestige and possibly lead to diplomatic recognition by Europe of the Confederacy.

Kentucky was much more heavily populated, had richer mineral resources, and was a major grain and livestock producing state. Yet Kentucky's primary importance was strategic. Bordered by the Ohio River to the north and the Mississippi River to the west, it stood as a buffer between the states of the Old Northwest and Confederate Tennessee and provided the main line of defense for the states of Ohio, Indiana, and Illinois. Kentucky also controlled access to several major river systems, including the Tennessee and the Cumberland that pointed south toward the heart of the Confederacy.

Missouri was also a major agricultural state producing vast quantities of grains and livestock. It also contained the major city of St. Louis, an important commercial center, and was the most populous of the border states. Strategically, Missouri protected the Union's western flank and guarded the western shore of the Mississippi River beyond the Confederacy's northern border. If allied with the Confederacy, it would threaten Iowa, Kansas, and especially Illinois; but more crucially, it would make Union control of both Kentucky and the Mississippi River much more difficult.

Rich in mineral and agricultural resources, containing a large white population, and controlling key transportation and communication networks, the border states were of vital importance. Had the border states seceded, the Union's resources would have been significantly reduced and the Confederacy's strategic advantages correspondingly increased. Lincoln himself questioned whether the Confederacy could be subdued militarily if the border states left the Union. "I think to lose Kentucky is nearly the same as to lose the whole game," he commented in justifying his cautious policy in that state. "Kentucky gone, we can not hold Missouri, nor, as I think, Maryland. These all against us, and the job on our hands is too large for us. We would as well consent to separation at once, including the surrender of this capitol."[3]

Historians understandably have pointed out that with such momentous consequences hanging in the balance, Lincoln's skillful handling of the border states is a notable example of his presidential leadership. "It was fortunate for the United States in the critical year 1861," Edward Smith wrote in praising his statesmanship, "that Abraham Lincoln understood perfectly the people of the Borderland. . . . [This knowledge] enabled him to frame surely the policies upon which the fate of the country depended."[4] Likewise, James Rawley began his book *Turning Points of the Civil War* with an analysis of the decision of the border states to remain in the Union. Speculating that the secession of the border states might well have changed the course of the war, Rawley carried his discussion only to the end of 1861, for by then, he argued, any possibility that the border states would join the Confederacy had ended.

This interpretation, however, does not analyze fully Lincoln's policies with respect to the border states. In examining the problem of the border states, historians generally have lost interest once these states unequivocally cast their lot with the Union. They have concentrated on the opening months of the struggle, from the call for troops to Lincoln's first annual message in December; and except for his efforts to get them to adopt a program of gradual emancipation have given only limited attention to Lincoln's policies concerning the border states during the remainder of the war.[5] Lincoln's policy goals, however, extended beyond preventing these states from seceding, and his purposes had not been completely achieved by the end of 1861.

I

Lincoln's border state policy blended several objectives. The first was to preserve or establish loyal governments in each of these states. In summarizing the administration's policy in Maryland in the early weeks of the war, General Nathaniel P. Banks, who was stationed in Annapolis in 1861, declared, "The secession leaders—the enemies of the people—were replaced and loyal men assigned to . . . their duties. This made Maryland a loyal State."[6] In devising his border state policy, as would be true later with his Reconstruction program, Lincoln always gave first priority to placing loyal men in control of the state government.

Lincoln's second objective was that each of these Union state governments take the lead in fostering loyalty among its citizens, controlling the civilian population, and marshaling the resources of the state behind the war effort. Lincoln did not shirk from his responsibility—as he saw it—to suppress disloyal activities among the civilian population, but he preferred to avoid such acts because they were controversial and politically embarrassing.[7] From his perspective, if suppression was necessary it was preferable for the state governments to take the lead in such activities.

Lincoln's third objective, closely related to the second, was to minimize the military occupation of these states so as to free troops for use at more critical points. A large occupying force diverted army units from the fighting, and by increasing friction between the army and the civilian population inevitably produced resentment. This was especially true in the western theater, where the fighting moved steadily away from Kentucky and Missouri.

Lincoln's final goal, which crystallized only after the first year of the war, was to end slavery in these states by voluntary state action. Anticipating a postwar Union without slavery, he wanted the border states to take the lead by adopting some form of gradual emancipation funded by the federal government. Foot dragging by the border states was an important backdrop to his decision to issue the Emancipation Proclamation, but even after taking this momentous step, Lincoln continued to appeal to the border states (which were exempt from the terms of the Proclamation) to end slavery.

It is against these goals, and not just the question of secession, that Lincoln's border state policies need to be evaluated. When these more ambitious policy objectives are considered, his record of leadership is less impressive. With respect to the border states, he was more successful in achieving some goals than others, and his program was more successful in some states than others. In broad terms, Lincoln's policies were fairly successful in Maryland, produced a mixed record in Kentucky, and were largely a failure in Missouri.

II

Following the outbreak of war, public sentiment in Maryland loosely followed the state's regional divisions. Western Maryland, an area of small farms with a diversified economy, was Unionist, while the major slaveholding regions of the Eastern Shore and Southern Maryland, where the tobacco economy was concentrated, were prosecession. Politically divided but with a vocal and militant secessionist minority, Baltimore, which contained a third of the state's population, held the balance of power.[8]

Lincoln's policies in Maryland resembled the proverbial iron fist in a velvet glove. The danger in the state to the Union cause, and the threat to the national capital, were immediately apparent. On 19 April a prosecessionist mob in Baltimore attacked the Massachusetts Sixth Regiment as it marched across the city to change trains on its way to Washington. In the ensuing melee, several soldiers and a number of civilians were killed. Worse still, the police commissioner ordered the railroad bridges outside the city destroyed and the telegraph lines cut, and Unionist Governor Thomas Hicks, who had earlier refused to call the legislature into session, wavered and implored the Lincoln administration not to send any more troops across the state. Hick's request threatened to isolate Washington and leave the capital unprotected.

Recognizing the delicate balance of opinion in the state, Lincoln resisted the impulse to force the right of transit and agreed temporarily not to send any more troops through Baltimore. Troops were still needed in Washington, however, and military authorities quickly devised a less direct route by sea and rail through Annapolis.[9] John Hay, Lincoln's private secretary, recorded the president's belief that "if quiet was kept in Baltimore a little longer, Maryland might be considered the first of the redeemed."[10]

Although Lincoln hoped to nurture pro-Union sentiment in the state, he took no chances. He authorized the military to suspend the writ of habeas corpus along any military line in the state. It was thus in Maryland that Lincoln, feeling his way in dealing with this unprecedented crisis, first suspended the writ and authorized arrests without trial.[11] Once Washington was secure, the army engaged in a massive display of force designed to overawe the civilian population by occupying Federal Hill in Baltimore. Before long, although the state government continued to function, Maryland was essentially under military occupation. Encouraged by this strong military presence, public opinion, initially inchoate and undeveloped, quickly swung to the Union side.[12] Once the emotions that erupted following the attack on Fort Sumter subsided, there was no possibility that Maryland would secede, but had it attempted to do so during these early weeks of war, Lincoln unquestionably would have used force to keep the state in the Union.[13]

When the state legislature assembled in May, it called for the recognition of the Confederacy, but under the watchful surveillance of the military it took no steps toward disunion. In the special congressional election in June, Unionist candidates polled 72 percent of the vote and triumphed in all six races. The fall election of 1861 was conducted in an atmosphere of intimidation as federal troops arrested prominent secessionist members of the legislature, guarded the polls in a few areas on election day, and seized disloyal citizens who tried to vote. Even so, critics overstated the extent of military intervention. John A. Dix, the commanding general of the Middle District, refused official requests to apply a loyalty oath and generally restrained the army's activities in order to avoid negative publicity.[14] Aided by Union soldiers who were given furloughs so they could vote, Unionist candidates were victorious, headed by Augustus W. Bradford, who was elected governor by a better than two-to-one margin. No doubt Bradford would have prevailed in any event, but federal actions helped swell his margin of victory.[15] Bradford's election removed any doubt that Maryland would remain in the Union. Throughout the war, the state was heavily garrisoned because of the need to protect the capital, but it posed no military threat to the Union. When Lee invaded the state in 1862, few Maryland residents welcomed him.

During the remainder of the war, relations between the federal government and the state revolved around two matters: arbitrary arrests and federal interference with free elections, and problems related to the institution of slavery. In addition, the Lincoln administration was drawn into the factional struggle for control of the burgeoning state Republican Party.

Complaints of federal interference in elections in Maryland were endemic during the war. A good example was the dispute between Governor Bradford and commanding general Robert C. Schenck over the latter's order imposing a test oath for voting in the 1863 election. Federal officials were irritated at the state's failure to enact an oath for voters, so Schenck announced that the army would enforce one he promulgated at the polls. Schenck, who had been elected to Congress from Ohio, claimed that his purpose was to prevent disloyal elements from voting, but he was equally interested in assisting the antislavery forces in the state. Bradford immediately protested to Lincoln about military interference with the election. After conferring with the general, the president modified Schenck's proclamation, designated General Orders No. 53, concerning the arrest of disloyal individuals, but let the oath stand. In his reply to the governor, Lincoln chided the state for failing to enact a loyalty oath and noted that under Schenck's order disloyal citizens could regain the right to vote by taking the oath. "I think that is cheap enough," he observed.[16] Lincoln's handling of this problem evidenced great political skill. He managed simultaneously to offer concessions to the governor, avoid undermining the military authority in the state, and publicly affirm his policy that "all loyal qualified voters in Maryland and elsewhere" should be allowed to vote without disturbance.[17] What interference occurred on election day resulted more from the zealousness and political ambitions of local officers than presidential policy.[18] Yet, relations between the state and federal government remained reasonably harmonious, and the issue of arbitrary arrests and interference gradually subsided. Indeed, for the 1864 election state officials stipulated a stricter loyalty test than Schenck had imposed in 1863, and the election passed with little federal disturbance.

The dispute over Schenck's loyalty oath was part of a larger struggle between radical Congressman Henry Winter Davis and Postmaster General Montgomery Blair, a conservative, for control of the Unionist party in Maryland. Wishing to retain the support of both men, Lincoln tried as much as possible to keep out of this fight, which he viewed as largely personal.[19] Again, he steered a middle course, taking a more radical stand on emancipation than Blair, whom he removed from the cabinet in 1864, yet unwilling to go as far as Davis and the radicals on this and related questions. While unable to stop the bitter factional struggle within the emerging Republican Party in Maryland, Lincoln's temperate actions also bore fruit. Unionist sentiment remained paramount in the state, and in 1864 Lincoln and the Republican Party gained a clear victory. The Republicans won control of the statehouse and the legislature and elected a majority of the state's congressmen. Most striking was Lincoln's victory. In 1860 he had received only 2,294 votes in the state; in 1864 he polled more than 40,000 votes and secured 55.1 percent of the popular vote (Table 2). Lincoln's personal triumph was testimony to his adroit management of affairs in Maryland.

III

When the war began, Kentucky, like Maryland, found itself torn between its loyalty to the Union and its cultural ties to the South.[20] Secession sentiment was stronger in Kentucky, however, and it was not possible to occupy the state militarily as was done in Maryland. Complicating the situation was the fact that the governor, Beriah Magoffin, favored secession. When Lincoln called for troops after the firing on Fort Sumter, Magoffin indignantly refused to supply any, and the state house of representatives officially adopted a policy of

TABLE 2. PRESIDENTIAL VOTE, 1860 AND 1864

State	1860		1864	
	Lincoln	Other	Lincoln	McClellan
Maryland	2,294	89,848	40,153	32,739
Kentucky	1,364	143,703	27,786	64,301
Missouri	17,028	148,490	72,750	31,678
Delaware	3,815	12,224	8,155	8,767

"strict neutrality." Union leaders such as John J. Crittenden endorsed the policy of neutrality as a temporary holding action; Kentucky's neutrality quickly became part of a game of maneuver between Unionists and pro-Confederates in the state for political supremacy.[21]

Confronted with Kentucky's neutral stance and pleas for restraint from Unionist leaders, Lincoln moved cautiously so as not to provoke public opinion in the state while waiting for the population's latent Unionism to assert itself. Varying his policy according to the situation, he realized that he could not force the issue the way he had in Maryland. A less restrained approach in the early months of the war might well have driven the state into the Confederacy.

In this difficult period, Lincoln avoided issuing any threats and used conciliatory language. He resisted the demands of Republican governors and editors to adopt a vigorous coercive policy against the state, and also the pleas of military commanders to seize the initiative and invade Kentucky.[22] Recognizing that the state's neutrality could not last long, Lincoln initially did not challenge it. He forbad the army to recruit volunteers in the state, declined to prohibit trade with the Confederacy, and promised Garrett Davis, a prominent Unionist, that he would not use force against the state if it did not resist the laws and authority of the United States. He repeated this pledge in another meeting with state leaders in July but was careful not to commit himself as to future action.[23] At the same time, he commenced shipping arms to Kentucky Unionists, and by early summer he authorized recruiting Union troops in the state. Time would demonstrate the wisdom of what James Russell Lowell, who demanded a militant approach, sarcastically termed Lincoln's "Little Bo Peep policy."[24]

While antislavery spokesmen such as Lowell fumed, Lincoln's pragmatic policy bore immediate dividends. In a special congressional election in June, Union candidates won nine of ten seats. Among those elected was Crittendon, the symbol of border state Unionism. Throughout the summer, both sides stepped up recruiting efforts in the state, but Lincoln continued to ignore Confederate activities in the state. In another special election in August to elect a new legislature, Unionists scored a resounding triumph, winning seventy-six of a hundred seats in the house; and with holdovers, twenty-seven of thirty-eight in the senate.[25] With Unionists in firm control of the legislature and the congressional delegation, it was only a matter of time until Kentucky's policy of neutrality was discarded.

A crisis suddenly developed, however, when John C. Frémont, the military commander in Missouri, issued on his own authority a proclamation freeing the slaves of all disloyal persons in Missouri. Kentucky Unionists immediately warned Lincoln of the potentially disastrous impact of Frémont's proclamation on public opinion in the state. Lincoln had already taken steps to revoke parts of Frémont's proclamation, but he subsequently emphasized its consequences for the struggle over Kentucky. "The Kentucky Legislature would not budge till that proclamation was modified," he explained, "and Gen. [Robert] Anderson telegraphed me that on the news of Gen. Frémont having actually issued deeds of manumission, a whole company of our Volunteers threw down their arms and disbanded. I was so assured, as to think it probable, that the arms we had furnished Kentucky would be turned against us."[26]

The decisive event that drove Kentucky out of its neutrality was not Frémont's rash act but the Confederate army's invasion of the state in September 1861. In quick order, U.S. forces under Ulysses S. Grant occupied Paducah, Kentucky, and the legislature demanded the withdrawal of the Confederate forces; when the Confederacy refused, the legislature requested federal aid to expel them. Lincoln promptly responded by sending additional troops to occupy the state, and Confederate forces were soon driven from Kentucky. Despite the establishment of a shadowy Confederate government and General Braxton Bragg's subsequent invasion in 1862, Union control of the state was never undermined. In his first annual message, Lincoln observed: "Kentucky . . . for some time in doubt, is now decidedly and, I think, unchangeably, ranged on the side of the Union."[27] His tactful handling of the state in these early months of the war contrasted sharply with Confederate leaders' imperious approach. As E. Merton Coulter concluded: "The South, too impatient to be tolerant and too impetuous to be tactful, lost the greatest prize of the West— Kentucky."[28]

This result left Governor Magoffin in a difficult position. Unionists distrusted him, and hence the legislature systematically hamstrung him and, as much as possible, simply ignored him. Eventually in 1862 he resigned after the legislature designated an acceptable successor. In 1863 Thomas Bramlette, the Unionist candidate, was elected governor by a commanding majority.

The outcome of the political struggle in Kentucky in 1861, however, did not end Lincoln's problems with the state. One point of irritation was trade. To prevent shipment of contraband to the Confederacy, the Treasury Department required permits for most goods and passengers. Applicants had to take an oath of allegiance and meet a stringent test of past loyalty. Complaints mounted that the permit system was used to punish anyone suspected of disloyalty or who ran athwart military officers. These protests reached a peak during the tenure of General E. A. Paine, who was finally removed for abusing his powers.[29]

More serious was the growing resentment over arbitrary arrests and military interference in elections. Lincoln's suspension of the writ of habeas corpus gave wide discretionary powers to military commanders, and he found it difficult to regulate their activities, especially on a day-to-day basis. The various raids of John Hunt Morgan, the flight of many guerrillas from Missouri to the state, and the continuing activities of bands of Home Guards, initially created to prevent secession in 1861, all contributed to the increase in violence and irregular fighting in 1864. In July 1864, Lincoln imposed martial law on the state, and it remained under this edict for the duration of the war.[30] The state suffered more disorder than Maryland, especially in 1864, and thus military intervention and suppression were more frequent.

The effect of these actions was to alienate Kentucky's Unionists from the administration. Governor Bramlette was particularly outspoken in his criticism. The Army's intrusion was especially marked in the 1863 election, and matters worsened again in the 1864 presidential campaign when several prominent Unionists, including the lieutenant governor, were arrested by military authorities. The situation required tact and forbearance, but the commanding general, Stephen G. Burbridge, who appealed to the small radical element in the state, was devoid of both. Early in 1865, Lincoln finally removed Burbridge and replaced him with General John A. Palmer, a much more capable administrator, but only the end of the war eliminated the problems that had produced such friction. As one Lincoln newspaper in the state commented, the president either had to change commanders "or give the whole of his time to the management of Kentucky affairs."[31]

It was Lincoln's policy on emancipation and black troops, however, more than arbitrary arrests or military interference with elections, that accounted for his unpopularity in the state. The Army's refusal to return runaway slaves produced inevitable friction with Kentucky slaveowners. And although at first Lincoln evidenced reluctance to accept black soldiers (on the grounds that it would turn Kentucky and the border states against the Union),[32] in 1863 he reversed this approach, producing such an angry protest in Kentucky that he agreed not to enlist blacks in the state if it met its draft quotas through volunteering. In early 1864, with enlistments lagging, Army officials in Kentucky began enrolling free blacks and slaves, and military authorities arrested several prominent state leaders for resisting recruitment of black soldiers. Black enlistments further alienated a public already disaffected with the administration.[33]

Lincoln's policies were only partly successful in Kentucky. More Kentuckians fought for the Union than the Confederacy, and when the rebel army invaded the state on several different occasions, it did not receive a friendly reception. In other respects, however, Lincoln's policies failed. Although Kentucky remained loyal to the Union, its congressional delegation strongly opposed the president. Lincoln never enjoyed much popularity in the state, especially after he adopted emancipation as a war aim, and Kentucky voted for George McClellan in 1864 by a decisive margin; indeed, Lincoln's proportion of the popular vote (30.2 percent) was the lowest he received in any of the twenty-five states that participated in the 1864 election (Table 2). The Republican Party remained weak in the state, primarily because large numbers of Unionists supported the Democratic Party over the slavery issue. Emancipation, black troops, military arrests, and suppression had all combined to unite Unionists and conservatives in the Democratic organization. Governor Bramlette, who supported Lincoln longer than most Kentuckians before breaking with him in 1864, warned the president that the extreme measures of his military commanders "have aroused the determined opposition to your reelection of at least three fourths of the people of Kentucky."[34] The Republican Party was confined to the most uncompromising Unionists and the most radical antislavery elements in the state.

IV

It was in Missouri, however, that Lincoln's policies achieved the least success.[35] More than any other border state, Missouri suffered from internal warfare, bitter political factionalism, and chaos and disorder during the war. The disappearance of many of the arrest records for Missouri precludes a precise tabulation, but it is clear that a staggering number of civilians were arrested for disloyal activity, and that the number of arbitrary arrests far exceeded that in any other loyal state.[36]

As in Kentucky, the onset of war in Missouri found a secessionist, Claiborne F. Jackson, in the governor's chair and a legislature that was more secessionist than the population as a whole. Jackson refused Lincoln's call for troops in April, but the secessionists were not strong enough to stampede the state out of the Union.[37] William S. Harney, commander of the U.S. forces in the state, reported that Unionists outnumbered secessionists in the interior of the state two to one and were a majority in St. Louis, gaining strength daily.[38] What was required to hold the state was a policy of tact and patience similar to that Lincoln followed in Kentucky.

The arrival of Captain Nathaniel Lyon, a stern antislavery New Englander with a small contingent of U.S. troops from Kansas, seriously weakened the prospects for a peaceful resolution. Even prior to his transfer, Lyon, who had aided the antislavery forces during the turmoil in Kansas, had concluded that "it is no longer useful to appeal to reason but to the sword, and trifle no longer in senseless wrangling."[39] Placed in the sensitive position of defending the St. Louis arsenal, the impatient Lyon began recruiting large numbers of volunteers while keeping a close watch on the secessionists. He soon formed a close alliance with former Congressman Frank Blair, the brother of Postmaster General Montgomery Blair and head of the Republican Party in Missouri. On 21 April, Lincoln, influenced by Frank Blair, recalled General William S. Harney, commander of the Department of the West, for consultations and put Lyon temporarily in charge of the troops in St. Louis.

The rash and impulsive Lyon lost little time in upsetting the delicate balance and throwing the situation into chaos by surrounding Camp Jackson, which posed no military threat, and capturing the state militia encamped there. Lyon's action was a major blunder: it achieved no crucial military end, provoked a serious riot in St. Louis by Confederate sympathizers, and, worst of all, drove many conditional Unionists over to the Confederacy. Quickly returning from Washington, Harney, who believed that precipitate application of force would make matters worse, worked to defuse the situation and allow Union sentiment to develop. To this end, he negotiated an understanding with Sterling Price, commander of the state militia, to maintain the peace. Harney bluntly informed the government that aggressive military force "could not secure the results the Government seeks, viz: The Maintenance of the loyalty now fully aroused in the State, and her firm security in the Union."[40]

Unconditional Unionists were dismayed at the Harney-Price agreement, while conservatives endorsed Harney's action. In Lincoln's cabinet, Attorney General Edward Bates defended Harney and condemned Lyon, while Montgomery Blair took the side of his own brother and of Lyon. In the end, under heavy pressure from the Blairs, the president once again removed Harney.[41]

Placed in command of the department, Lyon, who was devoid of common sense, promptly stirred up additional trouble. In a contentious four-hour meeting with the governor, he made clear his intention to use force against those he deemed disloyal. Jackson hastened back to his capital and issued a proclamation of war against the United States. Two days later, Lyon marched on the capital and put Jackson and other secessionist state officials to flight; skirmishing soon broke out between Lyon's forces and secessionists, who eventually organized a phantom Confederate state government with Jackson as governor. In less than two months, the reckless Lyon had plunged the state into a civil war that would never be completely suppressed during the next four years.

With the regular state government deposed, the state convention, which had been originally elected to consider secession, reconvened shorn of its secessionist members. It proceeded to declare the state offices vacant, dissolve the legislature, and establish a provisional state government with Hamilton R. Gamble, a conservative Whig, as governor. Gamble was the brother-in-law of Edward Bates. The provisional government was to serve only until November, when new elections would be held, but the election was postponed several times and the provisional government remained in power until January 1865, when it was replaced by regularly elected officers.

Lincoln meanwhile had appointed John C. Frémont, the famous western explorer and the Republican Party's first presidential candidate, commander of the western department. Frémont proved woefully incompetent as an administrator, military leader, and politician. He arrived the darling of the Blair clan, but their ardor began to cool when he failed to reinforce Lyon, who lost his life at the Battle of Wilson's Creek. At the same time, friction steadily mounted between Gamble and the aloof and imperious Frémont, who considered the governor a nuisance and refused to consult him.

Harried by guerrillas operating behind his lines and unable to drive Confederate forces out of the state, Frémont in desperation issued a proclamation on 30 August establishing martial law throughout the state and freeing the slaves of all disloyal masters in Missouri. Aware of the potentially disastrous impact this step would have on opinion in the border states, and unwilling to abdicate his responsibility as commander-in-chief to determine policy, Lincoln instructed Frémont to retract his proclamation. When the dimwitted but stubborn general refused, Lincoln publicly revoked it.[42] Frémont's fate was sealed: he had managed to alienate all but the most radical antislavery people in the state, and with virtually all factions clamoring for his head, Lincoln removed him a hundred days after he had assumed command.

The Confederate military threat to Missouri finally ended with the Union victory at the Battle of Pea Ridge in March 1862. Yet the removal of this threat did not bring peace and order to the state. Instead, Missouri remained under martial law, the legacy of Lyon's and Frémont's tenure, and guerrilla warfare raged across the state as partisans sought to even old scores or avenge new ones. Federal officials, reluctant to divert regular troops from the fighting, wanted the state government to handle the problem. The provisional government created a special force, the Enrolled Missouri Militia, to maintain order and put down the guerrillas, but it proved ineffective. Eventually in exasperation the army adopted the draconian solution of evacuating civilians from four western counties, a process that produced twenty thousand refugees. No policy pursued by the federal government, however, was able to end the fighting or eliminate the irregular bands of Confederate partisans.[43]

Following Frémont's removal, relations between the military and Gamble and the provisional government temporarily improved, only to soon deteriorate again. Disputes arose over control of the state militia and its relationship to federal troops in the state. As in the other border states, there was constant trouble over the army and slavery.[44] Solution at the local level of these problems, intensified as they were by personal hatreds and rival ambitions, was impossible. Lincoln's secretaries noted with regard to the state that "as a rule, serious local quarrels in any part of the country, whether of personal politics or civil or military administration, very soon made their way to President Lincoln for settlement." Yet, sorting through the "tangle of conflicting sentiment and irreconcilable factions" in the state from Washington was well nigh impossible.[45] Missouri affairs became a perpetual headache for the president.

Both Gamble and his opponents looked to the federal military commander for support and assistance in their struggle for state power. In a position that required tact, tolerance, and a delicate balancing of political interests, Lincoln's commanders were unequal to the task. Frémont failed miserably, and the new commander, Samuel R. Curtis, a former Iowa congressman, sided with the radical antislavery forces in the state against Gamble. Lincoln's tireless efforts to heal the breach and get the two men to work together were unsuccessful, so he finally removed Curtis in order to break up the quarrel. The new commander, John Schofield, threw the power of his command behind Gamble and the conservatives, which produced a radical outcry against him and eventually led to his replacement by William S. Rosecrans. Lincoln threw up his hands in frustration at the failure of his commanders to stay out of the state's politics.[46]

The Republican Party in Missouri was rent by bitter factionalism as radicals demanding the end of slavery battled against conservatives who gave priority to the Union issue. Charges and countercharges were hurled back and forth, and one delegation after another regularly trooped to the capital to win support in its battle for state supremacy. Caught between these rival groups, Lincoln and his military commander inevitably were unable to satisfy either side and became a target for both. In temper and spirit Lincoln was closer to Gamble and the conservatives, whereas on questions of policy, especially emancipation, he was closer to the radicals. Lincoln's unwillingness to take sides in the state's factional disputes led Gamble, in an outburst to Bates, to dismiss the president as "a mere intriguing, pettifogging, piddling politician."[47]

Gamble's death in 1864 left the conservatives disorganized and without a leader, and enabled the radicals to assume dominance. At the 1864 Republican convention, Missouri was the only state to oppose Lincoln's renomination, and even though the state supported him in the election in the fall (Table 2) and adopted emancipation in 1865, affairs in the state remained a persistent and insoluable problem for the president. The vicious irregular fighting in the state, the endemic political factionalism, and the large number of arbitrary arrests were all testimony to the failure of Lincoln's policies in Missouri.

V

The most sensitive problem Lincoln confronted in dealing with the border states was slavery. As has already been noted, he revoked Frémont's emancipation edict in 1861 with an eye to public opinion in the border states. In 1862 he negated another order freeing the slaves by one of his generals, David Hunter, in South Carolina. During this period, as the president carefully considered the problem of slavery and the Union war effort, he prodded the border states to abolish the institution by state action.

The first step he took in this direction was his message to Congress in December 1861, in which he recommended compensated emancipation in the border states.[48] He drafted a bill providing for compensated emancipation in Delaware, which had fewer than two thousand slaves, to serve as a pilot project for ending slavery in all the other border states. Lincoln's proposed bill was very conservative: it provided federal compensation to slave owners, authorized an apprenticeship system for minors, and ended slavery gradually over a thirty-year period. Nevertheless, hostility in the Delaware legislature was so strong the bill's supporters declined to even introduce it.[49] Delaware's response did not auger well for Lincoln's hopes that the border states would adopt emancipation.

When Congress took no notice of the proposal in his annual message, the president sent a special message on 6 March 1862, proposing federal funding for a program of compensated emancipation in the loyal slave states. He calculated that at the rate of $400 per slave, the expense to free all the slaves in the border states was less than the cost of the war for eighty-seven days.[50]

Four days later, he summoned the representatives of the border states in Congress to the White House, where he urged them to adopt a program of gradual compensated emancipation, noting that the controversies among the Union's supporters over slavery and its associated problems were "numerous, loud and deep." He repeated his argument that such a program would shorten the war.[51] The border state leaders present were generally skeptical, and when Congress subsequently approved a joint resolution agreeing to fund such a program, they remained opposed.[52]

Undaunted, Lincoln held a second meeting with border state leaders on 12 July 1862. Earlier, in annulling Hunter's proclamation, he had told the border state men, "You cannot . . . be blind to the signs of the times." Returning to this theme, he was earnest and forthright. He emphasized the great dissatisfaction his action had produced. "The incidents of the war cannot be avoided," he warned. "If the war continue long, as it must, if the object be not sooner attained, the institution in your states will be extinguished by mere friction and abrasion—by the mere incidents of war. It will be gone, and you will have nothing valuable in lieu of it."[53]

Despite Lincoln's plea, the border state leaders remained obdurate. A minority announced that they would urge the people of their states to consider Lincoln's plan, but the majority, including Crittendon and Garrett Davis of Kentucky, signed a report reiterating all their previous objections to emancipation. These objections were summarized by a Maryland Unionist who characterized emancipation as the beginning "of a great social revolution of labor and representation, in the midst of a political revolution."[54]

In the wake of the border state leaders' rejection of his second appeal, Lincoln decided to issue the Emancipation Proclamation. Yet even after he released the Preliminary Proclamation in September 1862, he continued to cling to the hope that the border states would adopt his program of gradual compensated emancipation. "Mr. Lincoln's whole soul is absorbed in his plan of remunerative emancipation," his old associate David Davis of Illinois reported after visiting Washington in November. "He believes that if Congress will pass a law authorizing the issuance of bonds for the payment of emancipated negroes in the border States that Delaware, Maryland, Kentucky, and Mo. will accept the terms."[55] He again recommended his plan in his annual message in December 1862. By this time, however, the initiative had to come from the border states themselves.

Public opinion in Maryland was generally hostile to the Emancipation Proclamation. Governor Bradford refused to sign an address of the Union governors approving Lincoln's action, and Congressman John W. Crisfield, one of the largest slaveholders in the state, publicly broke with the president over this question. The state's congressional delegation opposed the 1862 bill abolishing slavery in the District of Columbia, which the state had originally ceded to the federal government, and the Maryland House of Delegates denounced the law as a threat to the state and a violation of its rights.[56] Even so, opinion in the state slowly began to shift in response to the war's developments. The state's Union coalition, which united former Whigs, Know Nothings, and War Democrats, increasingly divided on the issue, and in 1863 the party split in two over the questions of emancipation and a new state constitution.

The 1863 election was a test of strength between the radical wing of the party, who called themselves the Unconditional Unionists, and their opponents. Led by Henry Winter Davis, the Unconditional Unionists favored immediate and uncompensated emancipation, black enlistments in the Union army, and a strict loyalty test in order to weaken the Democratic Party. The conservatives and moderates, led by Montgomery Blair, favored emancipation along the lines Lincoln had proposed, opposed black soldiers, and sought to win Democratic support. Capitalizing on popular frustration with the war and discontent over the policies on which it was being waged, the Unconditionals won a decisive victory in the fall election, carrying the one statewide office with 69 percent of the vote, winning four of the state's five congressional seats, and gaining control of the legislature.

Following the election, Lincoln counseled harmony in the Union ranks. Asserting that "I am very anxious for emancipation to be effected in Maryland in some substantial form," he indicated that although he preferred a gradual program, believing it would produce less confusion and destitution, he was not opposed to immediate emancipation. "My wish is that all who are for emancipation *in any form*, shall cooperate, all treating all respectfully, and all adopting and acting upon the major opinion, when fairly ascertained. What I have dreaded," he continued, "is the danger that by jealousies, rivalries, and consequent ill-blood . . . the friends of emancipation themselves may divide, and lose the measure altogether."[57] Divisions in the Unionist constituency, which extended beyond ideology to personal rivalries, were too deep to be healed by appeals to goodwill and common purpose.

Capitalizing on their new power, the radicals now moved to end slavery in Maryland. The voters approved holding a constitutional convention, and a majority of the delegates elected were emancipationists. The proposed new constitution abolished slavery in the state, subject to popular ratification. In an important move, the convention authorized soldiers in the field to vote on the proposed constitution. Referring to the upcoming vote on the antislavery constitution, Secretary of War Edwin Stanton told Lew Wallace, the new commanding general in the state, that "the President has set his heart on the abolition by that way; and mark, he don't want it to be said by anybody that the bayonet had anything to do with the election."[58] When antislavery forces requested his aid, Lincoln threw his influence behind the drive to ratify the constitution. In a public letter to a meeting in Baltimore, he endorsed the extinction of slavery in the state: "I wish success to this provision. I desire it on every consideration. I wish all men to be free."[59] In a close vote, the new constitution was approved, with the soldier vote providing the margin of victory for it and emancipation.[60] Although disappointed that the state had not taken this step two years earlier when he had urged it to do so, Lincoln was nevertheless pleased. In his final annual message, he hailed the "complete success" of emancipation in the state. "Maryland," he declared, "is secure to Liberty and Union for all the future."[61]

The emancipation forces prevailed in Missouri as well. Much as in Maryland, the conservative Unionists dragged their feet and failed to keep up with the advance of public opinion. The emancipationists won control of the legislature in the 1862 elections and steadily gained strength in 1863 and 1864. Emancipation became the most important issue in the state's politics. The radicals, known as the Charcoals, many of whom had been Republicans before the war, called for immediate emancipation. The reactionaries, or Snowflakes, opposed any interference with the institution, while the conservatives and moderates, led by Gamble and referred to as the Claybanks (because their stance was allegedly colorless), called for gradual emancipation. At the popular convention in 1863, the Claybanks, still in power in Missouri, influenced the delegates to approve a plan to end slavery in 1870 with terms of apprenticeship after that date. Lincoln criticized this plan, not because emancipation was gradual, but because it postponed the start for seven years. He told Schofield that he preferred a short period of emancipation and safeguards against slaves being sold in the meantime. "I have very earnestly urged the slave-states to adopt emancipation; and it ought to be, and is an object with me not to overthrow, or thwart what any of them may in good faith do, to that end."[62]

Dissatisfied with this program, the radicals kept up the agitation on emancipation, and in 1864 succeeded in getting a convention called to draft a new state constitution. In the fall election, the radicals won a majority of the delegates. The convention assembled in January 1865 and drafted a constitution that decreed immediate and unconditional emancipation. In the subsequent vote on ratification, solider ballots again tipped the scales in favor of the new constitution and emancipation.[63]

With more slaves than any other border state, Kentucky stubbornly clung to the dying institution to the bitter end. Precisely because slavery was stronger in Kentucky, Lincoln was convinced that if the state had responded favorably in 1862 to his original emancipation scheme, the war would have been brought to a close earlier. Instead, the state's congressional delegation opposed the president's plan for federally funded gradual emancipation, the legislature passed resolutions condemning the Emancipation Proclamation, and political leaders in the state denounced any move toward emancipation. Amendment of the Kentucky constitution was a particularly cumbersome process, but the state's failure to act was ideological rather than institutional. Kentucky Unionists remained bitter at what they perceived as Lincoln's betrayal of the original purpose of the war, and a majority refused to make any concessions or adjust to the changing world about them. After the Emancipation Proclamation was issued, a newspaper reporter declared that opinion was "universal" in the state that the president "has proved false to his platform, his pledges, and to his once ardent supporters and co-adjutors in the Border Slave States."[64] The situation did not improve over time. Indeed, defiant to the end, the legislature refused to ratify the Thirteenth Amendment in 1865. Lincoln's greatest disappointment concerning his policies in Kentucky was his inability to get his native state to budge on the question of slavery.

VI

How, then, do we account for the varying success of Lincoln's policies in these three states? Why was he reasonably successful in Maryland and Kentucky but not Missouri? The problem is more perplexing because enlistment records suggest that Unionism was stronger in Missouri than either of the other states (Table 3). Certainly there seems to have been less chance of the state seceding in 1861 than either Maryland or Kentucky.

In explaining Lincoln's difficulties in Missouri, James G. Randall provided a pat answer: the existence in the state of a powerful group of radicals was the source of all of Lincoln's problems.[65] The radicals were considerably stronger in Missouri than in Maryland, and they barely existed in Kentucky. But the division between Lincoln and the radicals was not as sharp as Randall contended. Indeed, Lincoln recognized that on questions of policy, he was closer to them than to their opponents. Shortly after meeting with a group of Missouri radicals, Lincoln remarked to his secretary, John Hay, "They are nearer to me than the other side, in thought and sentiment, though bitterly hostile to me personally. They are utterly lawless—the unhandiest devils in the world to deal with—but after all their faces are set Zionwards."[66] As Lincoln's comment suggests, more fundamental factors shaped the outcome of Lincoln's policies.

TABLE 3. ESTIMATED ENLISTMENTS FROM THE BORDER STATES

State	Union		Confederate
	Whites	Blacks	
Maryland	34,000	9,000	20,000
Kentucky	50,000	24,000	35,000
Missouri	80,000	8,000	30,000[1]
Delaware	10,000	1,000	1,000

Sources: James M. McPherson, *Ordeal by Fire* (New York: Knopf, 1982), 152–54, 185; Jean H. Baker, *The Politics of Continuity: Maryland Political Parties from 1858 to 1870* (Baltimore: Johns Hopkins University Press, 1973), 91.

[1] Another 3,000 fought as Southern guerrillas.

Perhaps the most obvious point to make, and the place to begin in analyzing this problem, is the importance of proximity. Maryland was closest to Washington, whereas Missouri was farthest away and Kentucky lay in between. Transportation and communication facilities were significantly better in the war than they were in, say, Andrew Jackson's time, yet the fact remained that the federal government in general best managed problems that were close at hand. Easy consultation with state political leaders, a surer grasp of public opinion, and a clearer sense of the problems were all consequences of shorter distances. Baltimore was "only a pleasant morning jaunt by rail from . . . Washington," Robert C. Schenck explained concerning his experiences as commander in Maryland, and thus no sooner did military officials take an action than "a delegation of influential Unionists at once hurried to the President."[67] The consequence was to keep Lincoln better informed about matters in the state and also to put the military under tighter executive control. No such close scrutiny was possible in Kentucky or Missouri, and as a result Washington displayed what Allan Nevins termed "a censurable myopia concerning the West."[68]

Lincoln's frustration with the situation in Missouri in 1861 is a case in point. He sent Postmaster General Montgomery Blair to St. Louis to advise Frémont. Frémont soon broke politically with the Blairs, and a crescendo of accusations between Frank Blair and Frémont descended upon the president. Uncertain of the true situation, Lincoln dispatched Secretary of War Simon Cameron and Adjutant General Lorenzo Thomas on a fact-finding trip. Rather than reserving the final decision to himself, as became his practice once he grew into his job, Lincoln authorized Cameron to remove Frémont if he thought it necessary.[69] This delegation of presidential responsibility betrayed his fundamental uncertainty about affairs in the state.

Exacerbating the situation in Missouri were the blunders of Union leaders in the initial weeks of the conflict. In this period, Lincoln relied primarily on Frank Blair, the leading Republican in the state, for advice. The hard-drinking Blair was not a good choice. Ambitious, outspoken, and passionate, he was often reckless and impulsive and offered highly colored advice. Hay, who was initially impressed with the Blairs, ultimately concluded that they "were not the safest guides about Missouri matters." He complained that despite his and other individuals' warnings, Lincoln continued to get "the greater part of his information from the Blairs & the Bates people who do not seem to me entirely impartial." While appreciative of the Blairs' early support for the president, Hay nonetheless believed that Lincoln placed too much reliance on them.[70]

Denouncing General William S. Harney's policy of moderation, Blair kept up a constant pressure to have the veteran soldier removed from command. Uncertain what to do, Lincoln initially wavered and then made a serious error in judgment by delegating the decision to Blair.[71] Armed with this presidential authorization to remove the general if in his opinion it was urgently necessary, Blair removed Harney from command and joined forces with Captain (soon Brigadier General) Nathaniel Lyon, with the disastrous consequences already noted. By the time Lyon was killed, serious damage had already been done to the Union cause. Frémont's utter incompetence merely magnified these problems. Lincoln's secretaries, John Nicolay and John Hay, who defended his vacillating policy, recognized the long-term consequences of this rupture in the Unionist ranks in Missouri: "The local embitterment in St. Louis beginning then ran on for several years, and in its varying and shifting phases gave the President no end of trouble in his endeavor from first to last to be just to each faction."[72]

Lincoln's inexperience and lack of knowledge was especially apparent in his handling of the Missouri situation in these early months. He made notoriously poor appointments and, lacking any real knowledge of the state or its politics, he relied on unsuitable advisers. Moreover, because Missouri was distant from Washington and removed from the major military theaters, Lincoln devoted less attention to the state. Without guidance from Washington about how to deal with a disloyal civilian population, Frémont acted on his own, instituting martial law and freeing the slaves of rebel masters. Historians have traditionally cited Lincoln's revocation of Frémont's edict as an example of his leadership concerning the border states, but it was probably the most unpopular act he committed during the first year of the war and left him badly damaged politically.[73]

As he gained experience, Lincoln took a stronger hand in supervising matters in Missouri, but he never fully comprehended the situation there. Particularly indicative of this failure was his well-meaning but futile proposal in 1865 to end the irregular violence in the state by appealing to the people to return home and agree to leave one

another alone. Detailing the flaws in Lincoln's plan, the new governor privately indicated that he had an "utter want of confidence in
its success" and asked the president to withhold it. From St. Louis
an astonished General Grenville M. Dodge was more blunt: "Allow
me to assure you that the course you propose would be protested
against by the State authorities, the legislature, the convention and
by nearly every undoubtedly loyal man in North Missouri," he telegraphed the president, "while it would receive the sanction of nearly
every disloyal, semi-loyal, and non-committed person there, all such
could, under the course live and should want to stay in that country,
while every loyal man would have to leave these counties."[74] Lincoln
persisted in this plan, with no good result.

The irregular nature of the loyal state government in Missouri presented yet another handicap. In Maryland, the state government was
controlled by the Unionists from the beginning, and their supremacy
was established beyond challenge by the fall elections of 1861. Like
Missouri, Kentucky had a pro-Confederate governor when the war
began, but even after Unionists secured control of the legislature,
they declined to oust him. Instead, they tied his hands so he could
not aid the Confederacy and eventually induced him to resign. As a
result, the state government retained its legitimacy throughout the
war, and in 1863 an unequivocal Unionist was elected governor.

In Missouri, however, Lyon's belligerence caused Governor Claiborne Jackson to ally openly with the Confederacy. Missouri Unionists
in the state convention declared the governorship vacant, but rather
than holding a popular election to select Jackson's successor, the convention, with only tenuous legal authority, selected Hamilton Gamble as governor. Initially, Gamble was to serve only until a regular
election could be held, but the Unionist majority in the convention
postponed the election several times because of the unceasing disorder in the state, and Gamble continued to hold the post until his
death in 1864. As a conservative, Gamble confronted what would
have been a severe and challenging situation even under the best of
circumstances, but his position was rendered infinitely more difficult
by the fact that he had never been elected by the voters. Such an
undemocratic procedure ran counter to the American political tradition; his moral authority undermined, Gamble could neither control
the Union party in the state nor the civilian population. Missouri had

no constitutionally legitimate government until the last few months of the war.[75]

If Gamble's irregular election weakened the authority of government in Missouri, the state's geographic location diminished the role of the U.S. Army, a potential prop for the state government. The inability of the Confederacy to mount any sustained threat west of the Mississippi after the Battle of Pea Ridge left the federal government anxious to devote as little military attention to the state as possible. A massive military occupation of the state, such as occurred in Maryland in 1861, and to a lesser extent in Kentucky, was not feasible in Missouri. Instead, Lincoln constantly complained about the number of troops he had to divert from more important objectives in order to control the state's civilian population. In refusing to disband the state's militia, which the state authorities created to preserve order, Lincoln explained, "I confess to a sympathy for whatever relieves our general force in Missouri, and allows it to serve elsewhere."[76]

Compounding these difficulties was the tradition of frontier violence in the state. Much more recently settled than Maryland or Kentucky, Missouri was much closer to the frontier stage of settlement, with its vigilante tradition and greater tolerance of personal violence. While also a problem in the pro-Confederate southern portion of the state, guerrilla warfare was especially pronounced in the turbulent, brawling western counties along the Missouri River. These counties had been in the forefront of the struggle to make Kansas a slave state in the 1850s. Relatively recently settled, they had become the major slaveholding area of the state by the 1850s, a factor that inflamed popular fears in the region. These fears, and the resulting bitterness stemming from the Kansas struggle, carried over into the war years and intensified. With an irregular state government and an ineffective military presence, these emotions soon erupted into personal violence. Once started, the strategy of retaliation and counterretaliation was impossible to stop. Moreover, it quickly spread across the border into Kansas, provoking retaliatory military raids from that state. Kansas troops invaded Missouri on several occasions and, remembering the long history of violence in their state, routinely plundered the civilian population, thereby increasing the animosity between the two states.[77]

Another difference that contributed to the Lincoln administration's difficulties in Missouri compared to the other border states was the state's past political history. Unlike Maryland and Kentucky, which had been Whig strongholds until the party's collapse in the 1850s, Missouri had been a Democratic state. Whiggery strengthened moderate Unionism in Maryland and Kentucky. In Missouri, in contrast, bitter factionalism erupted between former Whigs and Democrats in the Union ranks; this factionalism soon became more complicated, as the issue of emancipation broke the Union ranks further into radicals and conservatives.[78]

Aware that he needed the support and cooperation of all loyal Union men, Lincoln tried to steer a middle course. He told John Schofield when the latter assumed his new post as military commander in the state, "If both factions, or neither, shall abuse you, you will probably be about right."[79] Lincoln's moderation satisfied neither side. Confessing that he had been tormented with the state's factional quarrels beyond endurance, he complained, "Neither side pays the least respect to my appeals to your reason."[80] One consequence of growing radical strength was the abolition of slavery in Missouri, but it also produced a particularly virulent party factionalism that inflamed popular passions, crippled the state Republican Party, and strengthened their opponents. In Maryland, the radicals, although important, never commanded the support they gained in Missouri. And in Kentucky, the larger number of slaves, the stronger sentiment against emancipation, and the radical's failure to attract any prominent leader kept them impotent.

A final reason that contributed to the different experiences of these states was the existence of a Republican Party in Missouri before the war. This fact heightened Republican factionalism, drew the Lincoln administration into squabbles for state power, and made it easier for a radical faction to develop. In Maryland, and especially Kentucky, the party was more circumspect, being relatively weaker. As a result, the Lincoln administration worked closely with Unionists of other parties, which helped promote greater consensus.

Cleary the problems Lincoln confronted in these states were not all of his own making. Still, as president he made some serious mistakes in his border state policy. Perhaps Lincoln's biggest blunder was his early appointments in Missouri. Together, Blair, Lyon, and Frémont created a host of problems and controversies that continued long after Lyon's death and Frémont's removal. Lincoln's inexperience was woefully apparent. His handling of Kentucky, in contrast, was much more successful, and he was greatly aided by capable Unionists such as John J. Crittenden, Garrett Davis, James Speed, Leslie Combs, James Guthrie, and Robert J. Breckinridge.

Lincoln's effectiveness in dealing with subordinates is well illustrated in the cases of General Robert Schenck in Maryland and Samuel Curtis and John Schofield in Missouri. But being further removed from the scene and less certain of the situation, he gave Curtis and Schofield considerable leeway in policy matters, although he ultimately became frustrated that neither heeded his admonition that it was not "in the province of a military commander to interfere with the local politics or to influence elections actively in one way or another."[81] In Maryland, Schenck used his power to undermine the institution of slavery and in the process sometimes ran athwart of presidential directives. Aware of the situation, Lincoln, who on one occasion observed that Schenck was "wider across the head in the region of the ears," routinely summoned him to Washington, rewrote his orders, gave him much more explicit instructions, and kept him on a much tighter leash.[82]

Lincoln's problems in dealing with his generals highlighted one of the major causes for his difficulties: the hostile attitude of army officers, especially those from the North, toward the residents of the border states. The political ambitions of officers native to the state, such as Stephen Burbridge in Kentucky, were a further complication. In all three states, the army played a major role in destroying slavery, sometimes in accord with presidential policy or federal law, other times not. Viewing the people of the border states as at least quasidisloyal, Union generals erred on the side of overzealousness in making arrests and confiscating private property. With a few exceptions, the generals in command in Kentucky and Missouri lacked tact and common sense and often acted in an arbitrary and highhanded manner. Kentucky's early neutrality and persistent opposition to emancipation particularly discredited the state with the military. Governor Bramlette put his finger on the central problem in this regard when he bitterly complained: "We are dealt with as though Kentucky was a rebellious and conquered province, instead of being as they [sic] are, a brave and loyal people."[83]

Lincoln's record in dealing with the border states contained both successes and failures. Certainly keeping these states in the Union was Lincoln's greatest achievement during the first year of his presidency. Yet on other issues—emancipation, arbitrary arrests, the preservation of public order, and relations between civil and military authorities—his policies provoked greater resistance. He was especially plagued by the intractable situation in Missouri. To a much greater extent than either Maryland or Kentucky, that state proved impervious to Lincoln's presidential leadership. It left a dark blot on his otherwise generally positive record of accomplishments in the border states.

NOTES

1. In addition, approximately a half million whites lived in the Unionist regions of western Virginia and eastern Tennessee. See James A. Rawley, *Turning Points of the Civil War* (Lincoln: University of Nebraska Press, 1966), 11–12.

2. For this reason Delaware has been excluded from most of the discussion that follows. Even had Delaware's commitment to the Union been more qualified, it never could have functioned as a Confederate state as long as Maryland, which surrounded it, remained in the Union.

3. Abraham Lincoln to Orville H. Browning, 22 September 1861, in *The Collected Works of Abraham Lincoln*, Roy P. Basler, ed., Marion Dolores Pratt and Lloyd A. Dunlap, asst. eds., 9 vols. (New Brunswick, N.J.: Rutgers University Press, 1953–55), 4:532 (hereafter, Basler, *Collected Works*).

4. Edward C. Smith, *The Borderland in the Civil War* (New York: Macmillan, 1927), 141, 389–90; see also Allan Nevins, *The War for the Union*, 4 vols. (New York: Charles Scribner's, 1959–71), 1:119, 147.

5. A recent example of this approach is James A. McPherson, *Battle Cry of Freedom: The Civil War Era* (New York: Oxford University Press, 1988).

6. Mark E. Neely Jr., *The Fate of Liberty: Abraham Lincoln and Civil Liberties* (New York: Oxford University Press, 1991), 29.

7. Neely emphasizes the political liabilities of arbitrary arrests and military regulation of the press, courts, and elections (*Fate of Liberty*, 27–29). Smith likewise concluded: "It is doubtful if these measures were beneficial to the government" (*Borderland*, 394).

8. William J. Evitts, *A Matter of Allegiances: Maryland from 1850 to 1861* (Baltimore: Johns Hopkins University Press, 1974), 1–7; Jean H. Baker, *The Politics of Continuity: Maryland Political Parties from 1858 to 1870* (Baltimore: Johns Hopkins University Press, 1973), 8–11.

9. Nevins, *War for the Union*, 1:82–83; Lincoln to Thomas H. Hicks and

George W. Brown, 20 April 1861, Lincoln to Reverdy Johnson, 26 July 1862, Basler, *Collected Works*, 4:340, 5:343.

10. Tyler Dennett, ed., *Lincoln and the Civil War in the Diaries and Letters of John Hay* (New York: Dodd, Mead, 1939), 16.

11. Basler, *Collected Works*, 3:347.

12. Dennett, *Lincoln and the Civil War*, 18; John Nicolay and John Hay, *Abraham Lincoln: A History*, 10 vols. (New York: Century, 1886–90), 4:170 (hereafter, Nicolay and Hay, *Lincoln*); Nevins, *War for the Union*, 1:137–38.

13. While forbidding the Army to arrest the secessionist members of the state legislature prior to its assembling, Lincoln authorized Winfield Scott, the commanding general, to use force if they took any action hostile to the United States. Lincoln to Scott, 29 April 1861, Basler, *Collected Works*, 3:344. See also the account of Lincoln's interview on 4 May 1861 with a delegation from Maryland, in Nicolay and Hay, *Lincoln*, 4:172.

14. Morgan Dix, comp., *Memoirs of John Adams Dix*, 2 vols. (New York: Harper, 1883), 2:339–40; Baker minimizes the extent of federal interference in the November election (*Politics of Continuity*, 71–75).

15. Ibid., 62–75.

16. Augustus W. Bradford to Lincoln, 31 October 1863, Abraham Lincoln Papers, Library of Congress; Lincoln to Bradford, 2 November 1863, Basler, *Collected Works*, 6:556–57. Schenck's action is criticized in Charles Lewis Wagandt, *The Mighty Revolution: Negro Emancipation in Maryland, 1862–1864* (Baltimore: Johns Hopkins University Press, 1964), 159–63; and defended in Nicolay and Hay, *Lincoln* 8:460–61.

17. Thomas Swann to Lincoln, 26 October 1863, Abraham Lincoln Papers; Lincoln to Swann, 27 October 1863, Basler, *Collected Works*, 6:542.

18. For a judicious weighing of the evidence that minimizes the importance of military interference, see Baker, *Politics of Continuity*, 87–91. For a contrary view, see Wagandt, *Mighty Revolution*, 164–84.

19. Ibid., 190.

20. A dated and less than satisfactory account is E. Merton Coulter, *The Civil War and Readjustment in Kentucky* (Chapel Hill: University of North Carolina Press, 1926). Brief but more balanced is Ross A. Webb, "Kentucky: 'Pariah Among the Elect,'" in *Radicalism, Racism and Party Realignment: The Border States during Reconstruction*, ed. Richard O. Curry (Baltimore: Johns Hopkins University Press, 1969), 105–45. Rawley presents a good discussion of development in the state in 1861 (*Turning Points*, 9–45).

21. John J. Crittenden to Winfield Scott, 17 May 1861, in Nicolay and Hay, *Lincoln*, 4:233; Coulter, *Civil War in Kentucky*, 46. Another Unionist leader, Garrett Davis, assured George McClellan: "We will remain in the Union by voting if we can, by fighting if we must, and if we cannot hold our own, we will call on the General Government to aid us"; quoted in Nevins, *War for the Union*, 1:134.

22. Ibid., 133, 135–36, 139; Smith, *Borderland*, 280.

23. Lincoln to Simon B. Buckner, 10 July 1861, Basler, *Collected Works*, 4:444; Nevins, *War for the Union*, 1:133.

24. Quoted in Nevins, *War for the Union*, 1:136.

25. Coulter unsuccessfully attempts to minimize the importance of the Unionist victory in August (*Civil War in Kentucky*, 97–98).

26. Lincoln to Orville H. Browning, 22 September 1861, Basler, *Collected Works*, 4:532; James Speed to Lincoln, 3 September 1861, Abraham Lincoln Papers; Coulter, *Civil War in Kentucky*, 111–12.

27. Basler, *Collected Works*, 5:50. See James Speed to Lincoln, 22 December 1861, Abraham Lincoln Papers.

28. Coulter, *Civil War in Kentucky*, 80.

29. Lowell Harrison, *The Civil War and Kentucky* (Lexington: University of Kentucky Press, 1975), 98–100.

30. Basler, *Collected Works*, 7:426.

31. *Frankfort Commonwealth*, 24 February 1865, quoted in Coulter, *Civil War in Kentucky*, 213. Ulysses S. Grant concluded that "any officer of rank (not a Kentuckian) would be better than Burbridge, who has politics in his head" (ibid., 211).

32. Basler, *Collected Works*, 5:356–57.

33. Lincoln to Edwin Stanton, 28 March 1864, ibid., 7:272; Howard K. Beale, ed., *The Diary of Edward Bates, 1859–1866* (Washington, D.C.: Government Printing Office, 1933), 352.

34. Quoted in Coulter, *Civil War in Kentucky*, 186.

35. See William E. Parrish, *Turbulent Partnership: Missouri and the Union, 1861–1865* (Columbia: University of Missouri Press, 1963).

36. Neely, *Fate of Liberty*, 44–46, 128–29.

37. In the February election to select delegates to a state convention, Unionists of various stripes won 110,000 votes compared to 30,000 for secessionist candidates. When the convention met in March, it rejected secession by a decisive margin (Parrish, *Turbulent Partnership*, 9–14).

38. Nevins, *War for the Union*, 1:128.

39. Parrish, *Turbulent Partnership*, 16. See also Christopher Phillips, *Damned Yankee: The Life of General Nathaniel Lyon* (Columbia: University of Missouri Press, 1990).

40. William S. Harney to Lorenzo Thomas, 29 May 1861, quoted in Smith, *Borderland*, 250.

41. Lincoln to Francis P. Blair Jr., 18 May 1861, Basler, *Collected Works*, 4:372; Hans Christian Adamson, *Rebellion in Missouri: Nathaniel Lyon and His Army of the West* (Philadelphia: Chilton, 1961), 86–87; Blair to Lincoln, 30 May 1861, quoted in Nicolay and Hay, *Lincoln*, 4:222.

42. Lincoln to Browning, 22 September 1861, Basler, *Collected Works*,

4:532; Joshua F. Speed to Lincoln, 3 September 1861, Abraham Lincoln Papers. For Lincoln's modification of the proclamation, see Lincoln to Frémont, 11 September 1861, Basler, *Collected Works*, 4:517–18.

43. For the complicated history of the Enrolled Militia, see James A. Hamilton, "The Enrolled Missouri Militia: Its Creation and Controversial History," *Missouri Historical Review* 69 (July 1975): 413–32.

44. Michael Fellman, "Emancipation in Missouri," *Missouri Historical Review* 83 (October 1988): 36–56; John W. Blassingame, "The Recruitment of Negro Troops in Missouri during the Civil War," *Missouri Historical Review* 58 (April 1964): 326–38.

45. Nicolay and Hay, *Lincoln*, 6:380, 370. Even from the vantage point of several decades later, Lincoln's secretaries continued to be bewildered by affairs in Missouri during the war: "There is in the local history of Missouri such a confusion and contradiction of assertion and accusation concerning the motives and acts of both individuals and parties, such a blending of war and politics, of public service and private revenge, as frequently make it impossible to arrive at established facts or reach intelligent conclusions" (377).

46. Lincoln to Schofield, 27 May 1863, Basler, *Collected Works*, 6:234; Dennett, *Lincoln and the Civil War*, 95.

47. Gamble to Bates, 10 August 1863, quoted in Parrish, *Turbulent Partnership*, 160.

48. Basler, *Collected Works*, 5:48–49.

49. Ibid., 29–31; Nicolay and Hay, *Lincoln*, 5:206–8.

50. Basler, *Collected Works*, 5:144–46. See also Lincoln to Henry J. Raymond, 9 March 1862, Lincoln to James A. McDougall, 14 March 1862, ibid., 153, 160.

51. The contemporaneous account by Congressman John W. Crisfield of Maryland, who attended the meeting, is in Edward B. McPherson, *The Political History of the United States of America during the Great Rebellion* (Washington: Philip and Solomons, 1865), 210–11.

52. A bill to provide compensation to any of the border states that adopted emancipation died in the House in 1862 because their delegates in Congress opposed it and none of them came forward with an alternative plan.

53. Basler, *Collected Works*, 5:223, 317–19.

54. Wagandt, *Mighty Revolution*, 70. The border state objections are summarized in Nevins, *War for the Union*, 2:114, 148. The names of those signing the various reports are given in Nicolay and Hay, *Lincoln*, 6:111–12.

55. David Davis to Leonard Swett, 26 November 1862, quoted in Nevins, *War for the Union*, 2:235.

56. Wagandt, *Mighty Revolution*, 63–64. In an interview with Crisfield,

Lincoln told the Maryland congressman that while he objected to the timing of the bill and some of its terms, he intended to sign it because a veto would cause greater political trouble.

57. Basler, *Collected Works*, 7:226.

58. Lew Wallace, *Lew Wallace: An Autobiography*, 2 vols. (New York: Harper, 1906), 2:672.

59. Basler, *Collected Works*, 8:41–42.

60. The regular vote was 27,541 in favor and 29,536 against the constitution. Among soldiers, the tally stood 2,633 in favor and only 263 opposed (Baker, *Politics of Continuity*, 109n).

61. Basler, *Collected Works*, 8:52, 148.

62. Lincoln to Schofield, 22 June 1863, Lincoln to Stephen A. Hurlbut, 31 July 1863, ibid., 6:291, 358.

63. The constitution was approved by a margin of only 1,835 votes of 85,769 votes cast. Whereas civilians opposed the constitution by a vote of 40,640 to 39,675, Union soldiers from the state voted in its favor, 3,995 to 1,168.

64. *Cincinnati Gazette*, 10 January 1863, quoted in Coutler, *Civil War in Kentucky*, 161–62.

65. James G. Randall, *Lincoln the President*, 4 vols. (New York: Dodd, Mead, 1945–55), 2:15–16, 3:48–49.

66. Dennett, *Lincoln and the Civil War*, 108. For a general discussion of this point, see David Donald, "Devils Facing Zionwards," in *Grant, Lee, Lincoln, and the Radicals: Essays on the Civil War*, ed. Grady McWhiney (Evanston: Northwestern University Press, 1964), 72–91.

67. Wallace, *Autobiography*, 2:674–75.

68. Nevins, *War for the Union*, 1:309.

69. Simon Cameron to Lincoln, 12, 14 October 1861, Abraham Lincoln Papers; Lincoln to Samuel R. Curtis, 7 October 1861, Basler, *Collected Works*, 4:549.

70. Dennett, *Lincoln and the Civil War*, 94–95. With time and experience, Lincoln became more cautious in relying on Frank Blair and his family. For his later shrewd assessment of the Blairs, see Hay's entry for 9 December 1863 (133).

71. Lincoln to Francis P. Blair Jr., 18 May 1861, Basler, *Collected Works*, 4:372.

72. Nicolay and Hay, *Lincoln*, 4:216.

73. Nevins, *War for the Union*, 1:334–35, 340.

74. Lincoln to Grenville M. Dodge, 15 January 1865, Lincoln to Thomas C. Fletcher, 27 February 1865, Basler, *Collected Works*, 8:217, 319; Dodge to Lincoln, 16 January 1865, Abraham Lincoln Papers; Fletcher to Lincoln, 27 February (telegram and letter), Basler, *Collected Works*, 8:319–20.

75. Lincoln acknowledged this problem in a soothing letter to Gamble, 19 October 1863, ibid., 6:526–27.

76. Lincoln to Charles Drake and others, ibid., 503.

77. For descriptions of this partisan warfare, see Michael Fellman, *Inside War: The Guerrilla Conflict in Missouri during the American Civil War* (New York: Oxford University Press, 1989); Albert Castel, *A Frontier State at War: Kansas, 1861–1865* (Ithaca: Cornell University Press, 1958).

78. For Lincoln's analysis of the situation, see his letter to Charles Drake and others, 5 October 1863, Basler, *Collected Works*, 6:500.

79. Lincoln to John Schofield, 27 May 1863, ibid., 234.

80. Lincoln to Henry T. Blow and others, 15 May 1863, ibid., 218.

81. Dennett, *Lincoln and the Civil War*, 95.

82. Ibid., 105; Wagandt, *Mighty Revolution*, 123, 189; Nicolay and Hay, *Lincoln*, 8:459–60.

83. Quoted in Harrison, *Civil War and Kentucky*, 86–87; see also Basler, *Collected Works*, 5:426n–427n. Neely explains that one reason the Lincoln administration's record of arbitrary arrests did not generate a great popular outcry in the North was because most of those arrested were residents of the border states. Recalling the Baltimore riot, Kentucky's neutrality in the early months of the war, and Missouri's unsteady course, Northern public opinion simply did not care much about the fate of these states or its citizens beyond keeping them in the Union (*Fate of Liberty*).

9

Lincoln and Chase: A Reappraisal

John Niven

LINCOLN SCHOLARS and all who have a distinct interest in the Union's conduct of the Civil War are well aware of the differences that developed between the president and the politically ambitious Salmon P. Chase, his secretary of the treasury. Many have seen in these differences a conflict between the radical and conservative elements of the Republican coalition over control of the administration, over its conduct of war, and particularly over its policy on emancipation, civil rights for the freedmen, and the eventual reconstruction of the rebellious states. Lincoln, it has been well argued, sought a moderate position on these divisive points among the radicals in Congress, those within his administration, and their conservative counterparts. Chase, especially, has been cast as the leading radical in the cabinet, with Montgomery Blair, the postmaster general, as the leading conservative. Other members of an unusually able but fiercely contentious group are ranked somewhere in between these two poles.

There is sound evidence for making such judgments. But like all generalizations, they tend to oversimplify a complex series of events. Specifically, they overlook Chase's role as an indispensable manager of the nation's wartime economy through his financial and fiscal policies that dealt with an unprecedented and extremely difficult situation. Nor have these authorities considered Chase's personality, his majestic figure, his enormous self-confidence—just the right sort of person to deal with the rich, self-assured leaders of the eastern banking community. At the same time, he was a person with sufficient practical experience to cope with tough-minded members of the Senate and House finance committees in matters relating to the economy, as well as with temperamental cabinet colleagues. I think that

Lincoln quickly recognized these unique qualities and felt they were absolutely necessary for financing the war effort. Much later, after Lincoln had appointed Chase to the Supreme Court, he told Augustus Frank, a congressman from New York, that "Mr. Chase's ability and soundness on the general issues of the war there is, of course, no question. We have stood together in the time of trial, and I should despise myself if I allowed personal differences to affect my judgment of his fitness."[1]

The political in-fighting that has fascinated students of the Lincoln administration has also overshadowed an equally important aspect of wartime Washington: the unique relationship between Lincoln and Chase, which underwent considerable change during the three and one-half years of Chase's tenure in the cabinet. Lincoln remarked to his secretary, John Hay, that he had finally become so exasperated at Chase's political conduct while a member of his cabinet that he abruptly accepted Chase's resignation at a most inopportune time for the war effort. It was Chase's fourth letter of resignation. In recording this incident in his diary, Hay paraphrased Lincoln's reaction to Chase's letter: "You have been acting very badly. Unless you say you are sorry and ask . . . to stay, and agree that I shall be absolute and that you shall have nothing, no matter how you beg for it, I will go." Hay added dryly, "The President thought one or the other must resign. Mr. Chase elected to do so."[2]

Yet Lincoln continued to have high respect for Chase's abilities if not for his personal qualities, even when he took this disastrous decision. The patronage quarrel over Treasury appointments in New York City, which led to the acceptance of Chase's resignation, although clearly a skirmish between the radicals and the conservatives was, I feel, purely a skirmish which Lincoln could have headed off without extending and deepening the conflict. Of course, these were times of deep trouble for the president. The military situation in Virginia and western Georgia seemed stalemated despite heavy losses. But, politically, Lincoln was more secure than he had been a few months before, and would be two months later.

Thurlow Weed, Secretary Seward's political alter ego and a leading figure among New York's Republicans, made an interesting comment on this point. Writing to John Bigelow on 13 December 1863, Weed spoke of Chase's driving ambition for the presidency. "Mr. Chase's Treasury report is very able," he said, "and his huge banking machine will make him strong. But how pitiable it is to know his eye is single—not to the welfare of the country in an unselfish cause, but to the presidency. Mr. Lincoln says that he is 'trying to keep the maggot out of his brain.' "³ Weed, of course, was a political opponent of Chase within the Republican ranks, but his observation squares with evidence from many other sources, radical as well as conservative, that confirm Chase's passion for assuming the chief executive role.

Lincoln knew of Chase's ambition well before he appointed him to the Treasury post in March of 1861. Chase had been a candidate for the Republican presidential nomination in 1856, when he himself sought unsuccessfully the vice presidential nomination. Again, in 1860, when Lincoln received the presidential nomination, Chase along with Seward had been a leading candidate. The political ambitions of his rivals Lincoln assumed as a fact of life. His choices for his cabinet reflected the coalition nature of the new Republican Party. Lincoln was certainly not naive enough to expect in March of 1861 that partisans such as Seward and Chase would suddenly abandon their long-term goals.

Besides previous party affiliation and regional locales, Lincoln's perception of merit and ability counted much in his final selection. Unsure of himself as he faced the dread prospect of a divided Union, he felt he needed the counsel of the best minds and the most experienced administrators in the North. Both Seward and Chase had been in the public eye for the past decade. Both had been governors and United States senators from leading northern states. But, if anything, Chase commanded more attention from the president-elect than Seward. Chase had provided much of the intellectual and constitutional underpinnings of the free soil movement that eventually provided the ideology of the new Republican Party.

As early as 1833 Chase had done significant research and provided an original interpretation of the Ordinance of 1787, which declared all of the Northwest Territory to be free of slavery. He had published the results of his work in a short history of Ohio, which formed the introduction to his three-volume *Statutes of Ohio*. Lincoln must certainly have used this work in preparation for legal cases in which he was involved. His speeches during the fifties, including his debates with Stephen A. Douglas, indicate a thorough knowledge of the Ordinance of 1787. In all likelihood it was drawn from Chase's history and also from Chase's argument in the Van Zandt case that had been published as a pamphlet and distributed widely. Although the Van Zandt pamphlet is not among Lincoln's papers, it is reasonable to assume he received a copy. Chase sent copies to every member of the Congress to which Lincoln had been elected in 1846.[4] But, more important, Lincoln, like all free soilers, owed a great debt to Chase's legal and philosophical opinions on slavery. In particular, Chase made the argument that Lincoln and others adopted, linking the anti-slavery natural rights philosophy as expressed in the Declaration of Independence to the Constitution.[5]

Chase had gone to the very heart of the federal system with his elegant statement before the Supreme Court in the Van Zandt case. "The very moment a slave passes beyond the jurisdiction of the state in which he is held as such, he ceases to be a slave," Chase said, "not because any law or regulation of the state which he enters confers freedom upon him, but because he *continues* to be a man, and *leaves behind* him the law of force which made him a slave." Although others, Ben Wade for instance, had made similar points, no one had articulated the free soil position so clearly and so succinctly as Chase had in July 1842 and in early 1847.[6]

Chase may have lost the case, but his argument which led to a reinterpertation of the Constitution—especially Article IV, Section III on congressional power over the territories and the District of Columbia—was a significant contribution to the political formulation of Republican Party doctrine. Other definitions that Chase made of the original intent of the founding fathers on the subject of slavery that he had drawn from a careful study of *Elliot's Debates* and other basic sources certainly influenced the political action of free soil Whigs and Democrats, Lincoln among them.

Yet, curiously, Lincoln and Chase had not met each other until well after the Republican triumph in the presidential election of 1860. Chase had been one of the notable Republican politicians who had spoken in Illinois on behalf of Lincoln's campaign against Douglas for the United States Senate in 1858. Lincoln had been deeply grateful for his assistance. In a letter he wrote to Samuel Galloway, the influential Ohio educator and politician in July 1859, Lincoln remarked, "As to Governor Chase, I have a kind side for him. He was one of the few distinguished men of the nation who gave us in Illinois their sympathy last year." In the same letter, however, he thought Chase unsuitable for the presidential nomination and criticized the Republican convention in Ohio for its resolution urging the repeal of the fugitive slave law. A few weeks later Lincoln made speeches for the party in Columbus, Dayton, and Cincinnati, but missed meeting Chase who was himself on the hustings in other areas of the state.[7]

When the two men did meet face to face, it was under embarrassing circumstances. Lincoln had asked Chase to visit him in Springfield. Chase had just been elected to a second term in the United States Senate from Ohio when the invitation came. He arrived in Springfield on the evening of 3 January 1861, and sent word to the president-elect from his hotel that as soon as he had settled in he would call. Chase must have been somewhat surprised when Lincoln himself came to his room. Chase, handsome, dignified, and almost as tall as Lincoln, no doubt did little to ease what quickly became an awkward situation. For Lincoln had not as yet freed himself from a promise his managers had made at the Republican convention to bestow the Treasury portfolio on the current Republican boss of Pennsylvania, Simon Cameron. Lincoln opened the conversation with Chase when he said, "I have done with you what I would not perhaps have ventured to do with any man in the country. I sent for you to ask you whether you will accept the appointment of Secretary of the Treasury, without, however, being exactly prepared to offer it to you."[8]

It was not in Chase's nature to ease the president-elect's dilemma. Chase replied, loftily, that he had not sought any post, would not accept a subordinate position, and was not prepared at this time to say he would accept the Treasury Department if it were offered. Lincoln explained that he had offered the State Department to Seward, who had accepted. Had Seward declined, he would have named Chase to the post. At the time, Chase was no friend of Seward's, politically or otherwise, but he concealed his feelings on Seward's appointment. For the next two days, Chase conferred with Lincoln on matters of politics and public policy, but when he left for home he had not said whether he would accept the Treasury post if offered. Indeed, Chase impressed upon Lincoln that he felt he could serve the public better in the United States Senate.[9]

Between 5 January and 5 March, Lincoln managed to appease Cameron by offering him the War Department—a post Cameron accepted. Thereupon, Lincoln nominated Chase for the Treasury on 6

March, without consulting him. It was unanimously confirmed. Chase was absent from the Senate when the vote was taken, but on learning of it he immediately visited the president. He still withheld acceptance despite a virtual plea from Lincoln, who spoke of the extreme embarrassment that would result if Chase refused the office. Chase kept the president in suspense for a day before he accepted, a typical example of his self-important pose. But at this state of their relationship Lincoln was quite willing to blame himself for any hesitation on Chase's part. When Chase did accept, Lincoln was so relieved to have Seward and Chase in the cabinet at his side that it is doubtful that he ever gave Chase's position of reluctance a moment's thought.[10]

Of the two leading members in the new administration, Seward by far had the more impressive political and administrative career. Chase and Seward were college men, Chase a Dartmouth graduate, Seward a graduate of Union College in Schenecady, New York. Both men were prominent lawyers, but Chase's background and family connections were more distinguished than Seward's. Chase's father, a prosperous farmer, had been for many years a member of the New Hampshire senate. Chase's many uncles had attended Dartmouth, and two of them had enjoyed national renown. One uncle, Philander Chase, had been Episcopal Bishop of Ohio, founding president of two colleges, Kenyon at Gambier, Ohio, and Jubilee in Robin's Nest, Illinois, and president of a third, Cincinnati College. Another uncle, Dudley, had been a United States senator from Vermont and chief justice of that state's supreme court. Other close relatives were professional men and moved in the highest circles of New England society, which, in Lincoln's day and especially for northwesterners, represented high culture and wealth.[11]

Lincoln's background and education were in sharp contrast to Chase's, and to Seward's for that matter. Lincoln's amiable father, Thomas, could barely read and could write only with difficulty. His mother was illiterate. Lincoln was brought up in dire poverty where hard labor on one hardscrabble farm or another on the Kentucky and Indiana frontiers had been his daily lot until young manhood. He was very sensitive and secretive about his forebears. Although he was the essence of the successful self-made man in the new states of the Northwest, Lincoln never quite felt completely at ease in the company of highly educated individuals of wealth and fashion.

He had, however, sought and married a woman, Mary Todd, who was well above his station in life; and he had been hurt deeply by the opposition of her socially prominent relatives to their engagement and marriage. Lincoln presented to the outside world an air of homely confidence, mellowed by a natural bonhomie that stemmed from his western frontier background. He was shrewd in the ways of the open give-and-take that marked the upwardly mobile, small-venture capitalist and circuit-riding lawyer and politician of the Midwest at mid-century.[12] Lincoln probably never knew that Chase, this handsome, self-confident individual, had also borne his share of an insecure, poverty-ridden childhood and adolescence. Chase's father died bankrupt in 1817 when Chase was a child of nine. He had been shuffled from one family to another for the next three years and then was sent west, where he came under the exacting tutelage of his uncle, Philander Chase.

Bishop Chase was a tall, imposing, domestic tyrant whose constant insistence that his young nephew excel in all tasks was enforced by frequent beatings. Chase drew a devastating picture of his uncle in a letter to a cousin: "The Bishop never was qualified for the government of young men. His temper is too absolute and imperious; and he is apt to resort to the bastinado and the bowstring[;] . . . everyone who has been with him will bear testimony that his severity is great, excessive, and unnecessary." Yet the bishop's training, while deeply resented, was a formative force in modeling Chase's personality. Chase, too, had a bad temper, which he usually managed to control but which was more frequently concealed by an overbearing, self-rectitude that brooked no question.[13] His uncle certainly inculcated a driving ambition to excel, and his cruelty mixed with his overwhelming piety laid the foundations for Chase's self-deception about his own motives, as well as his consuming religiosity. One is tempted to attribute the dark side of Chase's character, his devious means to achieve what he considered rightful objectives, to an inbred remembrance of his uncle's wrath and his innate opposition to the kind of life the bishop had tried to impose upon him.

After the difficult years in Ohio and his graduation from college, Chase gravitated to Washington, hopeful that his Uncle Dudley, the senator, could secure a government clerkship for him. He was unsuccessful, but he did manage through his uncle's connections to establish a school that furnished him with a livelihood. At this point, Chase came under the influence of another person so decidedly different from his uncle the bishop that one can see the beginnings of another aspect of Chase's character, which we may take to be the brighter side of his personality.[14]

The individual was William Wirt, then attorney general of the United States, a genial, witty Virginian, who, besides being the foremost lawyer in the capital, was a novelist, a biographer, and the father of a bevy of beautiful daughters. Chase studied law with Wirt, but, more importantly, he and his charming family offered the awkward, sensitive young man the home he had never really known. Chase consciously modeled himself on Wirt, and it seems reasonable to attribute Chase's undoubted sincerity in his defense of human rights to Wirt's example.[15]

There is a Manichaean quality to Chase's personality that I think Lincoln recognized, although, of course, he would not have known the reasons for it. Chase himself testified to Wirt's influence, as he had earlier to the baneful example of the bishop, in a conversation with Admiral Samuel DuPont during the early fall of 1862; Chase alluded to his early life. As DuPont said in a letter to his wife, "Mr. Chase has great vigor of mind and [is] more easy and fluent than I judged him in the Senate. I think he is a statesman, and I could trace the effects of being as a young man under the influences and direction of a man like Mr. Wirt."[16]

A humane person, Lincoln had been attracted to Chase's courageous battle for human rights in the Ohio of the 1830s, 1840s, and 1850s. Lincoln shared with Chase a deep-rooted opposition to slavery. Lincoln found the institution both morally and socially repugnant in a nation professing democracy and equality of opportunity. But as a lawyer and a student of the Constitution, he was also a strong advocate of the federal Union, where the exercise of powers was divided between the central government and the states. In politics he had been a Whig. In many respects, however, Lincoln's views on the nature of the Union resembled those of northern Democrats who cherished states' rights as the basic determinant of social and economic institutions. He found Chase's political background, which fused Whig notions of morality and piety with a Democratic insistence on states' rights, quite compatible with his own views. Although far more pragmatic on the slavery issue than Chase, Lincoln had readily adopted Chase's linkage of the Declaration with the Constitution as an eminently lawful means of containing slavery wherever congressional power extended. Without disturbing the institution where it existed by state law, he looked forward to its eventual abolition through state power, eventually fulfilling the promise of the Declaration.

When the war began, Lincoln gave Chase complete freedom in developing and executing the financial policies necessary to support enormous expenditures. In fact, once Lincoln became assured of his ministers' capabilities, he gave them full reign in administering their respective departments. Despite a general consensus of historical opinion, and Lincoln's own profession that he was ignorant of financial and economic matters, I feel that he was quite as well-informed as any public man of his day, including Chase, on the broad outlines of finance and fiscal policy.

Contemporaries such as one of Chase's assistant secretaries, Maunsell B. Field, and his successors in the Treasury, Hugh McCulloch and George Boutwell, have criticized Chase for relying, in part, on fiat currency, or "greenbacks," instead of insisting on higher levels of taxation to finance the war effort.[17] Chase himself was uncomfortable with the inflation that resulted from his easy money policy, but he made the argument of necessity, one that present-day politicians make about the perils of taxation. Lincoln always backed up Chase in financial matters.

Chase's attitude toward Lincoln, as reflected in his diary and his correspondence, fluctuated between a grudging admiration and appreciation of the president's human qualities, and a consistent belief that given the opportunity he could do a much better job as chief executive. In his commentary on Lincoln, one can almost feel the tension between the brighter and darker sides of Chase's personality.[18]

Early in their relationship, Chase sensed Simon Cameron's administrative weaknesses and quickly moved in to manage the War Department. Lincoln, feeling his way on uncharted courses, let Chase play a prominent role in the military side of the war effort. The selection of Irwin McDowell, an Ohio man, to command the Union army at the first Battle of Bull Run was largely a result of Chase's influence. The appointment of General George B. McClellan to replace McDowell was again, in part, a product of Chase's involvement in War Department policy.[19]

Seward and others within the cabinet looked askance at Chase's encroachment of military powers. But Lincoln, who had come to realize Cameron's shortcomings, was willing, even glad, to tolerate Chase's assistance in this vital area. He was especially grateful for what he regarded as Chase's intimate knowledge of the situation in Kentucky early in the war. Chase saw to it that the Unionists in Kentucky were armed and organized to help repel the Confederate invasion of the state.[20] Chase was also influential in the replacement of Cameron with the energetic, able lawyer and former cabinet member, Edwin M. Stanton.

Chase had known Stanton for years. The short, combative lawyer was an Ohio native and had been associated with Chase politically. But Stanton had not been one of Chase's inner circle and was far more conservative on the free soil issue.[21] The two men established a good working relationship from the start, primarily because Stanton, while taking his cue from Lincoln on military policy, kept Chase informed. Chase continued to meddle in army movements and top appointments, but his virtual management of the War Department through Cameron had ended. Lincoln and Stanton, with the new general-in-chief Henry W. Halleck as an advisor, began to assume overall control. Still, the treasury secretary maintained his own sources of information, like Brigadier General James A. Garfield, General W. S. Rosecrans's chief of staff, until that commander's replacement after his defeat at Chicamauga. Chase constantly sought information from others in various theaters of operations, and he was not loath to give them the benefit of his advice. Until Chase's death in October 1862, fellow Cincinnatian Ormsby MacKnight Mitchell, the astronomer turned general, reported to him on military movements in Tennessee and northern Alabama, as did Erasmus D. Keyes, Joseph Hooker, and others of the Army of the Potomac.

As the war went badly for the Union, so Chase's frustration at his isolation from the military sphere quickened a driving ambition for the presidency. He sought to undermine Lincoln with the radical faction in Congress, significantly by blaming Seward, his cabinet rival, for undue influence over the president. The indirect object was to picture Lincoln as a weak and fumbling executive who should be replaced if the war effort were to succeed. He, Chase, was, of course, the logical alternative. Lincoln recognized the intrigue for what it was and circumvented it in the famous cabinet-congressional committee confrontation. At the same time, Lincoln demonstrated to his congressional critics that Chase had not been exactly forthright with them when he said that the cabinet was deeply divided on the conduct of the war. As Gideon Welles described the scene, "Secretary Chase indorsed the President's statement fully and entirely, but regretted that there was not a more full and thorough consideration and canvass of every important measure in open Cabinet."[22] For a time, Chase lost considerable credibility with the congressional radicals.

Throughout 1863, however, Chase continued to work for his objective, the Republican nomination in 1864. His popularity with the public was nurtured carefully through a campaign of press relations that featured him prominently as the indispensable financier. His policies, deemed highly successful in that mysterious world of banking and finance, impressed even hard-bitten politicians. In other ways, Chase sought to build a political machine through his extensive Treasury patronage. Chase always vehemently denied that his network of some fifteen thousand Treasury employees had political implications.[23] But his pose as a disinterested public servant fooled few and certainly not Lincoln. John Hay recorded a conversation he had with Lincoln in October 1863. Hay said that Lincoln seemed "much amused at Chase's mad hunt after the Presidency. He says it might win. He hopes the country will never do worse." But Lincoln in the same conversation recognized the darker side of Chase's character when he said that "like the blue-bottle fly, he lays his eggs in every rotten spot he can find."[24]

Chase's campaign collapsed in early March 1864, after Senators Samuel C. Pomeroy and John Sherman's ill-conceived, ill-timed, and scurrilous public attack on Lincoln backfired on the Chase candidacy. The president's supporters carried a majority of the Ohio legislature in repudiating the exaggerations and misstatements of Chase's informal campaign committee. Chase hastened to assure Lincoln that he had no knowledge of the documents and offered to resign, his third offer; Lincoln refused to accept his resignation. Their relationship, however, which early in the war had been quite cordial, was now correct but cool. From that time until the election in November, Chase, whose resignation was accepted on June 29, did not openly oppose the president. But he continued to maintain his exclusive control over his vast patronage apparatus and to resist any challenge in this area. It was ostensibly the New York City appointments that brought about the final rupture between the two men.

Out of public office for the first time in almost ten years, Chase looked to a high judicial appointment as an appropriate place for him to launch a campaign for the presidency in 1868. He knew that the eighty-seven-year-old chief justice of the United States Supreme Court, Roger B. Taney, was in failing health (he died on October 12), and Chase hoped to succeed him. With that object in mind, during the summer of 1864 Chase kept himself relatively free of the movement to force Lincoln out of the presidential race. And late in the campaign, Chase made numerous speeches in Ohio and other states in the Midwest in support of the president. Yet Chase had competitors for the judicial post, and Lincoln seemed to have some well-grounded fears that Chase would overly politicize the office.

From many points of view, Chase was the right person at the right time for the appointment that Lincoln made on 6 December 1864. The president had never doubted Chase's abilities, in fact he may have overrated them. In the last analysis, Lincoln had to decide between the dark and the devious in Chase's character and the bright and judicious aspects of a personality that could never understand why anyone should mistrust its motives. Lincoln did not live to see the sad triumph of the dark over the bright, as the chief justice vainly sought first the Republican nomination then the Democratic nomination for the presidency in 1868. Rutherford B. Hayes, who had known Chase for many years, spoke to this flaw in his nature: "Chase possessed noble gifts of intellect, great culture and a commanding presence. When this is said, about all that is favorable has been said. He was cold, selfish, and unscrupulous. . . . Political intrigue, love of power, and selfish and boundless ambition were the striking features of his life and character."[25] Hayes was not exactly an objective witness; his faction of the Republican Party in Ohio had been pitted against that of Chase and of Wade.[26] Lincoln was far more charitable and did recognize that Chase had qualities of mind and heart that, on occasion, rose above his perpetual quest for the presidency. I feel that he would have approved of Chase's statesmanlike role as an objective presiding officer in the highly charged partisan atmosphere of the Johnson impeachment trial. He would certainly have seen the brighter side of Chase's character as stated through Chase's opinion in *Texas v. White*: "The Constitution, in all its provisions, looks to an indestructible Union composed of indestructible states."[27]

NOTES

1. Quoted in Frederick J. Blue, *Salmon P. Chase: A Life in Politics* (Kent: Kent State University Press, 1987), 244, 245.

2. Tyler Dennett, ed., *Lincoln and the Civil War in the Diaries and Letters of John Hay* (New York: Dodd, Mead, 1939), 199.

3. John Bigelow, *Retrospections of an Active Life*, 5 vols. (New York: Baker and Taylor, 1909–13), 2:110.

4. Blue, *Salmon P. Chase*, 38.

5. See Chase's address to the Liberty Party convention held at Columbus, 9 December 1841, in Jacob E. Schuckers, *The Life and Public Services of Salmon Portland Chase* (New York: D. Appleton, 1874), 48, 49.

6. Schuckers, *Life and Public Services*, 63.

7. Roy P. Basler, ed., Marion Dolores Pratt and Lloyd A. Dunlap, asst. eds., *The Collected Works of Abraham Lincoln*, 9 vols. (New Brunswick, N.J.: Rutgers University Press, 1953–55), 3:378, 384, 394, 395, 425, 470, 471.

8. Schuckers, *Life and Public Services*, 201.

9. Ibid., 201–3.

10. Ibid., 207, 208.

11. Chase to John T. Trowbridge, 27 December 1863, 19 January 1864; Chase to John P. Bigelow, 23 September 1854; all in Chase Papers, Historical Society of Pennsylvania.

12. Stephen B. Oates, *With Malice Toward None: The Life of Abraham Lincoln* (New York: Harper, 1977), 4–15, 54, 55.

13. Chase to Joseph A. Dennison Jr., 5 November 1831, Chase Papers, Library of Congress; Robert B. Warden, *An Account of the Private Life and Public Service of Salmon Portland Chase*, 2 pts. (Washington, D. C.: Cincinnati, Wilstach, and Baldwin, 1874), 1:242; Charles D. Drake, MSS "Autobiography," 80, 81, Western Historical Manuscript Collection, University of Missouri, Columbia.

14. Chase to John P. Bigelow, 23 September 1854; Chase to Trowbridge, 19 February 1864, Chase Papers, Historical Society of Pennsylvania.

15. Salmon P. Chase, MSS "Diary," 5, 6 August, 17 September 1862, Chase Papers, Library of Congress; Schuckers, *Life and Public Services*, 421–23.

16. Samuel DuPont to Mrs. DuPont, in *Samuel Francis DuPont: A Selec-*

tion from His Civil War Letters, ed. John D. Hayes, 3 vols. (Ithaca, N.Y.: Cornell University Press, 1969), 2:256.

17. Maunsell B. Field, *Memories of Many Men and of Some Women* (New York: Harper, 1874), 275–79.

18. See, for example, David Donald, ed., *Inside Lincoln's Cabinet: The Civil War Diaries of Salmon P. Chase* (New York: Longmans, Green, 1954), 110, 119, 201.

19. Donald, *Inside Lincoln's Cabinet*, 12, 13; Chase to William Cullen Bryant, 4 September 1862, Chase Papers, Historical Society of Pennsylvania.

20. Chase to Trowbridge, 31 March 1864, ibid.

21. Chase to Jeremiah S. Black, 14 April 1870, Black Papers, Library of Congress; Benjamin P. Thomas and Harold M. Hyman, *Stanton: The Life and Times of Lincoln's Secretary of War* (New York: Knopf, 1962), 134–37.

22. Howard K. Beale, ed., *Diary of Gideon Welles: Secretary of the Navy under Lincoln and Johnson*, 3 vols. (New York: W. W. Norton, 1960), 1:194–98.

23. James G. Blaine, *Twenty Years of Congress*, 2 vols. (Norwich, Conn.: Henry Bill), 1:514.

24. Dennett, *Lincoln and the Civil War*, 110.

25. Blue, *Salmon P. Chase*, 242–46; Charles R. Williams, ed., *Diary and Letters of Rutherford Bichard Hayes*, 3 vols. (Columbus: Ohio State Archaeological and Historical Society, 1922–26), 3:242, 243.

26. Felice Bonadio, *North of Reconstruction: Ohio Politics 1865–1870* (New York: New York University Press, 1970), 100–102.

27. See the lengthy discussion of the case in Charles Fairman, *Reconstruction and Reunion 1864–88* (New York: Macmillan, 1971), 6: pt. 1, 628–67 (this vol. is part of an 11-vol. series entitled *History of the Supreme Court of the United States*, by various authors).

10

Lincoln and Seward in Civil War Diplomacy: Their Relationship at the Outset Reexamined

Norman B. Ferris

MOST HISTORIANS know William Henry Seward as one of the most eminent American secretaries of state. In his appraisal of the incumbents of that office, Alexander De Conde ranks Seward second in performance only to John Quincy Adams.[1] If ever an American political leader had a record of consistently working for territorial and commercial expansion entirely by peaceful means, that man was Seward.

Yet, according to practically every historian and biographer who has written at any length about him, one striking blemish appears on his record. During an interval of several months early in 1861, a bellicose Seward invented a "foreign war panacea" for solving the problem of Southern secession and was barely thwarted by President Abraham Lincoln from bringing about such a conflict. Either Seward was possessed of an almost insane truculence or he had anticipated John Foster Dulles's brinkmanship at the worst possible time. This apparent aberration in Seward's long record of constructive statesmanship is sometimes given more emphasis in textbooks than any of his other activities in the field of diplomacy. The impression thus created is one of instability, irresponsibility, and political ambition to the point of madness.

In 1976 I wrote *Desperate Diplomacy: William Henry Seward's Foreign Policy, 1861*, a volume that demonstrated how absurd was the traditional portrayal of Seward as a warmonger and that showed the myth's inception in the near-paranoia of the British minister at Washington—and in machinations against Secretary Seward by Massachusetts Senator Charles Sumner and other political opponents.[2]

Yet references still abound in histories and biographies to Seward's so-called "anglophobic outbursts,"[3] his "hair-trigger temper," his "rantings," his lack of "sobriety," and his "wild eccentricity" early in the war years, as well as his alleged plan "to bring on a world war," which Lincoln—"to his enduring credit, quietly filed away—and allowed Seward time to return to his senses."[4]

A recent edition of a popular college-level survey textbook refers to Seward's alleged "attempts to dominate Lincoln" and to the secretary's "initial blunders,"[5] while Thomas A. Bailey, in the tenth edition of his famous *Diplomatic History of the American People*, included the same imaginative version of Seward's " 'wrap-the-world-in-fire policy' " and " 'foreign war panacea' " that appeared in the third edition, published in 1946.[6]

Alexander De Conde's *History of American Foreign Policy* relates the familiar story of Seward's allegedly attempting to relegate Lincoln to a figurehead in his own administration, while pressing in a momentous memorandum for "a policy of hostility or war" against four European nations in order to "win back the loyalty of the seceded states and avoid civil war."[7]

It should therefore be apparent that the Seward foreign war panacea myth still flourishes.[8] Why is this untrue story still being repeated by historians? In part, I think, because many of them have merely echoed their predecessors rather than "going to the documents."

The greatest obstacle of all, however, to a sober, unbiased rethinking of the meaning and intent of Seward's diplomacy is, I believe, what I tend to call "the Lincoln factor." For example, two characterizations of me from Paul Holbo's review of *Desperate Diplomacy*: my "passing suggestions that Abraham Lincoln was hesitant or lacking in understanding" of foreign relations, and my "general neglect of the President detract[ed] from the book."

Exactly. Historians remain imbued with the notion that Lincoln *must* have been the central figure in, or at least the main influence on, American foreign policy during the Civil War years. This erroneous conception, advanced explicitly in four hundred and thirty-three pages by Jay Monaghan in *Diplomat in Carpet Slippers*, a book still cited frequently in bibliographies, is rendered implicitly in many specialized monographs that deal with Civil War diplomacy.[9]

Lincoln's greatness should not blind historians to the fact that during his presidency high officials in his administration (a majority of whom were hardly admirers of Seward), reputable journalists, well-informed diplomats, and leaders in Congress all repeatedly testified to their common belief that Seward was the chief executive's éminence grise. Were all of these eyewitnesses deluded when they assumed that Seward was in fact a kind of prime minister?

The Lincoln-Seward relationship during the entire Civil War period is a topic too complicated for thorough examination here. This discussion therefore is limited to the association of the two men in the early days of the administration, as they dealt with U.S. foreign relations. Lincoln himself depicted the nature of his relationship with his secretary of state in words clearly indicating a disposition to allow Seward to conduct foreign policy with a minimum of interference. As the president-elect told a European diplomat two days before his inauguration: "I don't know anything about diplomacy. I will be very apt to make blunders." And to a visitor who tried to influence him on a foreign policy issue, Lincoln asserted: "It does not so much signify what I think; you must persuade Seward to think as you do."[10]

Throughout the war years, Seward, while remaining a faithful subordinate to Lincoln, enjoyed the president's complete confidence. If Seward was in any sense a prime minister, it was because the chief executive desired him to play that role. Yet a myth persists to the contrary.

In 1890 Lincoln's two wartime private secretaries, John Nicolay and John Hay, published a massive biographical eulogy of their former chief, *Abraham Lincoln: A History*, in volume three of which appeared the chapter "Premier or President?"[11] The purpose of this chapter was to show how "the first real question of the Lincoln Cabinet . . . , 'Who is the greatest man?' " was solved by the president. Seward, who for almost four weeks had played "the leading part in the new Cabinet," was, it seems, overly ambitious. Allegedly he presented Lincoln on 1 April with a memorandum proposing that the president not only "by an arbitrary act plunge the nation into foreign war" but also "ask his rival [Seward] to rule in his stead."[12]

What had Seward said in this document? Nicolay and Hay reproduced his "Thoughts for the President's Consideration" verbatim.

First, the New Yorker had asserted, "We are at the end of a month's administration, and yet without a policy, either domestic or foreign." Although this had perhaps been "unavoidable" because of the need to fill crucial offices with loyal appointees while the Senate remained in session, further delay in giving attention "to other and more grave matters" might be dangerous.[13]

Let us analyze this much of the memorandum. Any historian who examines contemporary periodicals and manuscripts for the period knows that Seward was correct, both in suggesting that there was no perception—either in the nation or abroad—that the Lincoln administration had a coherent domestic or foreign policy, and in recognizing that practically all the president's time had been devoted to dispensing loaves and fishes to job applicants. Regarding this matter, Thornton Lothrop, hardly an apologist for the secretary of state, conceded that "Seward's paper only repeated the common talk of the time—the language of the newspaper press and the opinions contained in the private letters not merely of ordinary observers, but of well-informed and sensible persons."[14]

In his memorandum, Seward had next suggested that the new administration needed to demonstrate to the country that it was more concerned with preserving the Union than with the narrow party question of what to do about slavery. This was the only basis on which the North—Democrats, Constitutionalists, and Republicans alike, not only from the antislavery regions of New England and the upper Midwest, but also from the former Know-Nothing urban centers and the border states—could unite to combat the threatened slaveholders' rebellion. Many Americans regarded the military occupation of Fort Sumter in Charleston Harbor as a symbol of antislavery policy, hence, Seward advocated that Lincoln should order the evacuation of that post. At the same time, however, Lincoln should prepare for the outbreak of civil war, both by reinforcing every other "fort and possession in the South" and by readying a blockade of the Southern coastline.[15] Historians have debated whether Lincoln should have followed Seward's advice to evacuate Fort Sumter. There does appear to be almost unanimous acceptance of the wisdom of his remaining suggestions, all of which were eventually carried out with the president's approval.

Next, Seward offered recommendations under the heading "For Foreign Nations." The great powers of Europe were showing clear signs of a desire, if not an immediate intention, to intervene in Western Hemispheric affairs, both to help establish the Southern slave Confederacy amid the ruins of the federal Union and to restore European rule in Mexico and Central America.[16] How should the threat be met? Seward advised:

> I would demand explanations from Spain and France, categorically, at once. I would seek explanations from Great Britain and Russia, and send agents into Canada, Mexico, and Central America, to rouse a vigorous continental spirit of independence . . . against European intervention. And, if satisfactory explanations are not received from Spain and France, Would convene Congress and declare war against them.[17]

Was this "extreme belligerence," as Kinley Brauer has written, designed to provoke "a foreign crisis" to "reunite the American nations?"[18] Of course not. There is no real evidence, taking the memorandum in context, that Seward had anything of the kind in mind.

Seward had simply sought Lincoln's sanction for asking European envoys in Washington whether their governments intended to take advantage of the slaveholders' rebellion to intervene in American affairs, even as the great powers, acting in concert or in holy alliance, had been prone to do in diverse parts of the world earlier in the century. The French and Spanish seemed already to be mobilizing for armed incursions into Latin America. If the governments of France and Spain were already embarked on a policy of intervention and admitted this in their "explanations," then the U.S. government would of course have to defend its territory and its nearby vital interests. Otherwise, what use was the Monroe Doctrine? But a defensive war could not be waged constitutionally without the sanction of Congress. Meanwhile, it was only prudent to try to undermine movements already underway in Latin America to procure diplomatic recognition of the Confederacy,[19] and also to seek throughout the hemisphere for friends and allies who had a common revulsion "against European intervention."

All of Seward's foreign policy recommendations contained in his 1 April memorandum were carried out. His demands for explanations from all four European powers helped to persuade their leaders to exercise greater caution in dealing with the "American question" than they had at first exhibited.

Seward's agents and envoys in Canada and Latin America were so successful in seeking support for the cause of the American Union that no Western Hemispheric government ever recognized or overtly aided the Southern insurrection.

There was, of course, no need to "convene Congress and declare war" against Spain and France because the explanations of those two governments proved to be, if not entirely reassuring, at least sufficiently "satisfactory."

The final sentences of Seward's "Thoughts" of 1 April have inspired historians to emit accusations so intemperate that they would be laughable if they were not so universally accepted.

> But whatever policy we adopt, there must be an energetic prosecution of it. For this purpose it must be somebody's business to pursue and direct it incessantly. Either the President must do it himself, and be all the while active in it, or Devolve it on some member of his Cabinet. Once adopted, debates on it must end, and all agree and abide. It is not my especial province. But I neither seek to evade nor assume responsibility.[20]

Anyone who troubles to examine the text of the 1 April memorandum ought to see how obvious it is that this portion of it applies only to the category distinctly labeled "For Foreign Nations," clearly set off from the remainder of the document. To suggest, as so many historians have, that Seward was here trying to "take over the direction of government policy"[21] in general is to exhibit an inability to see what is plainly there. What the secretary of state was maintaining to a president who had already shown great diffidence to his opinions, especially on foreign policy questions, is not difficult to discern.

American foreign relations were in a perilous state and required full-time attention by a single directing force. Lincoln had little interest in foreign policy, and had many other problems with which to deal. The cabinet, consisting of long-time political rivals, was not cohesive. In meeting the threat from abroad, haste was requisite. Seward wanted two things: Lincoln's sanction for a concerted effort to *prevent* foreign war, and authority to make that effort without having it undermined by cabinet colleagues or jeopardized by the kind of vacillation already shown in regard to the Fort Sumter problem. Continued indications of weakness and indecisiveness on the part of the administration would tempt foreign adventurers. Seward wanted to show unity and strength; soon, with Lincoln's approval, he did.

Yet Frederic Bancroft, one of Seward's principal biographers, has characterized his memorandum of 1 April as "a reckless invention of a mind driven to desperate extremes," a mind "zealous to do what would be most certain to foment . . . a foreign war as the mainspring of his policy."[22] And Glyndon Van Deusen, Seward's most recent biographer, has declared that the New Yorker "was still clinging to the illusion that conflict with foreign nations could bring the South back into the national fold."[23]

What is the evidence supplied by historians to substantiate the presumption that the secretary of state actually "proposed to Lincoln a foreign war as a panacea for the country's ills?"[24]

In the face of his own awareness of Seward's lifelong aversion to foreign war, "except on the ground of necessary defence,"[25] Bancroft declares that, nevertheless, "Seward's theory of the unifying effect of foreign war had long revolved in his mind." Bancroft then offers two examples of this alleged theory: a speech in New York City on 22 December 1860, and a Senate address on 12 January 1861.[26] But close scrutiny of those two orations reveals nothing that justifies such an interpretation. As I related in *The Trent Affair*,[27] Seward's extemporaneous 22 December speech centered on the theme of American patriotism, which he claimed knew no sectional boundaries. He only mentioned a hypothetical foreign invasion to make the point that Northerners and Southerners, no matter how great their differences over slavery, would support each other in the face of an assault from abroad. As for the 12 January Senate speech, it requires a wild imagination indeed to read into that appeal for compromise and conciliation during the secession crisis any hint of a "foreign war panacea."

What evidence has been adduced by other historians for what Ephriam D. Adams declared was Seward's "insane scheme for saving the Union by plunging it into a foreign war?"[28] Van Deusen merely affirms that the secretary of state's reasons for desiring a foreign conflict "must remain, at least in part, a matter of conjecture."[29] And David Paul Crook, who writes that the "facts best fit the theory of brinkmanship," provides few "facts" beyond the speculations of Allan Nevins to back up his contention that what Seward desired was "a scare over war with Spain" to enable the U.S. Navy to reassert "federal authority over the Union forts on the Gulf of Mexico."[30]

But Nevins's theory (which he appears to have appropriated from Henry Temple) is not backed by reliable evidence. In the first volume of his *War for the Union*, Nevins claims that "it was war with Spain that Seward had primarily in mind. . . . The moment Washington opened war on Spain, Seward believed, the Cotton States would tremble lest Cuba become free soil. . . . To avert such a calamity, he hoped that Southerners would join the attack. . . . If France entered the war, the United States would also seize the French Islands."[31]

Where had Seward "disclosed these views"? Why, "in a number of confidential talks with Lord Lyons," the British minister. But Nevins actually bases his whole theory on a single document, a dispatch from Lord Lyons to the British Foreign Office that reveals no such "views" of Seward's. For supplementary documentation, Nevins confined himself to Bancroft, Nicolay and Hay, and James Ford Rhodes. Rhodes's book indeed describes the secretary of state's alleged plan to use a foreign war to reunite "the alienated sections" as "egregious folly," but Rhodes offers no documentation of the so-called "plan" other than a quotation from William Howard Russell's famous *Diary*. Russell, in turn, had accused Seward of "bombast," but, in no sense, warmongering.[32]

Allan Nevins, therefore, actually provides not a shred of real evidence in primary sources for his declaration that Seward's alleged proposal "that the North provoke a war with Spain and France to extricate itself from its difficulties, as criminal as it was stupid, must make Americans blush that they had a foreign minister capable of such an act."[33] And Nevins's contemporary Bruce Catton, in dismissing Seward's 1 April memorandum as "fantastic," an irritating imposition on a "busy" president by "an infatuated power seeker," shows equal powers of imagination. Like Nevins, Catton cites Nicolay and Hay among his authorities for the spurious story.[34]

Years earlier, in a biography of Seward published in the American Statesman series, Thornton Lothrop used such words as "wild" and "mad" to characterize what he called Seward's "incomprehensible" scheme which "came from the belief that a foreign war, or the prospect of one, would unite all our people, divert the attention of the South, . . . and put an end for the moment to all schemes of secession." What were Lothrop's sources for this idea? Solely Nicolay and Hay.[35]

The source of the foreign war panacea interpretation of Seward's 1 April memorandum must now be apparent. Printing that document for the first time, Nicolay and Hay attributed to the secretary of state a desire to "smother a domestic insurrection in the blaze and glory of a war which must logically be a war of conquest. . . . [Seward] would change a threatened dismemberment of the Union into the triumphant annexation of Canada, Mexico, and the West Indies."[36]

Except for the bare text of the memorandum, however, these authors provide not an iota of substantiation for their imaginative scenario, so inconsistent with Seward's well-known ideas, character, and history as a public man. In previous pages, however, these two biographers had cited as sources some articles by wartime Secretary of the Navy Gideon Welles, who had been a vehement political opponent of Seward's for some forty years. These articles had appeared in *The Galaxy* magazine after Seward's death and were largely devoted to a measured attack on his reputation. It was here that Nicolay and Hay, who (as they conceded) were trying in their biography to establish who in the Lincoln administration was "the greatest man," discovered how they might demonstrate Lincoln's superiority over Seward, whom they labeled his "rival."[37]

In Welles's articles, later expanded into a book entitled *Lincoln and Seward,* the former secretary of the navy drew on his padded, sanitized diary and his own sour recollections, as well as upon the reminiscences of fellow Jacksonian Democrats who had also been bitter political enemies of Seward's in the antebellum decades. The "first promoter of the Lincoln legend," according to John Niven, Welles's biographer, accused Seward of entering "upon his duties with the impression . . . that he was to be the *de facto* President." But Lincoln had exercised continuously "intelligent supervision" of Seward, even to the point, on one occasion, of having "expurgated, corrected, and improved" an "objectionable" instruction to Charles Francis Adams, U.S. minister at London.[38]

On and on go Welles's accusations and distortions, filling more than two hundred pages. Clothed in a paean of praise for Lincoln, the assault almost made it appear as if the real rivalry had not been between Welles and Seward, but rather between the president and his secretary of state. Welles's insidious polemic accomplished its purpose—to diminish the historical reputation of the only other man to serve eight years with him in the cabinets of both Lincoln and Andrew Johnson. Historians ever since have reflected the interpretations and parroted the unsubstantiated assertions contained in *Lincoln and Seward,* used as a source by Nicolay and Hay, by Charles

Francis Adams Jr. in his biography of his father and in influential articles in the *Proceedings* of the Massachusetts Historical Society, and by many other writers near the turn of the century. The impact of these works on later books and articles can be traced not only in footnotes and bibliographies but also in the language used to treat historical episodes. Thus did Lincoln's secretary of the navy, whose ideas and opinions had been so frequently rejected by the chief executive for those of Seward, have his ultimate revenge.

As an example of how Lincoln curbed the impetuosity of an irresponsible secretary of state, Welles referred to the president's editing of a diplomatic instruction. This document had probably been brought to Welles's attention by his friend Charles Sumner. It was soon to be published by Allen Thorndike Rice as a means of settling "the question of ascendency" among Lincoln and his advisers during "the war of the Rebellion."[39]

According to Rice, who as editor of the *North American Review* had built circulation for his magazine by publishing such documents of questionable authenticity as *The Diary of a Public Man*, he was in a position to reveal for the first time how Lincoln's corrections on Seward's draft instruction number ten to Adams, dated 21 May 1861, had "without question . . . saved the nation from a war with England, which, at that period, would probably have resulted in the establishment of the Southern Confederacy!" Those who still "claimed preeminence" for Seward over Lincoln, stated Rice, might now read convincing proof that the secretary of state had discovered in the president "a master who knew when to exact implicit obedience," as well as one who possessed "an insight into foreign affairs, . . . and a discrimination in methods of diplomatic dealing which entitle[d] the President," in comparison with Seward, "to the honors."[40]

To examine Lincoln's emendations in the facsimile provided in Rice's publications is to discover, however, nothing that justifies such extravagant language. One finds merely a few cautious but relatively unimportant alterations of terminology and several suggestions for omissions of material which Seward retained anyway. The most important passages which Lincoln suggested be left out were two. One began with the declaration "We are not insensible of the grave importance of this occasion. We see how . . . a war may ensue between the United States, and one, two, or even more European nations." The other passage, referring to the threat of British intervention in behalf of the Southern insurrectionists, declared that "when this act of intervention is distinctly performed, we, from that hour, shall cease to be friends and be forced to be enemies of Great Britain."[41]

Seward retained both of these warnings, substantially as he had first drafted them, in the instruction he sent to Adams, an instruction also published (minus one sentence) in volume one of the *Foreign Relations* series of U.S. diplomatic documents that Seward instituted later that year.[42]

According to Nicolay and Hay, however, Lincoln made a decisive deletion in this document, a change that would alter its impact on the British. He ordered Seward to omit the direction "to deliver a copy of it to the British foreign minister without further explanation" and instead to write to Adams that "this paper is for your own guidance only, and not to be read or shown to anyone." Although it is true that Seward partially acquiesced to the president's wish in this regard, it is also a fact that he directed Adams to "keep back nothing" contained in the instruction. It is therefore difficult to justify statements by historians, reflecting those originally made by Rice and taken up eagerly by Nicolay and Hay, to the effect that Lincoln somehow had a great impact on U.S. foreign relations by censoring Seward's 21 May instruction to Adams.[43]

The truth is, as Nicolay and Hay admitted, that it was Seward's "ordinary habit" to read his most important diplomatic instructions "to the president before sending them."[44] Even as Lincoln frequently sought Seward's advice about the wording of such documents as his inaugural addresses and the Emancipation Proclamation, so Seward welcomed the president's concurrence before issuing important state papers. On the occasion discussed here, Seward accepted some of Lincoln's editorial glosses and refrained from adopting others, even as Lincoln had done in regard to his First Inaugural Address, the most frequently quoted passage (the "mystic chords of memory" peroration) of which was urged on him by Seward.

It is, therefore, absurd to assert, as many historians have, that Seward's "reckless and inflamatory" instruction of 21 May was a "challenge" to Great Britain, which indicated "that the United States desired war," until Seward had his "teeth skilfully drawn" by Lincoln.[45]

Such an assertion makes as much sense as to say that Lincoln exhibited in the uncompromising tone of his draft 1861 inaugural address, which ended with the question, "Shall it be peace or a sword?"—a belligerent attitude toward the South; whereas through a long series of editorial alterations suggested by Seward and accepted by Lincoln, the address was transformed by Seward into a conciliatory act of statesmanship.[46]

While subscribing to the myth of Seward's jingoism, historians also seem to accept the idea that he was generally subdued for the rest of the Civil War, kept under close rein by President Lincoln. Nicolay and Hay provided an enduring impression. In dealing with Seward's 1 April memorandum, they wrote that Lincoln had "armed himself with his irresistible logic, his faultless tact, his limitless patience, his kindest but most imperturbable firmness." With a "hand of iron in a glove of velvet," he had written a reply that showed Seward "how serious a fault he had committed," after which the secretary of state had remained properly loyal and deferential for four long years to his chief, "not only without reserve, but with a sincere and devoted personal attachment." Thus, as E. D. Adams later put it, Lincoln's firm guidance had not only restrained his erratic underling, but had also induced him to make "a complete face-about in policy." As Brian Jenkins has written: "The daydream of a reunifying foreign war . . . faded from his mind."[47]

Charles Sumner's biographer David Donald has even suggested that this salubrious alteration of behavior was owing to the influence exerted through Lincoln by the senator from Massachusetts—that "under Sumner's watchful eye" Seward "grew mild and gentle in his conduct toward foreign powers."[48]

But Seward went through no such metamorphosis. All of his life he had maintained a strong aversion to war and a disposition to discuss, conciliate, and negotiate, rather than to bluster, boast, confront, and combat. As he explained to Charles Francis Adams, who had heard in London the contemporary rumors of Seward's alleged bellicosity toward England: "It has been an earnest and profound solicitude to *avert* foreign war—that alone has prompted the emphatic and sometimes, perhaps, impassioned remonstrances I have hitherto made against any form or measure of recognition of the insurgents by the government of Great Britain."[49]

The truth is that Seward realized a war between the United States and a European power would not only "set the world on fire," but would probably also wipe out democracy forever. His Senate

speeches during the 1850s often contained such sentiments. In letters, conversations, and diplomatic instructions, Seward referred frequently to the dangers of foreign war. On every occasion when an
injudicious word or an ill-thought-out policy might have led to a sev-
erance of diplomatic relations with one or more European governments, Seward was always on the side of peace. Indeed, in the case
of the *Trent* affair, it was the secretary of state who supplied the
decisive counsel that pulled the president, the rest of the cabinet,
and the nation back from the abyss of destruction.[50]

Before taking Seward into his administration, Lincoln had expressed as much admiration for the New Yorker as for any other public man. He had borrowed some of Seward's political ideas and
expressions, as he freely acknowledged, and he described his secretary of state to others, even after his own election to the presidency,
as still "the generally recognized leader of the Republican party."[51]

Seward, for his part, developed great respect and affection for the
ungainly Illinois lawyer. In a frequently misinterpreted passage from
a letter to his wife ("The President is the best of us: but he needs
constant and assiduous cooperation"), the secretary of state suggested
simply that Lincoln was an admirable but inexperienced man who
would be able to make good use of counsel from Seward and other
Washington veterans. That Lincoln himself recognized a need for
the New Yorker's advice and placed great value on it was reported
repeatedly by such contemporaries as Salmon Chase, Sumner,
Welles, and the Blairs, who bitterly resented Seward's special influence with the president. Indeed, Lincoln's dependence on Seward
was so well known that when John Wilkes Booth shot the president
in Ford's Theatre, his confederate Lewis Paine attempted to assassinate Seward that same night.[52]

Almost from the beginning of their official relationship, Lincoln
took great pleasure in Seward's genial company. On many occasions
he summoned Seward to the White House for a tête à tête, or ambled
alone across Lafayette Square to the Seward home for a relaxing visit,
or took the New Yorker on a carriage ride to visit a military unit or
spend a day simply "taking the air." There was indeed a remarkable
empathy between the two men, who shared such rare traits among
American politicians as utter honesty, magnanimity, compassion, the
inability to hold a personal grudge, and good-natured humor.[53]

Certainly, Lincoln would have been the first to agree that an instance of "Seward's folly" no more occurred in 1861 than it did in 1867. The cause of historical truth has been ill-served by the over-reaching of nineteenth-century admirers of Abraham Lincoln, whose gratuitous attempts to elevate the reputation of the sixteenth president by demeaning contemporary statesmen enabled a handful of venomous surviving Jacksonians successfully to undermine the reputation of the great Whig and Republican leader who had eclipsed them all.

I have traced the campaign of defamation against Seward through the surviving papers of Montgomery Blair, Salmon Chase, and Gideon Welles, three former Democrats who served with ex-Whig Seward in Lincoln's cabinet. The campaign began when a friend and political backer of Seward's, Thurlow Weed, published some autobiographical chapters in a popular magazine. Reading them, Welles became amazed at "the extraordinary influence which Seward had over both the Presidents under whom he served." This, Welles thought, had been "calamitous to the country." Both Lincoln and Johnson "were in a degree subject to him . . . he was constantly leading his chiefs into error." At once Welles initiated a correspondence with Blair and Chase, and also with Sumner, another former political opponent of Seward's, in order to "interchange views" about Weed's apparently "deliberate design . . . to falsify history" and to revenge himself on the four for thwarting Weed's attempt to get Seward elected president in 1860. "To some extent," Welles warned his correspondents, Weed had succeeded in creating "a prejudice against us." Welles needed help in an effort to "put these matters right."[54]

Early in 1872, Charles Francis Adams, former minister to Great Britain and a highly respected statesman, delivered a eulogy on Seward. That speech suggested that many of the ideas and policies for which Lincoln had received sole credit were actually influenced to a large extent by Seward, who had been the strongest intellectual force in the administration. Welles was indignant that what he had earlier condemned as Seward's constant meddling should now be represented as constructive leadership. Adams had implied that Seward "was chief in the [Lincoln] administration, and controlled . . . the measures and policy of the President." On the contrary, Welles retorted, Lincoln "was master of the situation, and . . . no member of the Cabinet was, I think, so often overruled and his propositions set aside as the Secretary of State." Welles himself "more than any other

was brought in conflict with Seward . . . but in every instance, I
believe, the President coincided in my views [a statement that under-
mines the credibility of anything Welles wrote about Lincoln and
Seward]. . . . Those of us who *know* the facts should correct these
errors." It was one thing for Welles to complain, in his diary and later
in letters to friends, that Seward had dominated Lincoln and Johnson; it was quite another matter for Adams to air the idea for the
general public and for the pages of history—at the expense of the
reputations of Welles himself, Blair, and Chase.[55]

As the year 1872 passed, Welles became virtually obsessed with
the conviction that old Jacksonian Democrats who had served in Lincoln's cabinet with Seward "should not permit history to be falsified,"
either by Weed's "fictitious memoirs of himself and Seward—
magnifying the deeds of each, and slyly traducing and defaming others," or by Adams's suggestion that Seward was "the controlling
mind" in the Lincoln and Johnson administrations. Other histories of
"our day" coming from the nation's presses he also judged to be
"most of them great humbugs." Welles decided to write his own version of history.[56]

Blair encouraged Welles's venture and persuaded Chief Justice
Chase to provide written sanction for Welles's role as spokesman for
the trio in correcting Weed's and Adams's alleged misrepresenta-
tions. The strategy adopted was indirect rather than forthright.
Welles would not openly attempt to vindicate the ideas and opinions
of the ex-Democrats versus those of Adams, Weed, and Seward, ideas
and opinions which Lincoln, guided by Seward, had so frequently
overruled. Rather, the approach was to a be an attack on the reputation of the deceased secretary of state, in which all of the latent ani-
mosities and frustrations of those who had been thwarted in their
desires to control the Lincoln administration and steer it in a state's
rights direction in domestic policy and toward a belligerent foreign
policy would emerge in such a way that the real quarrel would not
seem to be between Seward and them, but between Seward and
Lincoln. Thus a historical replay would be concocted in which the
nature of the cabinet contest of the early 1860s would be totally altered. Lincoln would be made the champion of the three disgruntled
cabinet survivors. "I would not intentionally do injustice to Seward,"
wrote Welles piously, "but the truth should not be perverted. We

who know the facts owe it to Lincoln, to the country, and to history that the mistakes of such a man as Mr. Adams should be corrected."[57]

Notices were published in the newspapers designed to elicit assistance from others. One former Democrat, Seward's predecessor as secretary of state, Jeremiah Black, responded. Black, described by Senator Henry Wilson as a "soured, disappointed, and vindictive" adviser to former President James Buchanan, whose "imbecile counsels" promoted Southern secession, wrote an emotional, inaccurate article stating that Seward had been personally responsible during the Civil War era for "the general decay of our political institutions." And what William E. Gladstone had described as "the greatest forensic effort in the English language," Seward's argument in the famous Freeman case of 1846,[58] Black labeled as "irrelevant trash" emitted by a lawyer who had disgraced the bar by "the odium of his conduct" in defending a Negro mass murderer in court. As a senator, Black declared, Seward had been "a mere demagogue," with "no convictions whatever." He was "narrow-minded, short-sighted, and destitute of . . . magnanimity."[59] Aside from its name-calling, Black's article, as Wilson pointed out, contained lie after lie—yet it was eagerly accepted by Blair and Welles as reinforcing their own attempt to destroy Seward's reputation. And although former U.S. Senator Truman Smith wrote Welles that "such a tirade of malignant abuse as that introduced by Mr. Black into the columns of the Galaxy" undermined the efforts of others to show that Lincoln was superior in "sagacity and plain common sense" to Seward, I have discerned no indication from Welles or Blair that either derived anything but pleasure from Black's scurrilous diatribe.[60]

The Welles and Blair families met in the summer of 1873 at Newport, Rhode Island, so that the two old politicians could confer in person about tactics while their offspring enjoyed the pleasures of the fashionable resort. Welles's anti-Seward, anti-Weed, anti-Stanton articles soon followed—also published in the Galaxy magazine. Blair was elated, terming them "a punishing blow to Weed & Adams." He was happy to find that many people agreed with him that the articles had made "a profound impression on the public mind." Seward's "pusillanimity" and "fulsomeness" had been conclusively demonstrated, and Lincoln had been shown to have suffered much from the New Yorker's presence in his cabinet. Best of all, Welles's writings were helping "enormously to perpetuate the principles of true democratic government" to which Blair and Welles had both devoted their lives. Andrew Jackson would have been proud of them.[61]

In his articles, Welles had originated the idea that "Seward *intended to be*, what Adams says, and I presume supposes he was, the directing and controlling mind of the administration." Seward, said Welles, had "contributed himself so much to that impression." But Lincoln, influenced "quietly" by Welles and Blair, had "never permitted him to go beyond his tether."[62]

Nicolay and Hay had needed a foil for Lincoln in the early chapters of their account of his role in the Civil War before they could bring George McClellan onto the scene. When they read in Welles's treatment of Lincoln and Seward that the secretary of state had intended to make the president his puppet, they found what they were seeking. They decided to join the cabal of ex-Democrats in putting the usurper in his place. This they accomplished by a careful selection of documents and by interpretations of the meanings of those documents based on the most unfavorable constructions of Seward's alleged motives and thoughts. Thus the mendacious Welles and the overbearing Blair projected their own traits onto the public impression of the dead Seward, and—in the guise of defending Lincoln against an allegation of a usurpation that would have been a joke to both the late president and his favorite adviser had they known about it—they managed to leave Seward's historical reputation in shambles.

NOTES

1. Alexander De Conde, *The American Secretary of State: An Interpretation* (London: Pall Mall, 1963), 171.

2. Some reviewers conceded agreement with this thesis, for example, Daniel Carroll in *Journal of American History* 64 (June 1977): 159–60; and, by implication, Thomas Farnham in *Journal of Southern History* 43 (August 1977): 459–60.

3. David Pletcher's review of Norman B. Ferris, *The Trent Affair*, in *Civil War History* 24 (September 1978): 271–72.

4. David Donald, *The Great Republic: A History of the American People* (Lexington, Mass.: D. C. Heath, 1981) 482–85.

5. Richard N. Current, T. Harry Williams, and Frank Freidel, *American History, A Survey*, 5th ed. (New York: Alfred A. Knopf, 1979), 379, 387.

6. Thomas A. Bailey, *Diplomatic History of the American People*, 10th ed. (Englewood Cliffs, N.J.: Prentice-Hall, 1980), 317–18.

7. Alexander De Conde, *History of American Foreign Policy*, 2 vols. (New York: Scribner's, 1978), 1:222.

8. Additional examples of the prevalence of that myth can be found in three reviews of *Desperate Diplomacy*: by Howard Kushner in *New York History* 58 (April 1977): 230–32; by Paul Holbo in *History, Reviews of New Books* 5 (November–December 1976); and by Ernest Paolino, who deprecated my "foredoomed effort to depict Seward as a pacific man," in *American Historical Review* 82 (1977): 183.

9. Jay Monaghan, *Diplomat in Carpet Slippers: Lincoln Deals with Foreign Affairs* (Indianapolis: Bobbs-Merrill, 1945).

10. Schleiden no. 30 to Breman Senate, 4 March 1861, Despatches of Rudolf Schleiden, copies in Library of Congress; George W. Curtis, ed., *The Correspondence of John Lothrop Motley*, 2 vols. (New York: Harper, 1900), 2:159.

11. This chapter was first published in *Century Magazine* 35 (February 1888): 599–616.

12. John Nicolay and John Hay, *Abraham Lincoln: A History*, 10 vols. (New York: Century, 1886–90), 3:444 (hereafter, Nicolay and Hay, *Lincoln*).

13. Ibid., 3:445.

14. Thornton Lothrop, *William Henry Seward* (Boston: Houghton Mifflin, 1899), 279–80.

15. Nicolay and Hay, *Lincoln*, 3:445–46.

16. Norman B. Ferris, *Desperate Diplomacy: William Henry Seward's Foreign Policy, 1861* (Knoxville: University of Tennessee Press, 1976), 5–11.

17. Nicolay and Hay, *Lincoln*, 3:446.

18. Kinley Brauer, "Seward's 'Foreign War Panacea': An Interpretation," *New York History* 55 (April 1974): 136. In this article Brauer mentions (145–47) Seward's "ungracious and undiplomatic outburst," probably resulting from "too much wine," on 25 March 1861, but I have shown in *Desperate Diplomacy* (213–14) that this story is not credible.

19. Lyons to Russell, 26 March 1861, British Foreign Despatches, Public Records Office 30/22/35.

20. Nicolay and Hay, *Lincoln*, 3:446–47.

21. Glyndon G. Van Deusen, *William Henry Seward* (New York: Oxford University Press, 1967), 283.

22. Frederic Bancroft, *The Life of William H. Seward*, 2 vols. (Glouster: Peter Smith, 1967), 2:134–36.

23. Van Deusen, *Seward*, 283.

24. Martin B. Duberman, *Charles Francis Adams, 1807–1886* (Boston: Houghton Mifflin, 1961), 267.

25. As I have previously written, "Seward abhorred war. He called it 'the bane of republics,' convinced that war . . . would inevitably transform them into despotisms. 'A democratic government,' he said, 'has no adaptation to war. . . . War, however brief its duration, and however light its calamities, deranges all social industry, subverts order, and corrupts public morals.' The first element of the country's happiness and security, then, was peace. War, by contrast, was 'the chiefest of national calamities, [and] so incongruous with the dictates of reason, so ferocious, so hazardous, and so demoralizing, that I will always counsel a trial of every other lawful and honorable remedy for injustice, before a resort to that extreme measure of redress; and, indeed, I shall never counsel it except on the ground of necessary defence. . . .' Nations were often debilitated by their wars; they were 'seldom impoverished by their charities' " (Ferris, "William H. Seward and the Faith of a Nation," in *Traditions and Values: American Diplomacy, 1790–1865*, ed. Norman A. Graebner [Lanham, Md.: University Press of America, 1985], 158, 173–74).

26. Bancroft, *Seward*, 2:136–37. Brancroft has been chided for not being "satisfied to tell the reader what Seward did or said, but [he] must track the action down to its motive source in the chambers of his soul" (Walter Allen, "William Henry Seward," *Atlantic*, December 1900, 850). Bancroft's collusion with Edgar Welles in doctoring the diary of Gideon Welles prior to publication is indicated in Howard K. Beale, ed., *Diary of Gideon Welles, Secretary of the Navy under Lincoln and Johnson*, 3 vols. (New York: W. W. Norton, 1960), 1:xxviii–xxxi.

27. Norman B. Ferris, *The Trent Affair* (Knoxville: University of Tennessee Press, 1977), 97–99.

28. Ephriam D. Adams, *Great Britain and the American Civil War*, 2 vols. (New York: Russell and Russell, 1958), 1:120.

29. Van Deusen, *Seward*, 281.

30. David Paul Crook, *The North, the South, and the Powers, 1861–1865* (New York: Wiley, 1974), 60, 63.

31. Allan Nevins, *The War for the Union*, 4 vols. (New York: Scribner's, 1959), 1:61–63; Henry Temple, "William H. Seward," in *The American Secretaries of State and Their Diplomacy*, ed. Samuel F. Bemis, 19 vols. to date (New York: Cooper Square, 1963–), 7:29–31.

32. Nevins, *The War for the Union*; Lyons no. 5 to Russell, 11 May 1861, FO115/260, PRO; James Ford Rhodes, *History of the United States from the Compromise of 1850*, 8 vols. (New York: Harper, 1907–29), 4:341–42; William Howard Russell, *My Diary North and South* (Boston: Burnham, 1863), 61–62.

33. Nevins, *War for the Union*, 1:vi.

34. Bruce Catton, *The Coming Fury* (New York: Doubleday, 1961), 288–91.

35. Lothrop, *Seward*, 278–82.

36. Nicolay and Hay, *Lincoln*, 3:444–45.

37. Ibid., 443; William R. Thayer, *The Life of John Hay*, 2 vols. (Boston: Houghton Mifflin, 1915), 2:20–21. Hay and Nicolay wrote their ten-volume *Abraham Lincoln* "in a spirit of reverence and regard" for the purpose of enhancing the "fame" of the sixteenth president (Thayer, *Hay*, 2:25, 45). One of Hay's biographers suggests that "the absence of so many points unflattering to the President" in the book "must have been intentional." Hay's diaries, on which so much of the book was based, "could have been written by a good press agent" (Anne H. Sherrill, "John Hay: Shield of Union" [Ph.D. diss., University of California at Berkeley, 1967], 106–8). James F. Rhodes, who relied heavily on the Nicolay-Hay volumes, nevertheless conceded that they were "partisan," with the two authors making "Lincoln out a saint" (*The McKinley and Roosevelt Administrations, 1897–1909* [New York: Macmillan, 1927], 121–23). And Tyler Dennett noted that Hay's eulogistic writings on Lincoln had made him "the Republican laureate," which aided him in obtaining high political offices in Republican administrations (*John Hay: From Poetry to Politics* [New York: Dodd, Mead, 1933], 142).

38. John Niven, *Gideon Welles, Lincoln's Secretary of the Navy* (New York: Oxford University Press, 1973), 577; Gideon Welles, *Lincoln and Seward* (New York: Sheldon, 1874), 76–77, 184–89.

39. Niven, *Welles*, 631; A. T. Rice, *Reminiscences of Abraham Lincoln by Distinguished Men of His Time* (New York: North American Publishing, 1888), liii–liv. See also A. T. Rice, "A Famous Diplomatic Despatch," *North American Review* 353 (April 1886): 402–10, and a thirteen-page facsimile supplement.

40. Rice, *Reminiscences*, liv.

41. Ibid., passim.

42. 37th Cong., 2d sess., 1862, S. Exec. Doc. 1, 87–90 (hereafter, S. Exec. Doc. 1).

43. Nicolay and Hay, *Lincoln*, 4:275; S. Exec. Doc. no. 1, 87–90, facsimile in Rice, "A Famous Diplomatic Despatch."

44. Nicolay and Hay, *Lincoln*, 4:269–70.

45. Brian Jenkins, *Britain and the War for the Union*, 2 vols. (Montreal: McGill-Queens University Press, 1974), 1:104; Duberman, *Adams*, 268; Adams, *Great Britain*, 1:126–27.

46. Roy P. Basler, ed., Marion Dolores Pratt and Lloyd A. Dunlap, asst eds., *The Collected Works of Abraham Lincoln*, 9 vols. (New Brunswick, N.J.: Rutgers University Press, 1953–55), 4:249–71; Nicolay and Hay, *Lincoln*, 3:319–43. Yet, historians fondly quote the twenty-five-year-old Henry Adams, ignoring his notorious penchant for hyperbole, as saying that Seward's instruction of 21 May left "no doubt" in his mind "that our Govern-

ment wishes to face a war with all Europe." He was "shocked and horrified," Henry Adams added, that the secretary of state seemed "guilty of so wicked and criminal a course." Opposed to this panicky exaggeration is the fact that the elder Adams obeyed Seward's instruction faithfully without any response from the British of belligerence or even irritation. Moreover, the American minister at Vienna, who had had many years of experience studying diplomatic documents, found Seward's 21 May instruction to Adams "unobjectionable in every way, dignified, reasonable, and not menacing, although very decided." And if ever an American was an anglophile, John Lothrop Motley merited that label. I have pointed out in *Desperate Diplomacy* that the probable causes of Henry Adams's outburst, and likewise of his father's anxious resolution to try to "prevent the mutual irritation from coming to a downright quarrel," were two. First, American newspapers, which arrived at the London legation simultaneously with Seward's instruction, contained reports of great hostility toward Great Britain throughout the United States. Second, the London *Times* that very morning had published an announcement that "in consequence of events which have convulsed the American Republic," a brigade of infantry was being sent to Canada. In such an atmosphere the two Adamses feared the effect of any remonstrance whatever. Other contemporary testimony that Seward's 21 May instruction was dangerously bellicose can be traced back to Senator Sumner, who seems to have been present when Lincoln went over the document and may even have himself contributed some of the emendations. Lord Lyons wrote the Foreign Office that Sumner had told him that "means had been found of alarming the President" that Seward's draft instruction had been, in its original form, "all but a direct announcement of war." As part of his campaign of slander against Seward on two continents, Sumner paid regular visits to Lord Lyons, to the French minister, Henri Mercier, and to the minister from the Hanseatic League of German States, Rudolf Schleiden, keeping them worried with assorted tales of Seward's alleged bellicosity toward England, which they dutifully transmitted to their governments. But Sumner, who in December 1862, led a Senate cabal in a vain effort to oust Seward from the cabinet so that he could replace him there, and whose distorted outlook may have actually imagined Seward as dangerously hostile to Great Britain, is hardly a reliable witness. After all, it was *Sumner* who had pressed for the forcible annexation of Canada, who made speeches in Congress during the Civil War far more anglophobe in character than anything Seward ever spoke or wrote, and who almost scuttled the Alabama claims negotiation with his demands for indirect damages. See Ferris, *Desperate Diplomacy*, 23–25, 51–52, 217–18; and David Donald, *Charles Sumner and the Rights of Man* (New York: Knopf, 1970), 21.

47. Nicolay and Hay, *Lincoln*, 3:447–49; Adams, *Great Britain*, 1:128; Duberman, *Adams*, 268; Van Deusen, *Seward*, 300; Jenkins, *Britain*, 1:224.

48. Donald, *Sumner*, 21, 25. For a similar interpretation see Rhodes, *History*, 3:425, but see my refutation of this theory in *Desperate Diplomacy*, e.g., 212.

49. Seward no. 42 to Adams, 21 July 1861, RG59, U.S. State Department archives; see Lyons to Russell, 20 July 1861, PRO30/22/35 for a similar explanation.

50. Norman Ferris, "William Henry Seward: Nineteenth-Century Advocate for Human Rights," an address delivered to the Chattanooga-area Historical Association, 1982, 12.

51. Ferris, "William Henry Seward," 12.

52. Ibid.

53. Ibid., 12–13.

54. Weed to M. Blair, 9, 21, 25 January 15 May 1871, 21 April and 18 November 1872, all in Blair Family Papers, folder no. 9, Library of Congress.

55. Welles to Blair, 21 April 1872, ibid.

56. Welles to Blair, 18 November 1872, folder no. 9, and Welles to Blair, 16 February 1872, folder no. 55, both in Blair Family Papers, Library of Congress.

57. Welles to Blair, 30 April 1873, Blair Family Papers, folder no. 9; Blair to Welles, 12 December 1873, Welles Family Papers, folder no. 69, both Library of Congress.

58. See Henry Cabot Lodge, "William H. Seward," *Atlantic*, May 1884, 690.

59. J. S. Black, "Mr. Black to Mr. Adams," *Galaxy*, January 1874, 107–21.

60. Welles to Blair, 19 September, 10 October, 22 December 1873, 19 March 1874; R. B. Warden to Blair, 10 May 1873, all in Blair Family Papers, folder no. 9; T. Smith to Welles, 22 December 1873, Welles Family Papers, folder no. 69, both Library of Congress.

61. Blair to Welles, 17 October, 9, 22, 28 November 1873, ibid.

62. Welles to Blair, 25 November 1873, 19 March 1874, Blair Family Papers, folder no. 9, Library of Congress, emphasis added.

11

Lincoln and Congress: Why Not Congress and Lincoln?

Harold M. Hyman

SINCE HERODOTUS, History's house has developed many rooms. Among diverse practitioners, even devotees of "retrospective futurology" have, recently, found shelter there.

I am not sure what "retrospective futurology" is.[1] But I believe strongly that the eminent political scientist Wilfred E. Binkley was not employing the technique adequately enough to forecast the Watergate tensions between President Richard Nixon and his party apparatus in Congress. In 1962, Binkley had noted that from the mid-nineteenth-century decades of the origins and rise of the Republican Party, "the genius of the party seems somehow to express itself most happily through Congress even to the present day." Binkley's statement appears in the 1962 revision of his significant 1937 book, *President and Congress*, in the important chapter on Lincoln and Congress. By the time Binkley's revised edition hit the stands, he had spent almost fifty years in research, teaching, thinking, and writing concerning presidential-legislative developments and relationships. Yet, after five decades of productive effort, he had to use the imprecise phrase "seems somehow" when estimating interactions between Lincoln and the Civil War Congresses, especially with respect to the apparent Capitol Hill focus of Republican Party affections in the 1860s.[2]

For a soberingly long time, reliable perceptions and insights into many aspects of Lincoln's Congresses have remained little improved from the murky quality of the writings of the 1930s. As an example of this continuing dimness, consider that Joseph Cooper, my history-minded Rice University political science colleague, in his 1968 monograph, insisted properly on "The Importance of Congress." But

he felt impelled to admit that "understanding of Congress's role in
the American political system and its significance for the successful
operation of that system remains quite backward." In a 1970 book on
the origins of standing committees in the House of Representatives,
Cooper skipped the Civil War years entirely, saying of them only that
they were "still largely shrouded in mystery due to a surprising lack
of scholarly attention [to] the development of [intra-congressional]
party mechanisms and leadership positions."[3]

I intend by the above remarks no snide criticisms of Professors
Binkley or Cooper severally, of political scientists particularly, or of
social scientists generally. Indeed, not only are political and social
scientists among my best friends, but I believe any historian is foolish
who is supercilious toward these spin-off disciplines.

To be sure, with rarest exceptions, including Binkley and Cooper,
political and social scientists are incurable presentists—if not futurol-
ogists. Like lawyers and judges, they mine the past briefly and curso-
rily in search primarily of a decorative footnote, paragraph, or page
in which to proclaim the impossibility of understanding the present
without awareness of the past. Cosmetic devotion done, the authors
of legal opinions, treatises, monographs, and articles in law and political and social science journals almost always ignore everything but
recent men, measures, and institutions. Such writers use history, in
the phrase of Professor Alfred H. Kelly, for "law-office" purposes,
and, to quote jurisprudent Jerome Frank, make "twistory" of history.[4]

Nevertheless, political and social scientists, and, to a lesser extent,
judges and lawyers, have presented to historians more challenging
insights, more usable hard data, and more impressive methodological
alternatives for the study of executive-congressional relationships
than have the great majority of "straight" historians. Until surpris-
ingly recently, historians, excepting a slim list of interdisciplinary
frontiersmen,[5] have increased our knowledge depressingly little
about significant, indeed basic, aspects of presidential-congressional
history, especially in the Civil War years.

Of those years, the late Professor James G. Randall, inquiring in
1936 if the Lincoln theme was exhausted, asked questions that, too
long unanswered, or, worse perhaps, accepted uncritically as final
judgments, deserve restatement:

> The subject of Lincoln's relations with Congress involves a whole bun-
> dle of questions. How does one account for the striking contrast be-

tween Lincoln and [Woodrow] Wilson in the matter of presidential leadership and initiative in legislation? Why were so few measures passed under Lincoln which could be termed administration bills, though such was normally true of important bills under Wilson? Why was Lincoln so bold in assuming power independently of Congress and yet so ineffective in exerting influence on Capitol Hill? Why was he so hesitant to use the veto? Why did he sign bills of which he disapproved, as in the case of the second confiscation act, [and] the West Virginia [admission] bill?[6]

Randall's research convinced him that the Civil War Congress "blundered in its military policies; . . .limped along in its schemes for war finance; . . . muddled things by its committee on the conduct of the war; . . . failed wretchedly in the matter of reconstruction; and . . . committed a glaring blunder in its fantastic scheme of confiscation."[7]

In the 1960s and 1970s, scholars have expressed doubts concerning the validity of those charges against the Thirty-seventh and Thirty-eighth Congresses. I am confident, however, that Professor Randall would have been pleased that the Lincoln theme is so clearly unexhausted, and would have welcomed the disagreements and applauded the derivative research. But I suggest also that he might have felt disappointment that his disciplinary heirs of the 1970s are still concentrating on questions and using research techniques that were familiar to him forty years ago. Our professional habit, again with exceptions, has been and is to add more titles to the incredibly long list of "Lincoln and . . ." studies. Similarly, biographies and monographs about prominent and not-so-prominent congressmen, cabinet officers, and high court jurists have continued to grow in number. Those studies are welcome in the sense that the great labors involved yield new nuggets—sometimes veins—of our recapturable past. But their accumulation is also depressing. That depression rises from the evident bravery of scholars who have tackled individual presidents and the entire presidency, individual justices and the entire Supreme Court, and individual congressmen—but never an entire Congress, much less the entire history of Congress, at least in book-length scholarly studies. Unlike the hapless Coxey, historians have kept resolutely off Congress's grass.

In terms of method and scope, the ever-increasing historical literature on our national decision makers has steered away from the history of our separate but unequal legislature—unequal at least with respect to scholarly attention. Historians have failed almost completely either to consider Congress as an institution or to analyze its major elements of governance in detail, much less in broad synthesis. In effect, historians have separated the tripartite branches of our national government far beyond the most extreme position advanced even by former President Richard Nixon and Professor Charles Alan Wright, his University of Texas Law School special counselor in the Watergate tapes controversy.

With glittering exceptions, scholars have been timid about tackling Congress and its internal components; they have been repetitive in what they have undertaken; and they have been unadventurous in method. Little wonder that, in the phrase of former United States Senator Joseph S. Clark of Pennsylvania, "the wonderful world of Congress" remains largely obscurred in terms of reliable historical scholarship. Again to cite Clark, Congress is "the sapless branch" of our national government.[8] Its internal operations are mysterious to laymen and even to law-men. The workaday machinery of Congress intrudes into general consciousness and the historical record primarily in periods of scandal or stress. The rest, to quote Shakespeare, "is silence."

Historians must accept some responsibility for the fact that in Herodotus's very house, one third of our nation's governance is ill-sheltered, ill-nourished, and ill-clad. I intend that observation to be no more an indictment of the traditional methods of most historians than of the seemingly more experimental practices of political and social scientists. My own work on Civil War and Reconstruction men, measures, and effects, if broadly inclusive in its definition of constitutionalism, has remained happily and stubbornly traditional, although several of my students learn and apply mass-data retrieval and/or legal scholarship techniques. Our shyness concerning the overall history of Congress makes the presentation of important new insights concerning Lincoln and his Congresses exceedingly difficult, if not improbable. We do not have in print (or, so far as I know, in preparation) a broad, scholarly, deeply penetrating history of Congress, or even a reliable, modern, usable history of a single Congress. "Congress under Lincoln" was the title of Professor John Y. Simon's Harvard dissertation on the Thirty-seventh Congress, and I suspect that he would agree now that the "under," if meant literally, is untenable.[9] The very title of my assignment for this meeting—"Lincoln and Congress"—indicates the near-reflexive priority we give to the White House end of Pennsylvania Avenue.

To be sure, until very recently a conference or even a paper on "Congress and Lincoln" would, I fear, have had a slim roster of qualified panelists from any discipline, especially history, from which to draw. I have no idea how much of an audience it might attract, but, playing futurologist, I guess it might be smaller than this one.

Suppose the chairman of this meeting had lost his moorings and given Congress first place over Lincoln in the program, so that my subject had to be "Congress and Lincoln." Are sessions imaginable on the immensely significant standing-committee development of the Civil War and Reconstruction years; on the related rise in importance of committee chairmen and the seniority system; on the legislative traffic controls exercised by House speakers and Senate presidents; on the two-party alignments in the Senate as distinguished from those in the House; or on congressional efficiency in lawmaking and executive watchdogging as compared to other Congresses, state legislatures, or foreign analogues? In light of the present condition of our data resources, can we tell anything new about these matters, or ask more important questions than Professor Randall posed forty years ago?

Among further queries that, in my opinion, want asking, I ask: What were the effects of changes in House and Senate rules of procedure made during the Civil War? Do we have *knowledge*, as distinguished from footnoted folklore, of the Civil War leadership roles of the most prominent senators and representatives, much less of the major committees or of the House clerk or Senate secretary? Are we secure in our scholarship about the intellectual sets of congressmen of both major parties concerning the limits of national involvement with state codes of law on race? Are we comfortable about the intracongressional effects of sectionalism, localism, or nationalism; about the length of Lincoln's reach in policy making; or about the proper role of judicial review in the mid-1860s? Have scholars yet addressed themselves to the task of determining the impact of lobbyists on legislators and legislation? Or examined the reaction of locally based political parties to the draft law of 1863?[10] Until we at least assemble the data needed to answer these questions properly, are we better equipped in 1974 than were scholars of the mid-1930s to respond to Professor Randall's queries and criticisms?

No one puts together a string of didactic questions in expectation of brief, positive replies. Partially affirmative responses are possible to some of them, however. Great scholars have attended brilliantly to presidential-congressional relationships in the Civil War years. In Illinois alone, Allan Nevins, Benjamin Thomas, James Randall and his student David Herbert Donald, among others, have set standards of quality and fashioned frames of reference that no one ignores and no one has surpassed. But as presently arrayed, even with contributions from political and social scientists, that literature has not allowed us to look hard across Pennsylvania Avenue from the White House into the marble fortress on Capitol Hill.

And this, I fear, is the message of my paper. For twenty-five years I have read, tried to learn, tried to teach, and written about Civil War and Reconstruction themes. Yet given the present state of sources, methods, and literature, I must acknowledge that another paper on Lincoln and Congress can merely crib from work by Binkley, Donald, George H. Haynes, Nevins, and Randall, from Professor Simon's and Dr. Bridges's fine dissertations, and from other available secondary literature.[11]

But I shall try, in three steps, to do something else. First, I hope to speak to some of Professor Randall's concerns about the relationships between Congress and Lincoln in which significant research is now maturing. Many seemingly disparate topics, subsumed under the "Congress-Lincoln" rubric, are implicitly connected; and all are concerned with basic institutional arrangements, procedures, and power structures of the Congress. This connective is affected by the alternative research methods employed, and, therefore, as my second step, I intend to comment on methods. Third, I shall venture a not-so-modest proposal aimed at encouraging further research into the Civil War Congresses and into congressional history generally.

To the first point. Professor Randall's mid-1930s catalog of alleged congressional excesses and failures stressed the lawmakers' ineffectiveness and excesses in matters of military power, war finance, and Reconstruction, particularly the "fantastic scheme of confiscation."[12] Not even Allan Nevins responded to all of those broad indictments. But he and other scholars have reviewed individual items in Professional Randall's gloomy roster.

Piecemeal recent judgments emerge from very close looks, sometimes through new methodological lenses, at bloc and party tensions;

goads, goals, and constraints; exciting elasticities; enfeebled rigidities; and allowable procedures. The consensus of those researchers concerning the quality of the Civil War Congress is more favorable than Professor Randall's dour declension.

Professor Randall's first criticism of the Civil War Congress centered on civil-military relationships and wartime finance, especially the performance of congressional committees. Post-World War II scholars, notably Michael Les Benedict, Charles A. Jellison, Fred Nicklason, and Hans Trefousse, have considered war finance and civil-military interactions as inseparable matters. They have noted the cooperative efforts of Lincoln and congressmen to control by means of committees the war-swollen military institution, while containing, if not always punishing, corruption in war-related contracts. Those scholars stress the pervasive and compelling Victorian sense of fiscal morality on Capitol Hill that, next to Unionism itself, justified, indeed compelled, resistance to secession and persistence in overseeing military operations and operators. Those scholars also indicate that, with Lincoln's hearty if covert approval, the House War Contracts Committee of 1861 (and its functional successor, the more famous Joint Committee on the Conduct of War) monitored the vast Union army. Civilian overseers developed controls unimaginable when the minuscule United States army had been the subject of congressional concern.

Prewar habits of governance plus politics in 1861 gave too-free rein to generals of conservative (McClellan) and radical (Fremont) persuasion. With respect to such tender questions as the timing and conduct of military offensives and the rendition of fugitive slaves to disloyal owners, Congress (like Lincoln) at first allowed field generals to blame battlefield failures on their nominal civilian overlords. Those committees, and Lincoln, sometimes overlooked and whitewashed defaulters in favor of maintaining party harmony and army goodwill, especially when emancipation and the recruitment of Negro soldiers became policy alternatives. Yet Lincoln's use of committees, and their recourse to him through timely leaks and pressures from Congress and the White House, helped civilians to cope with Fremont and chastise McClellan.[13] But the configurations of the Congress-Lincoln reciprocity are not yet fully clear.

A number of scholars have disagreed with Professor Randall's criticism of congressional action related to Reconstruction. Herman Belz,

Michael Benedict, Leonard Curry, Richard Curry, Willie Lee Rose, Hans Trefousse, and others, find, as I do, that Capitol Hill was a more rational and effective place than Professor Randall believed it to be.[14]

The relationship between the Civil War Congress and the judiciary has become strikingly clearer. The 1861 and 1862 Confiscation Acts, which Professor Randall called "fantastic," were, in the present consensus, rational, reasonable, and restrained measures that, along with other statutory and executive actions, laid the groundwork for an interconnected web of Reconstruction policies. The acts established judicial procedures whereby property of leading rebels could be seized and redistributed. Confiscation never had a chance, however, because it depended for enforcement on executive initiation of court prosecutions. Lincoln's hesitation about confiscating rebel property while the war was on, his death at the moment of the final contraction of the Confederacy, Andrew Johnson's decision not to enforce the statutes, and the intransigence of Southern whites combined to nullify the acts as tools of Reconstruction.

In the March 1863 Habeas Corpus Act, and in the July 1864 Wade-Davis bill, Congress again attempted to reconstruct states through the national courts. Professor Randall, despite his interest and expertness in state-to-national court jurisdictional aspects of the 1863 Habeas Corpus Act, virtually ignored congressional attention to that matter in the Wade-Davis attempt to regularize Reconstruction policy by statute.[15]

Recent scholarship stresses Congress's warm support for, rather than opposition to, the national courts. During the war, at the instigation of Congress, the national courts became forums of greater procedural and substantive fairness for national officers and freedmen who, in state and local courts, were denied the equal protection of states' laws. Viewed through the habeas corpus-jurisdictional lens, the improved clarity of the Civil War Congresses' vision of workable federalism, compared to prewar performance, is striking.

In all these statutes and bills, congressmen attempted a kind of Reconstruction-through-individual-litigation in the jurisdictionally augmented national courts, to follow military victory of course. That inexpensive solution did no violence to Victorian concerns about fiscal budget-balancing, and required no new, permanent, coercive bureaucracies. It also bypassed the unpalatable alternatives of the nation's doing nothing in the crumpling Confederacy in confirmation of battlefield sacrifices, or committing itself to a long-term military occupation.[16]

The second concern of this paper is that of method (I promise to avoid as much as possible the fearsome word "methodology"). The foregoing reestimations of the wartime adequacy of Congress are, with modest if significant and partial exceptions, largely traditional in method, at least in the sense of being literary analyses of manuscripts, other documents, and printed literature. The exceptions are quantified techniques that supplement authors' efforts to recapture, as examples, committee and floor action on particular pieces of legislation, leadership roles of individual legislators, and intra- and inter-party alignments in Congress. Those scholarly contributions are important, as are many others, but their constructive reconstructions of aspects of the Civil War Congresses are piecemeal because of the limitations of time, energy, and insight imposed by traditional methods.

Any veteran of Civil War legislative history research is familiar with the wearying task of turning the pages of the *Globe* and the serial set of congressional documents, and of deciphering the lost leads, fading footnotes, and puzzling parliamentary procedures. Some generally accepted, easily mastered quantified technique for exhuming significant, relevant facts from the congressional records is necessary as a basic refinement of our professional equipment, as for so long foreign-language reading proficiency was believed to be necessary.

I do not love for themselves the arcane techniques of the quantifiers and counters. I worry, as Professor Bertram Wyatt-Brown does, about "the grubbings of the punch-card set . . . the earnest scholars who work with small-scale units—from lame-duck sessions of Congress to dreary little towns on the New England coast. . . . [and] invariably . . . produce 'tentative' conclusions so delicately hedged that only another computer could translate the results into English."[17]

Some devotees of the cult of counting place technique refinements ahead of historical insights. So may behavioral-studies *aficionados*, legal-studies advocates, or even ordinary wordmen among historians.[18] Friends who are professional actors tell me their treasured cliché: "There are no small parts, only small actors." Regardless of research technique, those who ask trivial questions will evoke trivial replies.

But even Professor Wyatt-Brown has limited his pungent criticism to quantifiers of narrow vision, such as those who study a lame-duck session of a Congress. I take his point a step further. All researchers, including counters, need to attend now to the advice of Moncure D. Conway a century ago: "Sursum Corda!" ("Lift up your Hearts!") Look up, I suggest, to Capitol Hill. Apply all available research techniques, including mass-data retrieval, to *a* Congress, and to *the* Congress, on an adventurous scale, and present results in recognition of Samuel Eliot Morison's sage advice that history is, after all, a literary art.[19]

The danger in forgetting Morison's counsel is clear from a reading—or an attempt at reading—Thomas B. Alexander and Richard E. Beringer's useful and brave diagramming, *Anatomy of the Confederate Congress* (Vanderbilt University Press, 1972). One cannot really read the Alexander-Beringer book. It is, however, quantification that others may exploit, and the profession owes a debt to its authors. Ironically, from it we know more about voting patterns in the Rebel Congress than in its Potomac counterpart. But we still know distressingly little about the workaday performance of either legislature.[20]

An increasing literature attests to the possibility of happy issue from the marriage of counters and wordmen. From among a longish list,[21] I point especially to David Herbert Donald's pithy *Politics of Reconstruction, 1863–1867* (Louisiana State University Press, 1965), Joel Silbey's *Shrine of Party: Congressional Voting Behavior, 1841–1852* (University of Pittsburgh Press, 1967), and, already noted, Michael Les Benedict's *Impeachment and Trial of Andrew Johnson* and his *Compromise of Principle.* All are innovative, illuminating, readable combinations. E. L. Gambill's "Who Were the Senate Radicals?," Allan Bogue's "Bloc and Party in the United States Senate, 1861–1863," and Glenn M. Linden's " 'Radicals' and Economics Policies: The House of Representatives, 1861–1873," all in *Civil War History*, 1965–1967, are, I hope, precursors of book-length inquiries that I eagerly await.

As a discipline, history is closer now to a time when a Lincoln birthday observation will be in order on the theme "Congress and Lincoln." But an ominous cloud hovers over that otherwise brightening research vista. The presence of that threat creates both problems

and opportunities with respect to congressional history, and this is
the third part of my trilogy.

The nature of the problem is simply stated. It is the increasingly
unhappy unemployment and irrelevant-employment situation that
faces a distressingly large number of recent and soon-to-be Ph.D.s
from our graduate university history departments. Instead of adding
weight to the drive toward a scholarly recapture of the Civil War
Congress and other under-researched topics, the talent, training, and
energy of thousands of fine present and future colleagues are being
dissipated in bread-and-butter job substitutes for history positions.
Some unknowable number of history jobless will never return to
their proper work. Many others will never enter it. Bright undergrad-
uates in history are responding to dim job projections by crowding
into law and business schools. That response further depresses job
conditions in history departments as academic deans cut faculty numbers in proportion to sagging class enrollments.

Out of this rending problem comes opportunity. Now is the time
to develop large-scale pre- and postdoctoral employment alternatives
to teaching. Such alternatives should permit historians to sharpen
their special skills, encourage young people to enter and remain in
the discipline, and advance simultaneously the possibilities for systematic research into American history generally, including, of
course, that of Congress.[22]

Among the suitable, relevant, vital employment alternatives to the
teaching of college-level history and campus-connected research, I
suggest two projects that could instructively engage many hundreds
of pre- and postdoctoral candidates for many months or years, and
simultaneously advance the chances for viable "Congress and Lincoln" research and writing. First, a crying need exists for indexes,
suitable for use by historians, to be created for the published primary
sources of the United States government. Taken together, the *Congressional Globe* and *Record*, the serial set of congressional committee reports, *Messages and Papers of the Presidents*, *Statutes at Large*,
Revised Statutes, the *Reports* of the United States Supreme Court,
the *Federal Cases* of the lower United States courts, and the *Official
Records of the War of the Rebellion* form a mountain of books. Some
have never had indexes. Several that do have indexes are difficult
and deceptive to use because the indexes are categorized poorly for
historians. As one example merely, consider that the judicial records

of the 1850–1890 era list under the "master-servant" rubric a host of bedrock matters ranging from labor unionism to slave uprisings to freedmen's work contracts; the "fellow-servant" entry covers a multitude of industrial accident situations.

Obviously, states' analogues to these and other national government printed sources want also to be indexed. County, township, and city equivalents also exist, virtually untouched by scholars, waiting for users, or, tragically, not waiting in the sense that even printed records are lost if left too long unused.[23]

The sheer mass of material suggests a two-step indexing process. First, standard index categories must be established; that alone is a soberingly difficult and complex task. Second, in order that the process advance somewhat more swiftly than that of the dictionary of the French Academy, I suggest the use of mass-data retrieval technology. Obviously, if such technology is employed, indexers and users will have to learn computer techniques. Equally clearly, the need for adequate mass-data retrieval competence will require shifts in present graduate and even undergraduate training. But curricular shifts are not new to campuses.

Is the work involved in such an indexing program worthwhile? Consider, as only one example, in light of my "Congress and Lincoln" concern, the research capacity such index facilities would afford into the legislative development of the Confiscation Act. One index system could supply me with keys to committee actions, floor debates, and parliamentary maneuvers in both houses of Congress; supplemental comments from the *Appendix*; presidential actions and reactions; and judicial commentaries, if any.

The second step I should like Lincoln-centered inquirers and researchers to take is even more grandiose. I envision development of a nationwide computerized finding aid, a "union list" of manuscript and printed holdings in archives, historical societies, libraries, state and local government agencies, and public and private corporations—in short, a resurrected WPA Historical Records Survey, but on a far more systematic base.

Some efforts in that direction exist now, at least in planning or project application terms. The National Endowment for the Humanities has awarded a two-year grant to the American Antiquarian Society to compile an index—that is, a "union" finding aid—for documents written by prominent Americans of the 1763–1815 pe-

riod. Entries for that index would come from the approximately
twelve thousand catalogs published by auctions and dealers since
1867.[24] The National Endowment for the Humanities has also sub-
vented a project that I suggested, the Houston Metropolitan Archives
and Research Center, which has as its primary goal the creation of a
quantified catalog of manuscript and printed records in official and
private possession significant to the history of the Houston region.
The Center, with a staff of approximately five history Ph.D.s and ten
predoctoral students, will, I trust, help to prevent the destruction of
records of the metropolitan area and stimulate research in its history.[25]

It is also encouraging that ambitious commercial publishers are
aware of our research needs. A *Compendium of American Historical
Sources*, edited by Ronald A. Bremer, is supposed to come into print
within a year or so. According to an advertisement, a staff of six la-
bored five years to compile "the most important sources of information to the genealogist, the archivist, and the historian." Some of the
chapter titles are Organization and Record-Keeping, Correspondence, Migrations, Denominational Archives, Fraternal and Patriotic
Archives, Federal Records, Ethnic Archives, Court Records, Immigration, Naturalization, and Maps. There will, apparently, also be a
large bibliography and special chapters on state and county sources.[26]
I look forward to the completion of this aid.

In my opinion, now is the time to transcend even these commend-
able endeavors and give the nation a bicentennial commemoration
more worthy of its past than the pageants and other ephemera that
the American Revolution Bicentennial Administration appears unable to surmount.[27] Given the chance (and money), we can produce
a truly national, marvelously inclusive union catalog, a computer-
retrievable finding aid of unprecedented depth and scope that will
greatly accelerate useful scholarship.

Such a giant step is justifiable for diggers into congressional history. The politics of federalism and the democratization of politics
have spread the private papers of congressman as wide as the nation's
boundaries. United States representatives and senators are states'
men—a few become statesmen. City, county, and state party organi-
zations tie congressmen to localities.

Consider the significant but limited insight into the Wade-Davis
bill provided by a single letter that rests almost unused in the fine
holdings of the Huntington Library. This letter offers a rare opportu-

nity to know the self-image of the House Judiciary Committee in 1864. It was written by Indiana Representative Schuyler Colfax in response to a constituent who suggested that the House Judiciary Committee, of which Colfax was an active member, was conservative. In reply, Colfax for once broke his own rule against replying to insult.

> I have just noticed your allusion to the Committee of the Judiciary appointed by the House; and have conversed with Hon. James F. Wilson of Iowa, its Chair, about it. He is one of the must judicial men in the House, and was much surprised at our strictures as I was. He says that the [House] Com[mittee] have endorsed every radical proposition referred to them, and he regards it as the most radical Judiciary Committee he has been a member of. The *Senate* Judiciary Committee, which reported against and killed the Confiscation bill referred to it this session by the House Committee and shaped by the House, has the reputation of being a very conservative Committee. Ours has not.[28]

The foregoing letter is a very old-fashioned source. Until we use modern means to find and exploit such illuminating traditional sources, I fear that attempts at re-creating the history of Congress and of Lincoln must remain fragmentary and confusing. One day we must be able to locate the manuscript and printed collections that are concerned with the Civil War congressional committees, as well as with the other public concerns of the Age of Lincoln. Through exploiting a mechanized locator, we can husband energies, money, and time in favor of thinking, writing, and criticism, and thereby advance the substance of our responsibility. The very large task of preparing such a finding aid will afford large numbers of our fellow historians opportunities for career alternatives, and encourage the bright young people who now opt for other means of livelihood to reconsider history as a vocation.

Locating documents, the historian's most ancient duty, is worth lobbying for in state capitals and in Washington. The history of Congress is worth recapturing, because until we do we cannot know all the dimensions of the congressmen who were so concerned with the qualities of Lincoln's leadership. And until we recapture Congress we cannot know Lincoln. As Sophocles told us in *Antigone*:

> There is no art that teaches us to know
> The temper, mind, or spirit of any man
> Until he has been proved by government
> And law giving.[29]

NOTES

1. "An exercise in *Retrospective Futurology*, beginning in the spring of 1973 with a study of ancient Athens in the framework of the Graeco-Mediterranean world, will employ computer simulation and display. Richard Bellman and Robert Rosen will collaborate with John Wilkinson in this attempt to make an empirical analysis of history, conceived as a laboratory, in order to determine how policy trajectories in policy spaces were set and how emergent novelty arose." *Occasional Pamphlet* (Santa Barbara: Center for the Study of Democratic Institutions, 1972), 11.

2. Wilfred E. Binkley, *President and Congress*, 3d ed. (New York: Vintage, 1962), 135.

3. Joseph Cooper, "The Importance of Congress," *Rice University Studies*, 54 (1968): 53, and "Origins of the Standing Committees and the Development of the Modern House," ibid., 56 (1970): 116–17.

4. See, as example, Richard F. Fenno Jr., *Congressmen in Committees* (Boston: Little, Brown, 1973); George H. Haynes, *The Senate of the United States: Its History and Practice* (Boston: Houghton Mifflin, 1938); Alfred H. Kelly, "Clio and the Court: An Illicit Love Affair," *Supreme Court Review* (1965): 119–58; Jerome Frank, *Fate and Freedom: A Philosophy for Free Americans* (New York: Simon and Schuster, 1945), ch. 2. In 1964 the Carnegie Corporation financed a "Study of Congress" through the American Political Science Association; no accretion of useful scholarship has yet resulted.

5. Among historians who must be excepted from the categorization of insensitivity to these areas, I note especially Allan Bogue, "The Radical Voting Dimension in the U.S. Senate during the Civil War," *Journal of Interdisciplinary History*, 3 (1973): 449–74; Leonard P. Curry, *Blueprint for Modern America: Nonmilitary Legislation of the First Civil War Congress* (Nashville: Vanderbilt University Press, 1968); Michael Les Benedict, "Congressional Institutions and Radical Republicanism, 1863–73: Committees and Influence" (unpublished paper presented at the 1973 meeting of the Organization of American Historians); and Benedict, *A Compromise of Principle: Congressional Republicans and Reconstruction, 1863–1869* (New York: W. W. Norton, 1974).

6. James G. Randall, "Has the Lincoln Theme Been Exhausted?" *American Historical Review*, 41 (1936): 287–88.

7. James G. Randall, *Civil War and Reconstruction* (Boston: D. C. Heath, 1937), 381.

8. Joseph S. Clark, *Congress: The Sapless Branch* (New York: Harper, 1964), 51–79 (reprinted, in part, in Sidney Wise and Richard F. Schier, eds., *Studies on Congress* [New York: Crowell, 1969], 1–30).

9. John Y. Simon, "Congress under Lincoln, 1861–1863" (Ph.D. diss., Harvard University, 1960).

10. On the draft, see Eugene Murdock, *One Million Men: The Civil War Draft in the North* (Madison: State Historical Society of Wisconsin, 1971).

11. In addition to citations offered elsewhere (nn. 2, 4, 6, 7, 9, 12, 18) to relevant work by these scholars, see Roger Dean Bridges, "The Constitutional World of Senator John Sherman, 1861–1869" (Ph.D. diss., University of Illinois, 1971); Allan Nevins, *The War for the Union*, 4 vols. (New York: Scribner's, 1959–1971). Benedict's *Compromise of Principle* is a brilliant recent addition to Reconstruction literature and substantially advances it from the position of the last half century.

12. Randall, *Civil War and Reconstruction*, 381. See also the restatement in Randall and David Donald, *Civil War and Reconstruction*, 2d ed. (Boston: D. C. Heath, 1961), 291–92.

13. The list that follows is intended only to sample the relevant literature. Each suggests further reading and research. Benedict, *Compromise*, chs. 1–3; Fred Nicklason, "The Civil War Contracts Committee," *Civil War History*, 17 (1971): 232–44, esp. 235; Hans L. Trefousse, "The Joint Committee on the Conduct of the War: A Reassessment," ibid., 10 (1964): 5–19; Charles A. Jellison, *Fessenden of Maine: Civil War Senator* (Syracuse: Syracuse University Press, 1962); Benjamin P. Thomas and Harold M. Hyman, *Stanton: The Life and Times of Lincoln's Secretary of War* (New York: Knopf, 1962).

14. See, in addition to works cited in n. 13: Herman Belz, *Reconstructing the Union: Theory and Policy during the Civil War* (Ithaca: Cornell University Press, 1969); Belz, "The Wade-Davis Bill of 1864" (unpublished paper presented at the 1969 meeting of the American Historical Association); Willie Lee Rose, *Rehearsal for Reconstruction: The Port Royal Experiment* (Indianapolis: Bobbs-Merrill, 1964); Harold M. Hyman, *A More Perfect Union: The Impact of the Civil War and Reconstruction on the Constitution* (New York: Knopf, 1973); Richard O. Curry, "The Civil War and Reconstruction, 1861–1877: A Critical Overview of Recent Trends and Interpretations," *Civil War History*, 20 (1974): 215–38; Phillip S. Paludan, "The American Civil War: Triumph through Tragedy," ibid., 239–50.

15. See, in addition to n. 16, Herman Belz, "Henry Winter Davis and the Origins of Congressional Reconstruction," *Maryland Historical Magazine*, 67 (1972): 129–43; Gerald S. Henig, "Henry Winter Davis: A Biography" (Ph.D. diss., City University of New York, 1971), chs. 7–10. Cf. James G. Randall, "The Indemnity Act of 1863," *Michigan Law Review*, 20 (1922): 589–613; Randall, *Constitutional Problems under Lincoln*, rev. ed. (Urbana: University of Illinois Press, 1951), chs. 12–14; John Syrett, "The Confiscation Acts: Efforts at Reconstruction during the Civil War" (Ph.D. diss., University of Wisconsin, 1971); Michael Les Benedict, *The Impeachment and Trial of Andrew Johnson* (New York: W. W. Norton, 1973).

16. Stanley Kutler, *Judicial Power and Reconstruction Politics* (Chicago: University of Chicago Press, 1968); Catherine Tarrant, "A Writ of Liberty or a Covenant with Hell: Habeas Corpus in the War Congresses, 1861–1867" (Ph.D. diss., Rice University, 1972); W. M. Wiecek, "The Reconstruction of Federal Judicial Power, 1863–1875" (master's thesis, University of Wisconsin, 1966); Hyman, *A More Perfect Union.*

17. Bertram Wyatt-Brown, "Anti-Institutionalism in Antebellum America" (unpublished paper presented at the 1973 meeting of the Southern Historical Association).

18. Robert F. Berkhofer Jr., *Behavioral Approach to Historical Analysis* (New York: Free Press, 1969); Harold M. Hyman, "Law and the Impact of the Civil War: A Review Essay," *Civil War History,* 14 (1968): 51–59.

19. Moncure D. Conway, "Sursum Corda," *The Radical,* 1 (1866): 291–94; Samuel Eliot Morison, *History as a Literary Art,* Old South Leaflets, Series II (Boston: Old South Association, n.d.).

20. Such work as that of political scientist Richard Fenno (see n. 4)—which lays bare the alternatives, imperatives, and procedures of six House and six Senate committees between the years 1955 and 1966—has no counterpart for 1855–1866.

21. See William O. Aydolette, "Quantification in History," *American Historical Review,* 71 (1966): 803–25; Samuel P. Hayes, "Quantification in History: The Implications and Challenges for Graduate Training," *AHA Newsletter* (June 1966): 8–11; Jerome M. Clubb and Howard Allen, "Computers and Historical Studies," *Journal of American History,* 54 (1967): 599–607; Marshall Smelser and William I. Davisson, "The Historian and the Computer: A Simple Introduction to Complex Computation," *Essex Institute Historical Collections,* 104 (1968): 109–26. A convenient bibliographical base is Don Karl Rowney and J. O. Graham Jr., eds., *Quantitative History: Selected Readings—Quantitative Analysis of Historical Data* (Homewood, Ill.: Dorsey, 1969); see also Robert P. Swierenga, ed., *Quantification in American History: Theory & Research* (New York: Atheneum, 1970); and Roderick Floud, *An Introduction to Quantitative Methods for Historians* (Princeton, N.J.: Princeton University Press, 1973).

22. See the resolution of Gilbert Osofsky, member of the Midwest Radical Historians Caucus, "Minutes of the Business Meeting of the Organization of American Historians: April 13, 1973," *Journal of American History,* 60 (1973): 566–68.

23. Edward Papenfuse, "Finding Aids and the Historian: The Need for National Priorities and a Standard Approach," *AHA Newsletter* (May 1972): 15–19.

24. "News From the Field," *College and Research Libraries News,* 34 (1973): 229.

25. James B. Speer, Jr., "Houston Metropolitan Archives and Research Center," *Rice University Review*, 9 (1974): 11–15.

26. *American Libraries*, 4 (1973): 632.

27. See *AHA Newsletter* (May 1973): 16–17; "Nation's Birthday Celebration Spluttering Like Wet Fireworks," *Houston Post*, 25 October 1973, sec. DD, p. 6.

28. Colfax to N. G. Smithen, 18 May 1864, H M 23777, Henry E. Huntington Library, San Marino, Calif.

29. H. D. F. Kitto, trans.

12

Two War Leaders: Lincoln and Davis

T. Harry Williams

THEY WERE BORN within less than a hundred miles of each other in the same state and with less than a year's space between them in time, the two men who would lead the Northern and the Southern nations in the American Civil War and who have come in the historical and popular consciousness to represent two very different American traditions—the one the representative of a progressive modern culture rushing to meet the modern age, the other the embodiment of a static conservative culture clinging stubbornly to the ideals of a past age.

The two future opponents were born not only in a common geographical area and social environment but also in almost identical circumstances in that environment. Everybody knows that Abraham Lincoln was born in a log cabin in the Kentucky woods. But only some of the specialists know that Jefferson Davis also came into this life in a log house. The Davis dwelling was, it is true, somewhat larger than the Lincoln structure, but it was still a log cabin, the kind of house that most settlers built when they entered a wilderness frontier region. The size of the Davis cabin indicated that the Davises were somewhat better endowed with worldly goods than were the Lincolns, a cut above the latter economically and hence culturally and socially. The cut was not very high, however, and certainly not very significant. Thomas Lincoln, the father of Abraham, could not read and could barely write his name. Samuel Davis, the father of Jefferson, could both read and write, but his formal education was most scanty. Samuel owned more property than Thomas but not much more. Thomas was not the shiftless good-for-nothing fabricated by creators of the Lincoln myth. Although he was not well-to-do, he did fairly well by frontier standards, and his forebears in America and England were at least as prosperous as those of Samuel. Actually, neither father could be considered a successful man, and essentially both families belonged in the same economic and social category— yeoman farmer stock, movers who were constantly emigrating from one place to another hoping to find the elusive pot of gold in the new place, people who were, or wanted to be, on the way up, people who were, in the American phrase of the time, "on the make": in short, typical Americans of the time.

The two boys who were born in such proximity bore in their later years even a physical resemblance to each other. Or so it seemed to many observers. Why, some exclaimed, Lincoln and Davis looked almost enough alike to be brothers. In fact, as time went on a legend grew and was surreptitiously circulated that they were half-brothers. This fanciful tale was a direct outgrowth of the Lincoln myth that burgeoned so rapidly and abundantly after Lincoln's death. The reasoning behind it ran something like this. Lincoln had come from the lowest of surroundings and yet was a great man. Thomas Lincoln, therefore, could not have been his father. Who then was? His father must have been of distinguished stock, an aristocrat who lived in the area where Lincoln was born. A likely candidate leaped immediately to mind, his identity demonstrating that a Davis myth was also taking shape—it must have been that courtly and cultured representative of the planter class, Samuel Davis, who had transmitted his physical likeness to both sons. The propagators of this theory had not a scintilla of evidence to support it. They did not have even a good basis of logic. How did it happen that one son of an able father could be great and the other mediocre? They forgot, finally, that they were repudiating a fundamental principle of the American creed. In a country that prided itself on belief in a common-man's democracy, they were contending that an uncommon man could not surmount a common environment.

The supposed physical resemblance between Lincoln and Davis was largely imagined. Those who thought they saw it were overly impressed by certain obvious similarities in the two men—a thinness and boniness of face and frame, an expression of sadness and even melancholy on their faces, especially in repose. It is significant that those who fancied the resemblance were Americans and were perhaps looking too hard for it. Actually, the most penetrating contemporary descriptions of the two presidents were drawn by foreign observers who, though they may have looked with condescending eyes, looked without many preconceived ideas.

William Howard Russell, the English correspondent, wrote this sketch of Lincoln in 1861:

> Soon afterwards there entered, with a shambling, loose, irregular, almost unsteady gait, a tall, lank, lean man, considerably over six feet in height, with stooping shoulders, long pendulous arms, terminating in hands of extraordinary dimensions, which, however, were far exceeded in proportion by his feet. He was dressed in an ill-fitting, wrinkled suit of black, which put one in mind of an undertaker's uniform at a funeral; round his neck a rope of black silk was knotted in a large bulb, with flying ends projecting beyond the collar of his coat; his turned-down shirt-collar disclosed a sinewy muscular yellow neck, and above that, nestling in a great black mass of hair, bristling and compact like a riff of mourning pins, rose the strange quaint face and head, covered with its thatch of wild republican hair, of President Lincoln. The impression produced by the size of his extremities, and by his flapping and wide projecting ears, may be removed by the appearance of kindliness, sagacity, and the awkward bonhommie of his face; the mouth is absolutely prodigious; the lips, straggling and extending almost from one line of black beard to the other, are only kept in order by two deep furrows from the nostril to the chin; the nose itself—a prominent organ—stands out from the face, with an inquiring, anxious air, as though it were sniffing for some good thing in the wind; the eyes dark, full, and deeply set, are penetrating, but full of an expression which almost amounts to tenderness; and above them projects the shaggy brow, running into the small hard frontal space, the development of which can scarcely be estimated accurately, owing to the irregular flocks of thick hair carelessly brushed across it. . . . A person who met Mr. Lincoln in the street would not take him to be what—according to the usages of European society—is called a "gentleman": and, indeed, since I came to the United States, I have heard more disparaging allusions made by Americans to him on that account than I could have expected among simple republicans, where all should be equals; but at the same time, it would not be possible for the most indifferent observer to pass him in the street without notice.[1]

Another English observer, Edward Dicey, wrote of Lincoln in similar vein. Dicey conceded that Lincoln was not a prepossessing figure. "To say that he is ugly is nothing," Dicey recorded; "to add that his figure is grotesque is to convey no adequate impression." But after detailing the features that constituted Lincoln's ugliness, Dicey felt constrained to say: "Add to all this an air of strength, physical as well as moral, and a strange look of dignity coupled with all this grotesqueness, and you will have the impression left upon me by Abraham Lincoln."[2]

Russell also saw and described Davis, interviewing the Confederate president in his capitol at Montgomery just a short time after seeing Lincoln in Washington. Of Davis the correspondent wrote:

I had an opportunity of observing the President very closely: he did not impress me as favorably as I had expected, though he is certainly a very different looking man from Mr. Lincoln. *He is like a gentleman*—has a slight, light figure, little exceeding middle height, and holds himself erect and straight. He was dressed in a rustic suit of slate-colored stuff, with a black silk handkerchief round his neck; his manner is plain, and rather reserved and drastic; his head is well formed, with a fine full forehead, square and high, covered with innumerable fine lines and wrinkles, features regular, though the cheekbones are too high, and the jaws too hollow to be handsome; the lips are thin, flexible, and curved, the chin square, well defined; the nose very regular, with wide nostrils; and the eyes deep-set, large and full— one seems nearly blind, and is partly covered with a film, owing to excruciating attacks of neuralgia and tic. *Wonderful to relate, he does not* chew, and is neat and clean-looking, with hair trimmed, and boots brushed. The expression of his face is anxious, he has a very haggard, care-worn, and pain-drawn look, though no trace of anything but the utmost confidence and the greatest decision could be detected in his conversation.[3]

Russell, it seems to me, was saying something very perceptive and important about the two wartime leaders. As I read Russell, he was awarding the palm to the Northern president. The Englishman, conditioned by the precepts of his own society, naturally tended to judge American political figures by how they appeared in contrast to English figures, naturally tended to use as a measuring standard whether the American seemed to be by English or European "usages" a gentleman. Russell sensed immediately that not by any polite usage, including American ones, was Lincoln a gentleman. But he sensed also that in Lincoln's case the title was of no meaning or significance. He was saying, as was Dicey, I would contend, that here

was a man of raw but great power who transcended formal appella-
tions and did not care if he violated formal usages, a man who might
appear on the surface to be common but who was in reality of distinctly uncommon quality.

I would also contend that despite the apparent fair words, Russell
was not awarding very high praise to Davis. Of the Confederate, the
correspondent was saying: Here is a man of intelligence and determination, of good but not great quality, of some distinction of appear-
ance but of not much ability. Perceptively, Russell saw that Davis
was not a "natural" aristocrat, which is to say one of long family
standing, but a "nouveau" patrician, what a Virginia writer of our
own time, Clifford Dowdey, would call "the made article," but who
thought it was important to appear "like a gentleman," who had for
his own inner security, perhaps, to appear to be a gentleman.[4]

If Lincoln and Davis came from the same geographic area and
social and economic background, how did it happen that as war leaders they were so different, that they had different philosophies of the
use of power and used power in different ways? How can we say
that these two leaders of embattled peoples represented radically
different cultures or two diverging American traditions? Or are these
analyses of their leadership too facile and without real foundation?

Essentially they are correct. The two men did represent different
cultures, and the standards of their cultures influenced the way they
waged war. Lincoln and Davis were the products of different cultures
because in their youth they were wrenched away from the environment in which they had been born and thrust into societies that developed along drastically different lines. From Kentucky, a border
state between the North and the South that combined some features
of both sections, the Lincoln family moved first to Indiana and finally
to Illinois and thus came to rest in the section known then as the
Northwest, the Middle West of today, and in a society that already
exhibited most of the characteristics associated with what historians
like to call modern America—capitalistic, acquisitive, dynamic, democratic, pushing restlessly into the future.

The Davis family moved to Mississippi, to the section then known
as the Southwest, in the heart of the region that was about to become
known as the Cotton Kingdom, new, lush, lavish, where fortunes
could be made overnight by producing the white staple so desired in
the world markets. In the first phase of settlement, life in the realm

of cotton might seem to resemble that in any frontier area in the country. But it was a phase of fleeting existence. Slaves were brought in to cultivate cotton, large landed units were acquired by enterprising individuals, princely dwellings arose on these units or plantations, and soon in this new South the physical pattern of life duplicated, although more splendidly, the pattern in the older states of the seaboard South.

Not only did the cotton South reproduce the physical structure of life in the older South, it also adopted with proprietary zeal the social structure and culture of the older region, becoming, in fact, the most aggressive defender of that congeries of ideals called the Southern way of life. Thus the new South in which young Jefferson Davis spent some of his formative years did not remain "new" very long. It became "old" almost immediately, a part of the conservative, unhurried, unchanging South that in significant ways was outside the mainstream of American culture.

Because Davis was formed in such a society, his life before 1860 is in many respects more interesting to the historian than that of Lincoln, who was shaped in a society more typically American. In Mississippi the fortunes of the Davis family took a sensational turn for the better, all because of the efforts of one member, Joseph, a much older brother of Jefferson. Joseph became the holder of vast lands in the Natchez-Vicksburg area and in effect the head of the family. As the head, he determined that the younger Jefferson, whom he judged to be gifted with rare talents, should be trained to carry the family name to fame. Jefferson therefore received an unusually good formal education for a youth of his time and area. He attended a college in Kentucky; and then, having indicated a desire to be a soldier, was admitted to the Military Academy at West Point, the highest ranking institution of its kind in the country. He graduated with a reasonably good record and, as required by law, accepted a commission to serve for a specified period in the small regular army.

He was not entirely happy in his army service, which consisted of routine assignments in distant frontier posts, and after he married the daughter of his commanding officer, over the officer's opposition, he resigned his commission and returned to Mississippi. There he intended to pursue the life of a planter, managing one of the Davis units, and to prepare himself to go into politics by studying history and government. His young wife died almost immediately of a tragic illness, and it was only after a period of secluded grief that he resumed normal activities. He emerged from his retirement to remarry, serve in Congress, and then head a volunteer regiment in the Mexican War. At the battle of Buena Vista he led his unit to the field in a particular formation that he always believed had saved the day for his side. He never ceased to recall his action at Buena Vista, and in Richmond during the Civil War antiadministration wags quipped that the Confederacy was dying of an inverted V. A later critic sneered that at Buena Vista, Davis learned enough about war in five minutes to defeat the Confederacy.

But he did come out of the Mexican War something of a hero, and with friends and a strong-willed second wife to spur him on, he seemed likely to have an important political career. From then until the secession movement began, his career was almost an unbroken succession of advances. He was United States senator from Mississippi, spokesman of the South in the upper chamber, a power in the national Democratic Party, an advisor of presidents, and secretary of war, an office in which he demonstrated extraordinary administrative diligence and skill.

He stood on the eve of the Civil War as perhaps the foremost man of the South. He was intelligent and well educated and well read, was, in fact, very much the intellectual, impressed by what was said in the books, likely to be guided by the books, always convinced that he knew what was "logical" in a situation, ever ready to point out the logical to lesser men. Furthermore, he had traveled and knew other parts of the country better than most Southerners did, but his mental outlook was essentially Southern—limited and parochial. He knew little of what people in other sections felt or thought, and he did not know too much about the *feelings* of his own people. He had had much applause and little criticism. He was gracious to inferiors and polite to equals and probably did not realize that he had any superiors. He was about as perfect an embodiment of the culture of the South as can be imagined.

The facts of Lincoln's life before the war are so well known as to require less elaboration. Many of these facts have, however, been subjected to considerable misinterpretation. Thus it is widely believed that because Lincoln had little formal education he was an unlearned man. Actually, Lincoln had, through his own reading, acquired the basis of an excellent education. Very few young Americans of his time, few indeed of later times, would acquire, as he did, a mastery of English literary classics, the Bible, Blackstone, and Euclid. Lincoln was self-educated as a matter of necessity: there was no wealthy older member of his family who stood ready to provide him with a formal schooling. But the lack of such an education was not considered a handicap in his environment. Most boys in states like Illinois received only the rudiments of a formal education, a few grades at the most before they were put to work on the family farm. Lincoln was exceptional only in that he read after he went to work.

In similar fashion, Lincoln prepared himself to be a lawyer. He "read" law on his own under the guidance of a licensed attorney and then took and passed the examination for the bar. He became a highly successful lawyer, one of the best-known practitioners in his state. He won most of his cases, and while the fees in many of them were small, his remuneration in others was large. Contrary to one of the myths, he did not start out poor and remain poor. By the standards of his region, Lincoln was a moderately well-to-do man by the 1850s.

He could undoubtedly have become a wealthy man if he had given his main attention to the law. It was never his principal interest, however. Only one profession really attracted him, and it is no exaggeration to say that that one was a passion with him. Politics was the lifelong love of Abraham Lincoln. He was a natural or instinctive politician, a perfect example of the type, drawn to politics for various reasons but primarily because he was fascinated with it as an art, a great game for high stakes, exhilarating merely to practice. Such men may seek great ends in politics, but to them the profession may be an end in itself.

Lincoln did not attain before the war the formal distinction in politics that Davis did. He had held only two offices, a seat for several terms in the Illinois legislature and a place for one term in the national House of Representatives. But he was in politics almost continuously after he reached manhood and for a longer time than Davis was. Moreover, he was in it in a very different way, a more typically American way. Davis attained high office at practically his first try and without much trouble, because he was a war hero and a planter and, supposedly, a man born to lead. He retained his position for the same reasons, probably never understanding why he had been elevated. Lincoln had a more valuable experience for a man destined to lead a people in a crisis. He entered politics at what might be called the precinct or ward level, the lowest level, and then advanced to higher levels. He knew much more than Davis about the organizational side of politics, which is to say the practical side, and also the human side. He understood more perceptively than did Davis the limitations and the capacities of a democratic people.

One would search in vain to find among the tributes paid to Lincoln a commemoration of Lincoln the great politician. In the American lexicon, at least, the word politician has come to denote somebody who is a low and possibly venal character. We refuse to admit that the word means one skilled in the art of politics, that is, of government; we will not concede that politicians are, more than any others, the men who make it possible for the democratic system to function. The great politician may do more than make the system function. He may save it in a crisis or alter it to make it stronger or even, if he is disposed toward evil, destroy it. He has to have many attributes, but one he must have above all others. He must be ready to use power and to know when and how to use it. Although it was not apparent, Abraham Lincoln was such a politician in 1860. He was a man of great but unrealized ambition, a man of immense self-confidence, a man who was conscious that he possessed great inner powers of mind and character. A product of a society that was undergoing revolutionary change, he was capable in a given situation of acting like a revolutionary leader.

In recent years it has been the fashion to lay on Davis most of the blame for the failure of the Confederacy to conduct a more efficient war effort. The evaluations of him by historians have been almost uniformly critical and often unsparingly so. Allan Nevins, the most respected historian of the period, summed up the essence of current opinion when he wrote that Davis failed to execute the task entrusted to him, which was to create a nation. Davis failed, Nevins thought, because he did not realize his role, because he acted as though he was the head of an established nation, whereas he was really leading a revolutionary power struggling to become a nation.

Many of the criticisms of Davis, it has to be conceded, are deserved. For all his intelligence and education and experience, he demonstrated serious and even fatal faults as a war leader. One of these was a particularly grave handicap in a leader of a people fighting against a superior enemy, a people who had a particular need to be aroused to great efforts of devotion and sacrifice. He had no ability to communicate with the people of the Confederacy. Nothing that Davis said was ever quoted, whereas things that Lincoln said became a part of the American language. Davis's words were forgotten not because he was on the losing side but because he never said anything that people could remember. His sentences were too long and involved and legalistic to be remembered. Consider, for example, this passage from his inaugural address, one that is fairly typical of many of his state papers:

Our present political position has been achieved in a manner unprecedented in the history of nations. It illustrates the American idea that governments rest on the consent of the governed, and that it is the right of the people to alter or abolish them at will whenever they become destructive of the ends for which they were established. The declared purpose of the compact of the Union from which we have withdrawn was to "establish justice, insure domestic tranquility, provide for the common defense, promote the general welfare, and secure the blessings of liberty to ourselves and our posterity;" and when, in the judgment of the sovereign States composing this Confederacy, it has been perverted from the purposes for which it was ordained, and ceased to answer the ends for which it was established, a peaceful appeal to the ballot box declared that, so far as they are concerned, the Government created by that compact should cease to exist.[5]

Consider the effect of such words. They could never have brought men to their feet tingling with the sense of participating in a great adventure, nor could they have fired Southern hearts to sacrifice for a great cause.

Nevins has suggested that Davis spoke in this wooden, uninspiring style because he had no passion for anything, including the South, that he believed in the South in his brain but could not feel for it in his heart. The observation has merit, but it does not explain why Davis lacked the flame of passion. The answer may be that he simply was not a passionate person. It seems more likely, however, that the explanation is to be found in his personal and cultural background. Davis had never had to communicate with people, that is, to communicate with them in the sense of persuading or moving them. He proved to be unable to persuade or move people because he did not really know what people were like. He thought that other men were, in a lesser way, like him—responsive to theory, logic, scholarly and legal authority. He had not had to mingle with men in a fluid society, as Lincoln had, and he did not have the intuitive understanding of human nature that would enable him to overcome his lack of experience.

Just as he could not communicate with people in the mass, Davis could not communicate with them as individuals, even with his civil and military leaders. That is to say, he could not deal with them in such a way as to bring out the best in them, to really lead them. It is revealing that he tended to surround himself with advisers who were of average and even mediocre capacity. The only first-rate man in his cabinet was Judah P. Benjamin, and Benjamin was never permitted to exercise the influence that his ability entitled him to. He had to spend an inordinate amount of time and energy in maintaining a relationship with his superior that would enable him to hold his place. Davis selected only one first-rate military leader, Robert E. Lee, and Lee too had to exercise enormous tact just to get along with the president. It may be argued that Davis put so many ordinary people around him because he had no superior people from whom to choose. But it is also possible that there was a kind of subconscious deliberation governing him, that some unsureness in himself impelled him to place "little" men in his entourage. Certainly his conduct was in marked contrast to Lincoln's procedure in selecting advisers. No fear of being overshadowed showed in Lincoln. He appointed to his cabinet William H. Seward and Salmon P. Chase, who had been his recent rivals for the Republican nomination and who thought they were bigger men in every way than the president was. Lincoln needed them to help him execute his task of preserving a nation, but he did not name them solely because he altruistically wanted results. He was supremely confident that he could bend Seward or Chase or any other of his advisers to any purpose.

Those Confederate leaders who did not choose to propitiate Davis either quarreled with him continuously or resigned their offices or suffered official subordination or removal. Whatever the result, their usefulness to the cause was lessened or lost. The story of Davis's relationship with other prominent Confederates could be written as a study in acrimony and broken friendships. Most historians have placed on Davis the onus for these bitter brawls. One biographer, H. J. Eckenrode, said that Davis was a sensitive and vain man who would stand to the last on a wrong decision. The president was "maddened by reproof, shriveled by ridicule," Eckenrode continued, and looked on criticism "as a sort of crime." Clifford Dowdey, Davis's severest critic among Southern writers, wrote that Davis could never admit that he was wrong because the correctness of his opinions was the only thing he had to be proud of. David M. Potter, commenting on the same quality in Davis, said: "He seemed to feel that if he were right that was enough; that it was more important to vindicate his own rectitude than to get results." Douglas S. Freeman, more friendly to Davis than most, could still admit that he was too sensitive, too inclined to claim to the hilt all his due authority. Freeman further noted a distressing tendency to dispute theoretical points merely to win a "logical" victory. Here Freeman was referring to Davis's long, lecturing letters, most of them written to generals, pointing out where the officers were wrong and where the president was right. Davis seemed to think that people would be glad to get these letters, would be gratified to have their errors identified and analyzed.[6]

Davis did exhibit the faults attributed to him by historians. But it would be unjust to leave it that these were merely the expression of a peevish or petulant man. Worse, it would blur our understanding of history, would prevent us from seeing an aspect of Southern culture that helps to explain the failure of the Confederate venture. Davis was what he was because his culture had made him that way. Practically every Confederate leader was of the planter class or subscribed to its ideals. And practically every representative of the planter class was a man very much like Davis. The plantation system produced men who were haughty, imperious, accustomed to giving orders but not to receiving them, used to working with inferiors but not with peers or superiors, not used to working under supervision or on a rigid routine. There was, moreover, something in plantation culture that produced men of little discipline. Possibly the enforced conformity of thought on slavery had the effect of causing men to let their passions run unrestrained in other areas. Whatever the cause, plantation men had difficulty in subjecting themselves to the discipline that modern war demands; indeed, the Southern people as a whole did not do nearly as well in submitting to this discipline as the Northern people did. When Davis and other leaders quarreled, they were only expressing a weakness that was common to their class. If Davis had been a greater man, he might have managed to exercise more patience and tolerance. But he could hardly have acted much differently from what he did. Nor could any man who might conceivably have been chosen president instead of him acted any better.

The most frequent recent criticism of Davis is that he failed to realize that his task called for him to act like a revolutionary leader. This is what Professor Nevins meant when he said that Davis failed to recognize his role. Professor Potter defined what the role required: a revolutionary leader must concentrate on the essential and disregard the irrelevant; he must concern himself with overall leadership and leave detail to subordinates, and he must have a ruthless desire for success and be willing to adopt innovations that will bring success.

It is the opinion of practically every current commentator that Davis did not come up to these standards. He proceeded in almost every situation as though he was the head of a going nation. One example will illustrate his approach. In some parts of the Confederacy opposition to the war reached such proportions that the suspension of civil law and the imposition of martial law were clearly called for. The Confederate Constitution, like the United States Constitution, was vague as to what branch of the government had the right to revoke the writ of habeas corpus. Davis assumed that the right must rest with Congress. He asked that body for permission to suspend, and the legislators, after lengthy debate, granted him a restricted permission. It is instructive to note how Lincoln proceeded in an identical situation. He assumed that the right to suspend must rest with the branch able to act most quickly in an emergency, namely, the executive or, specifically, the president. So he invoked martial law under the guise of the war powers of the president. It was incidents like these that caused an official in the Confederate War Department to write in his diary: "All the revolutionary vigor is with the enemy. With us timidity—hair splitting."[7]

But the best example of Davis's conservatism is the way he proposed to fight the war. The defensive strategy the Confederacy adopted and adhered to for four years, except for a few departures, was almost completely a Davis creation. It has been argued in his behalf that he had no choice as to strategy, that the North flung offensives at the Confederacy all along its line and the South had to meet the thrusts, that the Confederate government had to try to hold every foot of its territory or lose popular confidence. There is merit in the arguments; and it should be noted that Davis said on several occasions that if he had not been forced to resort to the defensive, he would have gone over to the offensive. Yet the fact remains that in the first two years of the war, when the striking power of the Confederacy was at its greatest strength, the offensive was hardly employed. For all his lip service to the offensive, Davis did not really like it as a strategy. He seemed to think instinctively in defensive terms, seemed to have a fixation about holding places. A defensive strategy appealed to him, for one reason because it was so logical (it would show the North and the world that the South did not want war) and Davis would think of logic before he would of success.

Men in the Confederate government who observed Davis with some perception were aware of his deficiencies. They ascribed his failure to formulate an overall view of the war to his preoccupation with administrative detail. He had to approve every decision connected with army matters, even down to the appointment of minor officers. A member of his cabinet confided to his discreet diary that the president feared "details may be wrongly managed without his constant supervision." A War Department official complained in his diary that Davis constantly concerned himself with "little trash" that clerks should handle.[8]

Historians have usually explained this obsession with the irrelevant and unimportant by saying simply that Davis was a good and a natural administrator. Some have suggested that his experience as secretary of war was bad for him, that in that office he found that he was so good at handling detail he could not give up the habit, that Davis as president never rose above the level of secretary of war. One can agree that Davis was a first-rate administrator. One can also agree with the generally held view that skill in administration is not a necessary or even desirable quality in a war leader. When we think of Davis expending time and energy over some minor matter, we inevitably contrast him with Lincoln, who technically was a poor administrator, who detested detail, but who always kept the overall picture of the war in mind.

But to say that Davis did not have an overall picture because he liked administration is an inadequate explanation of his failure. It is setting up an effect as a cause. Davis liked to busy himself with small things because he was happier with them than with large things. He disliked the new, the unorthodox. Even when he permitted offensive

operations, he refused to give the commanders the forces they desired, as he refused Lee before Gettysburg. He would not dare to
achieve a great result, he would not dare to gamble for victory. But
for this he should not be criticized. The kind of war a nation fights is
an expression of its culture. Davis, the leader of the Southern nation,
was only translating the ideals of his culture. The South—the Confederacy—was conservative in every fiber of its being. It looked to
the past as a retreat from the modern world, and it looked to the past
in war and it fought a conservative war. Davis's role may have called
for him to be a revolutionary, but he could not by nature have been
one. No other man who could have been elected president could
have been a revolutionist. The Southern system could not have produced such a man. And if by some accident a revolutionist had been
selected president, the Southern people could not possibly have understood what he was trying to do.

The Confederate official who complained that all the revolutionary
vigor was with the enemy spoke accurately. It is an apparent anomaly
that the government that was the established and legal one, and that
claimed to be engaged in suppressing a rebellion, itself employed
ruthless, remorseless, and at times illegal means to achieve its purpose. But the anomaly is easily explained. The society of the North
had been for a long time and still was in a state of change, of change
so great that it can justly be called revolutionary. The industrializa-
tion of the economy, as example, was in full swing when the war
began, although its transforming effects would not be fully seen until
after the conflict. Ever since the 1830s, dozens of reform societies
had been actively at work to alter this or that aspect of society, to
remake America in a more perfect image, to inaugurate change, it
sometimes seemed, just for the sake of change. The Northern mind
was curious, experimental, innovative, future-looking—in a word,
modern. The North was, in contrast to the South, centralistic—in its
economy, in its society, and in its thinking about government. It was
a society that was willing to allow power to government.

Inevitably such a society would wage a war that was like itself. It
would be but lightly committed to doctrine, it would develop new
ways of war, it would centralize its war effort. And it would be able
to do all these things with an ease and facility that the conservative
South could never hope to achieve. This society or culture of the
future would find that it could do other things under the stress of

war. It placed a high value on its own worth, and it had an inordinate urge to survive. Consequently, it would let nothing stand in the way of its purpose. It would permit its government to repress opposition to the war by the blunt, effective method of imprisoning objectors under martial law—an estimated 14,000 men and women were thus jailed during the conflict, many of them being held without ever being brought to trial. And it would allow, would indeed expect, the government to dispense with the conventions and rules if that were necessary to bring victory, to cut around the corners of legality if that would hasten the outcome.

Practically every author who has written about the Civil War has paid tribute to the leadership of Lincoln. He had many qualities to arouse admiration. He was highly intelligent. He possessed great moral strength, immense determination, and a vast stock of patience. He was superbly skilled at getting along with people and managing people. He was a master of words, and he spoke with words that stirred his people and that still have the power to stir the hearts of men today. He had, it is now almost universally agreed, a firm grasp, a better one than most of his generals, of the overall nature of the war and of what was required to win it. He strove constantly to define the purposes of the war in the highest terms, to lift those purposes to the loftiest level: the victory would not be for a section or a nation but for the family of mankind.

All these praises we willingly accord to Lincoln. But there is one quality about his leadership that we do not seem to want to recognize, or if we recognize it, we do not want to emphasize it, and certainly we do not analyze it. We do not say, or do not say very frankly, that one reason Lincoln was a great war leader was that he was willing to use power. It is true that in the books his uses of the war powers are detailed: that he called for troops to suppress the rebellion, which was equivalent to a presidential declaration of war; that by executive proclamation he set up a naval blockade of the South; that he increased the size of the regular army without congressional authorization, which was a violation of the Constitution; that he allowed money appropriated by Congress for one purpose to be used for a different purpose, which was another violation of the Constitution; that he suspended civil law without clear constitutional sanction; and that finally by executive edict he declared free the millions of slaves in the Confederacy.

The acts are outlined, but they are never related to the man. The usual comment is that Lincoln was exercising powers inherent in his office. One could easily get the impression that he exercised them because they were there and he had to use them, that any man in the office would have acted in much the same way. Yet a moment's reflection will convince anyone that it might have been very different. One can think of a number of men who might have been placed in the presidency who would not have gone nearly as far as Lincoln did. One can also think that had one of these men sat in the office the war might well have turned out differently.

How, then, are we to explain Lincoln and his use of power? It is evident that he was a product of his culture, that coming out of a society that was capable of revolutionary change he was capable of employing revolutionary methods. He once said, as Davis never could have said, that he was not so scrupulous that he would let nine parts of the Constitution be destroyed because he would not violate one part. This cultural, this "sociological," explanation of Lincoln is revealing. But it is not completely satisfying. It does not take the full measure of this strange, deep man, who, when he was very young, gave in a public lecture a description of how a dictator might rise in America—and who in the midst of his warning became so carried away with the man he was depicting that he obviously, although subconsciously, identified himself with the dictator.

We should admit that Lincoln was a great man and leader—but that one of the qualities of his eminence was that he was a great politician, a great power artist. Men like him, men who love power, have done much evil in the world. They have also done great good. It has been the fortune of the democracies that in threatening crises such men have appeared to lead. Nobody can explain why they appear or why democracies have the wisdom to accept them and place them at the head of affairs. All we can do is be thankful that they come.

NOTES

1. William Howard Russell, *My Diary North and South* (Boston: Burnham, 1863), 37–38.

2. Edward Dicey, *Six Months in the Federal States*, 2 vols. (London: Macmillan, 1863), 1:220–21.

3. Russell, *My Diary*, 173, emphasis added.

4. Clifford Dowdey, *Lee* (Boston: Little, Brown, 1965), 154.

5. Lynda Lasswell Crist, ed., *The Papers of Jefferson Davis*, 9 vols. to date (Baton Rouge: Louisiana State University Press, 1971–), 7:46–47.

6. H. J. Eckenrode, *Jefferson Davis: President of the South* (New York: Macmillan, 1923), 118; Dowdey, *Lee*; David M. Potter, "Jefferson Davis and the Political Factors in Confederate Defeat," in *Why the North Won the Civil War*, ed. David Donald (Baton Rouge: Louisiana State University Press. 1960), 105; and Douglas Southall Freeman, *R. E. Lee: A Biography*, 4 vols. (New York: Scribner's, 1934–35), 2:4–7.

7. Edward Younger, ed., *Inside the Confederate Government: The Diary of Robert Garlick Hill Kean* (New York: Oxford University Press, 1957), 101.

8. Younger, *Inside the Confederate Government*, 100.

3
THE LINCOLN LEGACY

13

Lincoln, the Rule of Law, and the American Revolution

Phillip S. Paludan

THE ELECTION OF 1864 was an important one, perhaps the most important this nation has ever had. It was important primarily because it was happening at all. In the midst of this country's bloodiest war—a war that would ultimately take more than 600,000 lives (one out of every eleven men of service age), a war that quite literally often pitted brother against brother—the people of the North were going to walk, not march, to the polls and cast their ballots; they might even decide to repudiate the war itself, to throw Lincoln out and put in his place the Democratic Party candidate, George B. Mc-Clellan. If they did so, they might be said to be declaring that the United States would be the disunited states of America—two nations where there had been one. Many believed that in voting against Lincoln they would be saying that the Constitution had failed. Almost certainly if Lincoln lost, the slave's hope for liberty would end. The election was hotly contested, and as far as Lincoln knew he might just lose it. In fact he predicted that he would lose.[1]

On a small farm near Sturbridge, Massachusetts, John Phillips knew how he was going to vote. Phillips was a Democrat of the Thomas Jefferson school, and in 1864 he was 105 years old. The first presidential candidate he had voted for was George Washington.

Election day came in the fall of 1864, and John Phillips got on his horse and rode alongside his son, who was only seventy-nine at the time. Together they rode into Sturbridge to the polling place at the town hall. They got off their horses and walked into the hall through a door bordered by two flags—both of them the Stars and Stripes. When Phillips entered the hall, the people there stood up and took off their hats. He was the oldest man in town, and maybe the oldest man in the nation. To them, he was a symbol of the Revolution of 1776. He had lived the Revolution that they only read or talked about.

Massachusetts did not have the secret ballot in 1864, and Phillips was offered his choice: he could take a ballot with McClellan's name on it and vote for the Democratic Party and all it stood for, or he could vote for Lincoln and all the Republican Party stood for. Phillips stepped forward. Bystanders paused to hear what he would say. "I vote," he said, "for Abraham Lincoln." It was a resonating moment, more important than any single vote out of the more than 2.3 million Lincoln received, for at that moment the revolutionary generation touched Lincoln and endorsed his efforts.[2]

Not every person of the revolutionary generation would have voted for Lincoln; perhaps many would have repudiated him. Certainly the Confederacy had doubts about whether or not Lincoln deserved such support. Yet those who voted for Lincoln in 1864 must have believed that the symbol did match reality—that Lincoln was in fact the descendent of the revolutionary tradition, and that he was leading the fight to preserve what the blood of 1776 had been spilled to create. Lincoln himself thought so: "Four score and seven years ago our fathers brought forth on this continent, a new nation, conceived in Liberty, and dedicated to the proposition that all men are created equal. Now we are engaged in a great civil war, testing whether that nation, or any nation so conceived and so dedicated, can long endure."[3]

Lincoln had been thinking about the central issues of the American Revolution for many years before his 19 November 1863 address at Gettysburg. "I have never had a feeling politically," he said in February 1861, "that did not spring from the sentiments embodied in the Declaration of Independence." He had often wondered, he added, what kept the revolutionary soldiers struggling in their fight for independence. He thought it was the Declaration. Something more than just separation from England; rather, a hope that they were giving not only liberty to themselves but hope to the world that some day all men, everywhere, should have an equal chance.[4]

As Lincoln thought about 1776, two themes emerged. Both would be important in his response to the Civil War crisis, and both have a message for people one hundred years later. The themes are, first, veneration for the rule of law and, second, preservation of the revolutionary ideals.

Lincoln's respect for the rule of law focused on the importance of law and order in a democratic society. In his 4 July 1861 address he put the question squarely: "Must a government, of necessity, be too *strong* for the liberties of its own people, or too *weak* to maintain its own existence?" Where was the line between liberty and order? How could a nation guarantee order without crushing the very liberty it sought to preserve?[5]

Lincoln made his first statement on that question in 1838, and his emphasis then was on order. In January of that year the Young Men's Lyceum of Springfield had asked him to speak on "The Perpetuation of Our Political Institutions." Lincoln prepared his talk in an atmosphere charged by recent incidents of civil disorder. Mobs had murdered Negroes in Mississippi, burned a black man to death in Missouri, shot and killed an abolitionist editor in Alton, Illinois, and terrorized directors of a bank in Baltimore. To be sure, Lincoln was a Whig and therefore opposed Andrew Jackson as "a concentrated mob," but his objections to mob control were not political only.[6]

In his speech to the Lyceum, Lincoln did, of course, call for a halt to mob violence—not so much because of injustice to the victims (though that was appalling) as because of the example of lawlessness that mobs set. Soon, he believed, the decent, law-abiding, law-respecting people of the nation would lose faith in the ability of the government to preserve order.

An even greater danger, Lincoln believed, was that in such a situation, a tyrant might appear—not that the many would generate anarchy, but that one man would establish a tyranny of misrule. Lincoln feared that the best citizens would see the excesses of mobs as proof that democratic government could not work. The government of the country would then be "left without friends, or with too few, and those few too weak, to make their friendship effectual." At such a moment the ambitious man, the man whose ambition overwhelmed his devotion to the existing system, would gain power, "seize the opportunity, strike the blow, and overturn" the nation's political system.[7]

Lincoln faced a potentially telling rebuttal, however. In the American Revolution there had been mobs in the streets, as well as the repudiation of an existing form of government—government unmaking on a large scale. Hundreds of thousands of Americans had devoted themselves to demonstrating that the British form of rule did not work. Yet that disorder had not spawned a tyrant. Did not history therefore repudiate Lincoln? Was not his argument the sort of political blather one could expect of a Whig seeking to curtail the triumph of Jacksonian democracy? Was Lincoln not merely turning occasional outbreaks of violence into an excuse to throw Democrats out of office? Did not the success of 1776 expose Lincoln's rhetoric as shallow and politically expedient?

There is no question that political expedience was involved in Lincoln's remarks. He was not a saint. He was an ambitious young Whig politician. The Democrats were in office; the Whigs were not. What he said had political purpose. But it also reflected significant insight into the meaning of the American Revolution. Far from invalidating Lincoln's argument, history—viewed as the passage of time instead of as a frozen moment—showed the quality of his vision. For the date was not 1776. It was 1838, and the meaning of the Revolution was different.

The revolution of 1776 had not produced a tyrant because, as Lincoln put it, "the jealousy, envy, and avarice, incident to our nature, and so common to a state of peace . . . were, for the time, in a great measure smothered and rendered inactive; while the deep rooted principles of *hate*, and the powerful motive of *revenge*, instead of being turned against each other, were directed exclusively against the British nation." But by 1838, as Lincoln said, the "state of feeling" that had prevailed during the Revolution "*must fade, is fading, has faded*, with the circumstances that produced it." The Revolution survived in memory as a historical event, but the ideals of those who lived it—rather than reading and hearing about it—were gone. By 1838, time had done what invading armies could not do. The men whose convictions had brought on the Revolution were passing away. Those pillars of the temple of liberty, as Lincoln called them, were crumbling, and the temple would also fall unless something was done to hold it up.[8]

What, then, would save the Republic? Were the passing of time and the ambitions and avarice of man to be the undoing of the nation that Lincoln would later call "the last best hope on earth"? Lincoln thought not. A solution was available—a solution discovered by the revolutionary generation: government of laws and not of men. Reverence for law and the constitutional system would save the Republic. If reverence for law could become the *"political religion"* of the nation, Lincoln said, its people would find salvation from disorder.[9]

Lincoln spoke to perhaps the most compelling of the American traditions—that a country should be ruled by laws, and that legal-constitutional institutions should demand respect and devotion. In a society based on the individual pursuit of benefit—a society exalting individual rights and selfishness in both the economic and political spheres, a society of great geographic and economic mobility, with no rigid class lines to equal those of Europe, no established church, no enforced doctrinal purity—what was to keep that society from flying apart? Lincoln had the answer—respect for legal institutions, for all laws, for the due legal process of doing things, and for fellow citizens as lawmakers and law-respectors. If a government made by and for the people could not earn respect, what in the name of heaven could hold it together. In a nation that encouraged, as no other did, the individual search of millions for different personal ends, what would happen if its citizens did not devote themselves to unity of means? Lincoln understood profoundly the nation's devotion to its legal institutions and the order of law. He knew that the people, faced with threats to order, were likely to follow the man who promised order. Lincoln saw that the nation's greatest danger was not anarchy but the compulsion to be saved from anarchy.[10]

Lincoln's solution to the problem of a potential tyrant arose out of that same attachment to the order of law. He proposed devotion to laws as the nation's *"political religion."* Perhaps he meant that a people could protect themselves from an order-espousing tyrant by devoting themselves to laws, not men, and to the legally established political processes. Such devotion would prevent any one man from promising to maintain order by ignoring or circumventing the law. Lincoln understood the ambitions of men. His own ambition was a "little engine that knew no rest," as his friend William Henry Herndon put it. And perhaps Lincoln's very self-knowledge gave him a devotion to the nation's restraints on such ambitions.[11]

Whether his understanding of order in a democracy grew out of personal insight or political awareness or a combination of the two, his conclusion was the same—the salvation of the nation depended on nurturing and sustaining a devotion to the legal-constitutional system established during the revolutionary era.

Lincoln's veneration for the rule of law is one aspect of the connection he has with the Revolution of 1776. But he also recognized that the Constitution was worthy of devotion because it was a constitution of liberty—one created to give life to the ideals of the Declaration of Independence. When Lincoln saw those ideals in danger, when he saw the spirit of 1776 repudiated, he was energized into action.

In 1820 the United States Congress passed the Missouri Compromise, which prohibited slavery above 36° 30' latitude (the territories acquired in the Louisiana Purchase) and provided that Missouri would enter the Union as a slave state and Maine as a free state. Most people believed that the Compromise was a resolution of the slavery issue in the territories. The government had committed itself to protecting slavery in one place and allowing freedom to grow in another. To men like Lincoln that settlement was in accord with the ideals of the Revolution. It was a settlement that had to be made, but one that did not give national approval to slavery. Lincoln believed that the founders of the nation believed that slavery was an evil, an evil that would die out in time. He thought that they had sanctioned slavery in the Constitution because without it there would have been no Constitution at all. But they hoped and perhaps believed that that necessary evil would eventually fade away.[12]

In 1854 it became apparent to Lincoln and to thousands of others that a basic issue of the Revolution of 1776 was, in fact, being repudiated. The Kansas-Nebraska Act of 1854, which allowed slavery to expand above the 36° 30' line, seemed to give the endorsement of the national government to the idea that slavery was not an evil to be quarantined.

Lincoln charged that the Kansas-Nebraska Act had changed the moral stance of the nation. "Near eighty years ago," he said, "we began by declaring that all men are created equal; but now from that beginning we have run down to the other declaration, that for SOME men to enslave OTHERS is 'a sacred right of self-government.'" Lincoln noted that one senator, on the floor of Congress, had recently called the Declaration of Independence a "self-evident lie"—and no one had rebuked him. Had such a statement been made at Independence Hall in 1776, Lincoln insisted, "the very door-keeper would have throttled the man, and thrust him into the street."[13]

The ideals of the revolutionary era seemed to be dying with the men who had first espoused them. To that point Lincoln on several occasions quoted his political idol Henry Clay. Clay, a slaveholder himself, nevertheless believed that slavery would and should decline and die, and opposed those who defended human bondage. As Lincoln put it, "Henry Clay once said of a class of men who would repress all tendencies to liberty and ultimate emancipation, that they must, if they would do this, go back to the era of our Independence, and muzzle the cannon which thunders its annual joyous return; they must blow out the moral lights around us; they must penetrate the human soul, and eradicate there the love of liberty; and then and not till then, could they perpetuate slavery in this country."[14]

Lincoln saw the moral lights around him going out. In 1857 the United States Supreme Court issued the Dred Scott decision. It had two major points: First, Congress could pass no law that interfered with the right of slaveholders to take their slaves into the territories (an endorsement of the principle of the Kansas-Nebraska Act); second, no black man could be a citizen of the United States. The right to citizenship, as Chief Justice Earl Warren would later observe, is the most important right of all. It is the right to have rights. But in 1857 Chief Justice Roger Taney insisted that the revolutionary generation, the men who wrote the Constitution, did not believe that blacks were part of the national political body.

The decision outraged Lincoln. He insisted that the revolutionary founders had in fact seen blacks as members of the political community. Blacks had voted in New Hampshire, Massachusetts, New York, New Jersey, and even in North Carolina, during the revolutionary era. As a further indication of the low esteem in which slavery was held in that era, most states also made it easy for masters to free their slaves.

But how things had changed. As Lincoln said, "In those days, our Declaration of Independence was held sacred by all, and thought to include all; but now, to aid in making the bondage of the negro universal and eternal, it is assailed, and sneered at, and construed, and hawked at, and torn, till, if its framers could rise from their graves, they could not at all recognize it." The black man's plight seemed symbolic of the disdain for liberty current in the land.

> All the powers of earth seem rapidly combining against him. Mammon is after him; ambition follows, and philosophy follows, and the Theology of the day is fast joining the cry. They have him in his prison

house; they have searched his person, and left no prying instrument
with him. One after another they have closed the heavy iron doors
upon him, and now they have him, as it were, bolted in with a lock of
a hundred keys, which can never be unlocked without the concurrence
of every key; the keys in the hands of a hundred different men, and
they scattered to a hundred different and distant places; and they stand
musing as to what invention, in all the dominions of mind and matter,
can be produced to make the impossibility of his escape more complete than it is.[15]

Less eloquently Lincoln expressed his feelings to a correspondent:
"When we were the political slaves of King George, and wanted to
be free, we called the maxim that 'all men are created equal' a self
evident truth; but now when we have grown fat, and have lost all
dread of being slaves ourselves, we have become so greedy to be
masters that we call the maxim 'a self-evident lie.' The fourth of July
has not quite dwindled away; it is still a great day—*for burning fire-
crackers*!!!"[16]

The secession crisis of 1860–61 brought together the two aspects
of Lincoln's devotion to revolutionary traditions: concern for the rule
of law and apprehension about the survival of the ideals of 1776.

On the Fourth of July 1861, Lincoln articulated the two concerns
in a discussion of the right of revolution, made in response to declarations by secessionists that they were now doing four score and five
years later what the founders had done in 1776. The secessionists
argued that they had been oppressed by a central power, and were
therefore seeking autonomy—the right to be let alone, to live as they
chose.

Lincoln unknowingly had been preparing himself all his adult life
to answer that assertion. Yes, he insisted, there is a right of revolution.
And the people may revolt against tyranny. But the crucial question
was, "What are you making a revolution for?" When a revolution
took place for a morally justifiable cause, then revolution was a moral
right. But when exercised without such a cause, it was "simply a
wicked exercize of physical power." What was the cause, then, for
which the South was revolting? Lincoln thought he knew. He saw
that the Southern states had hoisted the banner of the Declaration of
Independence, but argued that it was not the banner of '76. "Our
adversaries have adopted some declarations of independence," he
told Congress in July 1861, but "unlike the good old one, penned by

Jefferson, they omit the words 'all men are created equal.' Why? They have adopted a temporary national constitution, in the preamble of which, unlike our good old one, signed by Washington, they omit, 'We, the People,' and substitute 'We, the deputies of the sovereign and independent States.' Why? Why this deliberate pressing out of view, the rights of men, and the authority of the people?" Protection of the rights of men and the authority of the people had justified the Revolution of 1776 and made it more than a "wicked exercize of physical power."[17]

Perhaps Lincoln's denial of the right of revolution to the Confederacy was only a rhetorical coup. More compelling to him was the fact that secession—especially secession by gunfire—struck at the only security the generation of 1776 had been able to pass on to its descendants—the institutions, the laws, and the Constitution. The men of the Revolution were gone, but their laws and institutions remained. And those had to become the "political religion of the nation." Lincoln insisted that any attempt to form a Confederacy by destroying the Union was illegal. There were no lawful means and no lawful justification for secession.

The South had been denied no legal right in 1860, Lincoln insisted. No responsible official had threatened to touch slavery in the slave states. The right of Southerners to hold property there (the only clear legal right they had over the slaves) was not in jeopardy. Furthermore, the secessionists were not, despite their protestations to the contrary, respecting the Constitution at all. They were rejecting the constitutionally established means of changing the results of an election—that is, winning the next election. At best, secession was replacing the electoral process. At worst, bullets were replacing ballots. But secession was not a constitutional device and not a legal recourse. It was not law; it was "the essence of anarchy."[18]

Throughout the prewar era Lincoln had seen evidence that the ideals of the American Revolution no longer enlisted the devotion of his generation. Since the Kansas-Nebraska Act, and probably earlier, Lincoln had been reinforced in his belief, expressed in the 1838 Lyceum address, that the idealism of the generation of 1776 was fading. All that remained of that idealism was the nation's constitutional-legal institutions. And secession now mortally endangered those. Lincoln could not and would not allow those institutions to fall.

And thus the war came—four long years fought, as Winston

Churchill later would say, to the last desperate inch. You know the result—the principle of battle by ballot triumphed over battle by bullet. The idea that all men are created equal prevailed over the idea that some men have the right of winning their bread from the sweat of other men's faces. The nation was a little further on the road to securing for all people the rights to life, liberty, and the pursuit of happiness. The Constitution and the institutions it nurtured had triumphed. The principles of the Declaration were close to realization. That, after all, was why John Phillips of 1776 had voted for Abraham Lincoln in 1864.

NOTES

1. Roy P. Basler, ed., Marion Dolores Pratt and Lloyd A. Dunlap, asst. eds., *The Collected Works of Abraham Lincoln*, 9 vols. (New Brunswick, N.J.: Rutgers University Press, 1953–1955), 7:514 (hereafter, Basler, *Collected Works*).

2. Ibid., 8:118.

3. Ibid., 7:23.

4. Ibid., 4:240.

5. Ibid. 426.

6. Ibid., 1:108–15; Joel Parker, *A Charge to the Grand Jury upon the Importance of Maintaining the Supremacy of the Laws* (Concord, N.H.: Marsh, Capen & Lyon, 1838); Leonard Richards, *Gentlemen of Property and Standing: Antiabolition Mobs in Jacksonian America* (New York: Oxford University Press, 1970); David Grimsted, "Rioting in Its Jacksonian Setting," *American Historical Review* 77 (1972): 361–97; Nicholas B. Wainwright, ed., *A Philadelphia Perspective: The Diary of Sidney George Fisher*, ed. Nicholas B. Wainwright (Philadelphia: Historical Society of Pennsylvania, 1967), 154–58.

7. Basler, *Collected Works*, 1:111–12.

8. Ibid., 114–15. For a general description of the widespread national disquiet over the demise of the revolutionary generation, see Fred Somkin, *Unquiet Eagle: Memory and Desire in the Idea of American Freedom, 1815–1860* (Ithaca, N.Y.: Cornell University Press, 1967).

9. Basler, *Collected Works*, 1:112–15.

10. I have elaborated the importance of legal institutions for pre-Civil War society in "The American Civil War Considered as a Crisis in Law and Order," *American Historical Review*, 77 (1972): 1013–34.

11. On Lincoln's personal ambition as a source for his views of democ-

racy, see Edmund Wilson, *Patriotic Gore: Studies in the Literature of the American Civil War* (New York: Oxford University Press, 1962), 99–131.

12. Basler, *Collected Works*, 2:272–75.

13. Ibid., 275.

14. Ibid., 3:29.

15. Ibid., 2:404.

16. Ibid., 318.

17. Ibid., 4:438. See also Thomas Pressly, "Bullets and Ballots: Lincoln and the 'Right of Revolution'," *American Historical Review*, 67 (1962): 647–62; in that excellent article Pressly emphasizes Lincoln's relationship to the revolutionary tradition and his criteria for justified and unjustified revolutions. In this essay I have tried to change the orientation by placing Lincoln's views within the context of his concern for the rule of law and his belief that the revolutionary heritage of 1776 could only be secured through a respect for legal-constitutional institutions.

18. Basler, *Collected Works*, 4:267–68.

14

The Use and Misuse of the Lincoln Legacy

John Hope Franklin

I CANNOT USE the hallowed phrase, "Here I have lived," but I can say that I am happy to be back in the Land of Lincoln, where I spent sixteen of the best years of my life. My ties to this state continue to be strong, and it is a source of great pleasure to be back among friends of many years. It is a great honor to be present on this occasion sponsored jointly by the Abraham Lincoln Association. It is a hallowed occasion, made so not only because of the giant whose birthday we celebrate, but also because of the manner in which, through the years, it has been celebrated here.

Almost all of you, if indeed not all of you, have heard speeches on the sixteenth president of the United States covering every conceivable aspect of his life and related, in one way or another, to every conceivable problem in the community, the nation, and the world. I was particularly sensitive to what the members of the Abraham Lincoln Association might have heard through the years on this occasion that would surely accord them the title of the world's leading authorities on the misuse as well as the use of the Lincoln legacy. Before taking too much for granted, I decided to look at the addresses that had been delivered before this august body to make certain that I would not embarrass myself, as well as previous speakers, by choosing the announced subject for this evening's talk. If the members of the association had, indeed, been subjected to the misuse of the Lincoln legacy, I promised myself that I would notify Judge [Harlington] Wood that I had decided to speak on another topic.

When I had gone through the speeches, I reproached myself for having entertained such an apprehension. The talks were, almost without exception, admirable examples of the kind of remarks that should be made on such an occasion. There is nothing particularly remarkable about that when one is reminded that each year, with one notable exception, the association has been extremely careful in the selection of its speakers. And because, in its wisdom, the association has selected such luminaries as Paul Angle, Carl Sandburg, Benjamin P. Thomas, Andrew C. McLaughlin, T. V. Smith, and Allen Nevins as its speakers, one can learn from their speeches and writings about the use—not the misuse—of the Lincoln legacy.

The proper use of the Lincoln legacy was made in his address in 1936 before this association by the distinguished philosopher, T. V. Smith of the University of Chicago. Lincoln lighted life, he said, with two great virtues, simplicity and magnanimity. "He pitied where others blamed; bowed his own shoulders with the woes of the weak; endured humanely his little day of chance power; and won through death what life disdains to bestow upon such simple souls—lasting peace and everlasting glory. How prudently we proud men compete for nameless graves, when now and then some fool of fortune forgets himself into immortality."[1]

Lincoln early became a symbol and an inspiration to those who chose to use his legacy, as well as those who chose to misuse it. When school children were first taught the meaning of the Emancipation Proclamation or to recite the Gettysburg Address or to appreciate the sublimity of the words in the Second Inaugural, there were others who kept his memory alive for other purposes. One would have thought that Lyon G. Tyler, the fourteenth child of the tenth president of the United States, could have found more important things to do with his enormous energies than to stoke the fires of the Southern hatred against Abraham Lincoln. The tasks of editing the *William and Mary Quarterly* and *Tyler's Historical Quarterly* were not sufficient to occupy his time, so he spent countless hours, days, weeks of his long life in the effort to incite Southern resentment against the martyred president. Lincoln established despotism, Tyler argued, by waging a cruel and barbarous war on Southern civilians. The Emancipation Proclamation was a criminal act, and because of it, Lincoln was the "true parent of Reconstruction, legislative robbery, negro supremacy, cheating at the polls, rapes of white women, lynching, and the acts of the Ku Klux Klan."[2] In another of his ravings, Tyler said that Lincoln was vulgar in his personal habits, weak and deceitful in character, and, in any case, dominated by the radicals of his party.[3] What he expected to gain by this remarkable misuse of the Lincoln legacy was a persistent Southern rejection of Lincoln as a folk hero in the former Confederacy.

Not all white Southerners, however, shared the view of Lincoln that Lyon G. Tyler expressed. Indeed, some embraced him fully and sought to claim him as a patriot, standing in the finest traditions of the South. That is what J. K. Vardaman did in 1914 when he declared in Congress that he had made a "very careful study of Mr. Lincoln's ideas on this question [racial equality] and I have often said, and I repeat here that my views and his on the race question are substantially identical."[4] This was uttered by the man who had said that the Negro was an industrial stumbling block, a political ulcer, a social scab, "a lazy, lying, lustful animal which no conceivable amount of training can transform into a tolerable citizen." He would not be deterred, Vardaman said, if lynch law occasionally resulted in the punishment of an innocent Negro. "We would be justified in slaughtering every Ethiop on the earth to preserve unsullied the honor of one Caucasian home."[5] For Vardaman to indicate that he and Lincoln shared "substantially identical" views on the race question was to sully both the name and memory of one who would certainly have been outraged to have been associated in any way with such wild and irresponsible views as those expressed by Vardaman.

Thomas Dixon Jr., whose novels formed the basis for the epic film, *Birth of a Nation*, did all that he could to claim Lincoln as a Southerner fully in sympathy with the Lost Cause. In one of his several works dealing with the era of Reconstruction, *The Clansman*, the following scene is described: When a Southern lady told President Lincoln that she was delighted he was a Southern man, he asked her how she knew:

> "By your looks, your manner of speech, your easy, kindly ways, your tenderness and humor, your firmness in the right as you see it, and, above all, the way you rose and bowed to a woman in an old faded black dress, who you knew to be an enemy."
>
> "No, madam, not an enemy now," he said softly. "That word is out of date."
>
> "If we had only known you in time."[6]

For Dixon, it was not Lincoln's humanitarianism or humility or belief in democracy that elevated him to greatness. Rather, as in the case of Vardaman, it was the racism they thought they saw in Lincoln that ennobled him and made him a Southerner. This is what the White Citizens Councils thought they saw in Lincoln when they placed a large advertisement in the *New York Times* and other newspapers on his birthday in 1968. Under the caption "Lincoln's Hopes for the Negro," the organization gave selected quotations from Lincoln calling for the separation of the white and black races and for the colonization of blacks outside the United States.[7]

If the perceived racism of Lincoln endeared him to the Vardamans, the Dixons, and the White Citizens Councils of the South, that same perceived racism repelled some black Americans in more recent times. Malcolm X declared that Lincoln did more to "trick Negroes than any other man in history." He was not at all clear on what the trick was.[8] Julius Lester, the author of *Look Out Whitey, Black Power's Gon' Get Your Mama*, called Lincoln a colonizationist and "hesitant emancipator." Blacks, he declared "have no reason to feel grateful to Abraham Lincoln. Rather they should be angry at him," presumably for not doing more for them.[9] In 1968, Lerone Bennett, the historian and senior editor of *Ebony*, asked the question, "Was Abe Lincoln a White Supremacist?" and answered with an emphatic "Yes." Lincoln must be seen, Bennett argued, "as the embodiment, not the transcendence of the American tradition, which is, as we all know, a racist tradition."[10]

In seizing on statements and even policies pursued by Lincoln at a given time in history, neither Malcolm X nor Lester nor Bennett recognized the flexibility of Lincoln and his capacity for growth. Beginning with his simple revulsion to slavery when he saw it in New Orleans in 1831, he gradually embraced the numerous factors that were the components of freedom and equality. Among these were the divestiture of all the attributes and trappings of slavery, the respect and dignity due a citizen of equal standing before the law, economic opportunity, political and social equality, and enjoyment of the franchise. By 1865, Lincoln had come to regard all these as important for the freedmen if they were to live among other free men. The failure to recognize the attributes of flexibility and the capacity for growth in Lincoln and, instead, to treat him as a static, stunted figure is to misuse the legacy that he has left for all of us.

In defining the role of government in society, persons of varied views and philosophies have enlisted the aid of Lincoln to advocate the neutrality of government or its increased role or, indeed, the restriction of that role. During the Great Depression, when the needy, the unemployed and the powerless appealed to government to rescue them from their misery, there were those who insisted that Lincoln would be opposed to such action. "The voice of Lincoln speaks today," said Dr. Joseph R. Sizoo. "Could he walk the paths of life it would be to make a plea for lowliness. What we shall eat and drink and wherewithal shall we be clothed has become to many people their only concern in life. Take materials things away from them and their very motive for living seems lost. . . . We have come to say that poverty breeds crime and have apparently forgotten that out of poverty God has brought the leaders, the thinkers, the poets, and the saviors of the world. . . . Do not be afraid of hard times. Through these the rebirth of our better selves will come."[11] This voice of Lincoln spoke out in February 1932! It is difficult to believe that Lincoln at any time in his life would argue that poverty was a precondition for becoming a leader, thinker, poet, or savior of the world. It was not terribly courageous of Dr. Sizoo to summon Lincoln and use him as his mouthpiece to express views that he did not care to utter as his and his alone.

Along the same line, Lincoln has been used to bolster up our economic system. There could hardly be any debate that he stood for free enterprise, its supporters insist. Ralph McGinnis of Eastern Illinois University made the classic case for Lincoln's support of the free enterprise system by recalling that Lincoln had said, "In all that the people can individually do for themselves, the government ought not to interfere."[12] It is to be doubted that this places Lincoln firmly in the camp of those who were purists when it came to the free enterprise system. Had he been in that camp, it would have been difficult for him to justify his employment by the Illinois Central Railroad, which had come into existence as a result of a munificent grant of land and other perquisites by the United States government, and had prospered because the state of Illinois exempted it from taxation for six years. Indeed, the largest fee that Lincoln ever earned—five thousand dollars—was paid by the Illinois Central in a case that Lincoln won for the railroad, a ruling that successfully resisted the claim of McLean County that it could tax the railroad.[13] One can cheer the prosperity and success of the Illinois Central, but when a corporation was as heavily subsidized by the federal and state governments as it was, it cannot claim that its success was due to free enterprise. If Lincoln stood for free enterprise, it was the kind of free enterprise that many American corporations favor when they get subventions, tax exemptions, and many other tokens of assistance from the government.

Anti-Communists insist that Lincoln has always been one of their strongest supporters. At the height of the cold war, a leading editor of a western newspaper went so far as to bring Lincoln into the anti-Communist fold. Were he alive today he would be no appeaser of "imperial communism," he insisted. "As a world figure, whose significance for all nations and all peoples has steadily grown, Lincoln's greatness arises out of his role as a secular prophet of democracy. There were many timid, frightened men in Lincoln's day. That cowering breed is still with us. In the face of the Soviet menace, they would have us scurry to cover." He quoted Lincoln as saying, "Our reliance is in the love of liberty, which God has planted in our bosoms. Our defense is in the preservation of the spirit which prizes liberty as the heritage of all men, in all lands everywhere."[14] This may all be quite true, but Lincoln was not called upon to focus his attention primarily on foreign affairs. His experience and his activities in that field were, indeed, quite limited. It is not possible to know how he would have functioned during, say, the Napoleonic period or during either of the great world wars. To cast him in the role of a sophisticated internationalist of whatever views is to engage in play-acting and to obscure his remarkable achievements in the arena where he was called upon to function.

If the anti-Communists claimed him as their very own, can anyone blame the women if they enlist his aid in seeking passage of the Equal Rights Amendment? As one of the leaders said in her speech at Gettysburg a decade ago: "I am pretty sure he liked women. He neither put them on a pedestal nor condescended to them."[15] She repeated a story she said she had recently heard, which I suspect this audience heard not so recently. The story is not the most tasteful, but since she told it at the shrine at Gettysburg, I may be indulged in relating it here. Lincoln once left his hat in a chair, and a lady of considerable proportions sat on it. When she arose, Abe surveyed the wreckage and said, very mildly, "Madam, I could have told you that my hat would not fit before you tried it on."[16] The speaker went on to say that it was a matter of record that Lincoln was not surprised when a woman asked to be appointed chaplain to a Wisconsin Regiment. He passed the request to the secretary of war with the notation that he had no objection to it. Lincoln would have appreciated a speech, she said, that had been given by the president of Chatham College, a speech undercutting the pseudo-arguments advanced by opponents of equal rights for women in business: such claims that women would not remain in a job because they would marry and leave, that a woman simply could not wear two hats and do a decent job even in one role, and that the independent, self-directed woman is the kind who would wreck her own home and perhaps someone else's as well. She said, "I can almost hear Abraham Lincoln making short work of these myths because in so many ways he was ahead of his time."[17] On the face of it, they were myths that were as absurd as they were spurious, especially as we view them through the prism of the greatly improved status of women today. But if that speaker could almost hear Lincoln advocating women's rights or the Equal Rights Amendment, I can only say that her aural sensitivity is remarkable to the point of being downright miraculous.

One of the rather remarkable and perverse ways in which the Lincoln legacy has been associated with many of the disorders of our society was suggested in remarks by Melvin E. Bradford of the University of Texas at Dallas. Until he was mentioned in 1981 for a possible appointment as chairman of the National Endowment for the Humanities, Bradford was a rather obscure English professor known more for his critical comments on Southern writers like William Faulkner and Eudora Welty than for his views on the great public policy issues of our time. Overnight, as a result of the scrutiny of his background, he achieved a measure of notoriety by insisting that Abraham Lincoln had contributed significantly to the unrest in contemporary America. His appointment to the Endowment was blocked, but he continued to reiterate his views on Lincoln's contributions to our present confusion. Lincoln, he stated, was the first Puritan president who "recited as a litany the general terms of his regard for universal human rights," while intending all along to go no further than the "rigid racism of the Northern electorate" and his own feelings would allow. Then, in his delineation of the power of the Lincoln legacy, Bradford made a quantum jump in reasoning and evaluation. In Bradford's view, Lincoln's political religion derived from the Declaration of Independence and elevated equality into a fundamental axiom of our political culture. In so doing, said Bradford, Lincoln produced a recipe for continuing turmoil, since "the Northern habit has become national" and anger is to be expected from those who have received "a promissory note that contains . . . the condition that it need never be paid." Following the course that Lincoln charted, he concluded, "we are more likely to arrive at the final plain of desolation than to a happy port in the New Zion of the Puritan vision."[18]

One can understand, although not necessarily admire, those who, in celebrating Lincoln's birthday, undertake to associate him with whatever causes they espouse or views they seek to promulgate. It is as though on this special occasion one expects to be forgiven for making extravagant statements regarding the Great Emancipator. There have been many who should seek such amnesty. A favorite Lincoln birthday orator a generation ago was Senator Edward Martin of Pennsylvania. As he went about the country speaking and then reproducing his speeches in the *Congressional Record*, one cannot be certain whether his distaste for the Truman administration exceeded his love for Lincoln. The important thing was that Lincoln also abhorred the travesty of government that the Truman administration represented. "Abraham Lincoln trusted the people of the United States," Martin declared in 1951. "One of his outstanding characteristics was his undeviating faith in the capacity of freemen to govern themselves. Government that is not responsive to the people must degenerate into dictatorship." Then, forgetting Lincoln for the moment, Martin launched into a full-scale indictment of the Truman administration. It had lost the confidence of the American people, was riddled with corruption, and was characterized by Communist infiltration and appeasement of the Soviet Union. Then toward the end, remembering the occasion, he made his peroration as Lincolnesque as he could: "For the survival of freedom we must renew our allegiance to the fundamental principles that have come to us from the founders of our Republic. And then, God willing, we shall bind up the nation's wounds and do all which may achieve a just and lasting peace among ourselves and with all nations."[19] Instead of saying, "Consider the source," one is inclined to say, "Consider the occasion."

It would be difficult to find an occasion when a greater effort was made to associate Abraham Lincoln with an unpopular cause than the effort made by a recent president of the United States. In the winter of 1974 the Watergate revelations had implicated President Richard Nixon himself, and he was a very troubled man who found it more and more difficult to maintain his equanimity. On the morning of 12 February 1974, he turned up unannounced at the Lincoln Memorial and delivered a speech to the few hundred people who happened to be there to pay tribute to Lincoln on his birthday. "Why, why is Lincoln, of all the American Presidents, more revered not only in America but in the world," Nixon asked. "He freed the slaves, saved the Union, died of an assassin's bullet just at the height of his career. He had humility, humor, feeling and kindness, and perhaps more than anything else the strength, the poise under pressure."

Warming to his subject and seeking to draw a parallel, Nixon continued, "When we examine the American Presidents, it is quite clear that no President in history has been more vilified, or was more vilified during the time than Lincoln. Those who knew him . . . have written that he was deeply hurt by what was said about him and drawn about him, but on the other hand, Lincoln had the great strength of character never to display it, always to stand tall and strong and firm no matter how harsh or unfair the criticism might be." In concluding his remarks, Nixon said, "Even Lincoln would have marvelled if he were living today. This nation now the strongest nation in the world, the richest nation by far in the world, and a nation greatly respected all over the world, and the question he would have asked, as we must ask ourselves, is how will history look back on our time."[20]

This effort on Nixon's part to draw a parallel did not quite come off. The parallel was flawed, for it ignored history regarding the circumstances and events with which Lincoln coped as well as Lincoln's character and approach in dealing with them. It did not come off, moreover, because it was a tasteless and self-serving effort to make Nixon himself innocent by association. The significance of the event is that it shows the length to which desperate men will go in misusing the Lincoln legacy.

Perhaps these examples are sufficient to suggest the persistent misuse of the Lincoln legacy. One of the few pleasant results of such an exercise is to show how the bright light of Lincoln's character is a quality with which almost everyone wishes to be associated. This includes the rich and poor, the black and white, the happy and the wretched, the guilty and the innocent. Even if some tend to misuse the Lincoln legacy, that very act is an affirmation of its importance and of its enduring quality. And that misuse is instructive to all of us as how best to observe this birthday. No one said it better than Congressman Paul Findley a few years ago: "The spirit of liberty is the legacy of Lincoln. We must resolve to preserve and perpetuate this spirit."[21]

NOTES

1. Thomas Vernor Smith, "A Philosopher Looks at Lincoln," Abraham Lincoln Papers Delivered before Members of the Abraham Lincoln Association at Springfield, Illinois, on 12 February 1936, p. 67.

2. Lyon Gardiner Tyler, *A Confederate Catechism: The War of 1861–1865*, 5th ed. (Holdcroft, Va.: Privately published, 1930), 16.

3. Lyon Gardiner Tyler, *John Tyler and Abraham Lincoln, Who Was the Dwarf?* (Richmond, Va.: Richmond Press, 1929), 20–21; Michael Davis, *The Image of Lincoln in the South* (Knoxville: University of Tennessee Press, 1971), 131–32.

4. U.S. Congress 63d Congress, 2d sess., 1914, *Congressional Record* 51:3040.

5. Albert D. Kirwan, *Revolt of the Rednecks, Mississippi Politics: 1876–1925* (Lexington: University of Kentucky Press, 1951), 146–47.

6. Thomas Dixon Jr., *The Clansman* (Lexington: University Press of Kentucky, 1970), 31–32.

7. "Lincoln's Hope for the Negro," *New York Times*, 12 February 1968, sec. 1, p. 36.

8. Malcolm X, quoted in Robert Penn Warren, *Who Speaks for the Negro?* (New York: Random House, 1965), 262.

9. Julius Lester, *Look Out Whitey, Black Power's Gon' Get Your Mama* (New York: Grove Press, 1969), 58.

10. Lerone Bennett, Jr., "Was Abe Lincoln a White Supremacist?" *Ebony*, February 1968, 42.

11. Dr. Joseph R. Sizoo, *The Voice of Lincoln* ([Washington, D.C.:] Privately published, 1932), 6

12. Ralph Y. McGinnis, ed., *Quotations from Abraham Lincoln* (Chicago: Nelson-Hall, 1977), 41.

13. See John J. Duff, *A. Lincoln: Prairie Lawyer* (New York: Rinehart, 1960), 312–18.

14. U.S. Congress, 82d Congress, 1st sess., 1951, *Congressional Record* 97, pt. 2, app.: 857–858.

15. U.S. Congress, 93rd Congress, 2d sess., 1974, *Congressional Record* 120, pt. 5: 7016.

16. P. M. Zall, ed., *Abe Lincoln Laughing: Humorous Anecdotes from Original Sources by and about Abraham Lincoln* (Berkeley: University of California Press, 1982), 134.

17. Same as footnote 15.

18. Melvin E. Bradford, *Remembering Who We Are: Observations of a Southern Conservative* (Athens: University of Georgia Press, 1985), 145–56.

19. U. S. Congress, 82d Congress, 1st sess., 1951, *Congressional Record* 97, pt. 2, app.: 906.

20. "Remarks of the President at the Lincoln Memorial on the 165th Anniversary of Abraham Lincoln's Birth," *Loyal Legion Historical Journal* 30 (February 1974): 3.

21. U.S. Congress, House, "Lincoln, Lover of Liberty," 94th Congress, 2d sess., 1976, *Congressional Record* 122:3010.

ABOUT THE CONTRIBUTORS

EUGENE H. BERWANGER is a professor of history at Colorado State University, Fort Collins. He is author of *The Frontier Against Slavery: Western Anti-Negro Prejudice and the Slavery Extension Controversy* (1967) and *The West and Reconstruction* (1981).

CHRISTOPHER N. BREISETH is President of Wilkes University. His other contribution to Lincoln studies is "Lincoln, Douglas and Springfield in the 1858 Campaign," in Cullom Davis, et al, eds. *The Public and Private Lincoln: Contemporary Perspectives* (1979).

DON E. FEHRENBACHER (1920–1997) was the William Robertson Coe Professor of History and American Studies at Stanford University. Author of numerous books, he won the Pulitzer Prize in History in 1979 for *The Dred Scott Case: Its Significance in American Law and Politics*. His last book, co-authored with his wife Virginia, is *Recollected Words of Abraham Lincoln* (1996).

NORMAN B. FERRIS is a professor of history at Middle Tennessee State University. He is author of two books on William Henry Seward's diplomacy: *Desperate Diplomacy: William H. Seward's Foreign Policy, 1861* (1976) and *The Trent Affair: A Diplomatic Crisis* (1977). He is now writing a full-length biography of Seward.

JOHN HOPE FRANKLIN is the James B. Duke Professor Emeritus of History, Duke University. He is author of numerous books, including *The Emancipation Proclamation* (1963), *From Slavery to Freedom: A History of Negro Americans*, 7th ed. (1994), and *George Washington Williams: A Biography* (1985). President William J. Clinton awarded Franklin the Presidential Medal of Freedom in 1995.

WILLIAM E. GIENAPP is a professor of history at Harvard University. His book *The Origins of the Republican Party, 1852–1856* (1987) won the Avery O. Craven Award. He is at work on a one-volume biography of Abraham Lincoln.

JOHN T. HUBBELL is a professor of history at Kent State University. He is director of the Kent State University Press as well as editor of the distinguished journal *Civil War History*. With James W. Geary, Hubble co-edited *A Biographical Dictionary of the Union* (1995).

HAROLD M. HYMAN is William P. Hobby Professor of History at Rice University. A noted authority on constitutional and legal history his books include *Era of the Oath: Northern Loyalty Tests During the Civil War and Reconstruction* (1954) and *A More Perfect Union: The Impact of the Civil War and Reconstruction on the Constitution* (1973).

JAMES M. MCPHERSON is Edwards Professor of American History at Princeton University. Author of numerous books, his *Battle Cry of Freedom* (1988) won the Pulitzer Prize. His most recent book is *For Cause and Comrades: Why Men Fought in the Civil War* (1997).

JOHN NIVEN (1921–1997) was a professor of history at Claremont Graduate School. Author of numerous biographies, his last was *Salmon P. Chase: A Biography* (1995). He served as editor of the highly regarded documentary project *The Salmon P. Chase Papers*.

PHILLIP S. PALUDAN is a professor of history at the University of Kansas. His books on the Civil War are *Covenant with Death: The Constitution, Law and Equality in the Civil War Era* (1975), *Victims: A True Story of the Civil War* (1981), and *"A People's Contest": The Union and Civil War, 1861–1865* (1988). His book *The Presidency of Abraham Lincoln* won the prestigious Lincoln Prize in 1995.

MICHAEL VORENBERG is an assistant professor of history at the University at Buffalo, State University of New York. He worked as a research assistant on David Herbert Donald's *Lincoln*. His dissertation, "The Civil War Politics of Emancipation and the Thirteenth Amendment," was directed by William E. Gienapp.

T. HARRY WILLIAMS (1909–1979) was the Boyd Professor of History at Louisiana State University. A prolific author of studies on Lincoln and the Civil War, his most memorable works include *Lincoln and the Radicals* (1941) and *Lincoln and His Generals* (1952).

ARTHUR ZILVERSMIT is a professor of history at Lake Forest College. He is author of *The First Emancipation: The Abolition of Slavery in the North* (1967) and editor of *Lincoln on Black and White: A Documentary History* (1971).

ABOUT THE EDITOR

Thomas F. Schwartz became curator of the Henry Horner Lincoln Collection at the Illinois State Historical Library in 1985. In 1993 he was appointed Illinois State Historian. He is author of more than fifty articles, reviews, chapters, and electronic reference entries dealing with Abraham Lincoln and Illinois. Schwartz curated several major exhibitions and co-curated with John Rhodehamel the nationally acclaimed *"Last Best Hope of Earth": Abraham Lincoln and the Promise of America.* He is the editor of the *Journal of the Abraham Lincoln Association,* adviser to the *Journal of Illinois History,* curator of the Electronic Lincoln Presidential Library, and heads the historical content team for the proposed Abraham Lincoln Presidential Library in Springfield, Illinois.

INDEX

36–37; and Lincoln, 10–12,
35–56; and Lincoln's cabinet, 41,
46; meeting with blacks, 42,
72–73; newspaper reactions to,
43–44; opposition by Central
American countries, 44; proposed
sites, 41; reaction of Frederick
Douglass, 42; support in Congress, 40; at Vache Island, 46–47,
54n32
Colored National Convention, 78
Confederacy, 174, 199; conservatism
of, 224; defensive military strategy, 222–23
Confederate Constitution, 222
Confiscation Acts, 59–60, 72
Congress: black suffrage, 29; historical research, lack of, 192–208;
need for new data about, 196; re-
lationship with Lincoln, 192–208;
support of judiciary, 199. *See also*
scholarship; Thirty-eighth Con-
gress; Thirty-seventh Congress
Congressional Record, The, 249
Constitution, 222: reinterpretation,
159; and slavery, 118
Conway, Moncure D., 29, 201
Cooper, Joseph, 192
Cornish, Dudley, 63
Crisfield, John W., 140
Crittendon, John J., 130, 139
Crittendon Compromise, 110
Curtis, Samuel R., 137

Davis, David, 139
Davis, Garrett, 139
Davis, Henry Winter, 140
Davis, Jefferson, 74, 114: communication difficulties, 218; Confederate leaders, 220–21; conservatism
in war strategy, 222–23; criticisms
of, 213–14, 218–19, 221; education compared to Lincoln's,
216–17; family background compared to Lincoln's, 210–11,
214–15; and Lincoln, 210–30;
military background, 215–16; military strategy, defensive, 222–23;
personality, 216, 218–19; physical
description compared to Lincoln's, 212–13; political background compared to Lincoln's,
217–18; southern culture, influence of, 215, 221, 224; terms for
peace, 114; threat against black
soldiers, 74; understanding of role
in Confederacy, 218; war leader,
218–19, 220–21
Davis, Joseph, 215
Davis, Mrs. Jefferson, 95
Davis, Samuel (father of Jefferson),
210–11
Declaration of Independence, 108,
236: foundation of Lincoln's political philosophy, 116–17
De Conde, Alexander, 170–71
Delaware: gradual emancipation,
24; status as border state, 122
Democratic Party in Illinois, 38
Dicey, Edward, 212
Diplomacy, Civil War, 170–91. *See
also* Seward, William Henry
Dixon, Thomas, Jr., 244
Donald, David Herbert, 28, 197,
201
Doolittle, James R., 39
Douglas, Stephen A., 4: Lincoln-
Douglas debates, 5–6, 37; slavery
extension, 116
Douglass, Frederick, 30, 69–86,
82n1: address at Freedmen's Me-
morial Monument to Lincoln, 80;
black recruitment, 65–66, 71; col-
onization, 42, 72; and Constitu-

Gamble, Hamilton R., 135, 137–38, 146–47

Garfield, James A., 165

Garnet, Henry Highland, 42

Garrison, William Lloyd, 29

Gibbs, C. C., 50

Gladstone, William E., 185

Grant, Ulysses S., 63, 80, 98

Great Emancipator, The: called racist by black scholar, 3–20, 16n3; colonization, 10–12; commitment to Emancipation Proclamation, 8; criticisms of, 4; Hampton Roads Conference, 9, 15; historians' interpretations, 3–20; Lincoln-Douglas debates, 6–7; moral leadership, 7–10; as politician, 7, 9–10; popular image as, 5; radicals, 14; reconstruction policy, 4, 10–13; Wadsworth letter, 13–14, 16–17n8; white supremacy, 3–5. *See also* colonization

Greeley, Horace, 8, 25, 61: apparent breakdown, 112; focus on many goals, 107; inconsistency of goals, 115; peaceable secession, 109; peace overture to Confederates, 113–14; recruitment of black soldiers, 61; "The Prayer of Twenty Millions," 61; urges attack on Richmond, 112

Habeas Corpus Act, 1863, 199

Hahn, Michael, 14, 29, 76

Halleck, Henry W., 63

Hampton Roads Conference, doubts about, 9, 15

Harney, William S., 134–35, 145

Harpers Ferry, 70

Hay, John, 48, 108, 127, 157, 172, 177, 186: opinion of Francis P. Blair, Jr. & Sr., 144–45; and William T. Seward, 177, 186

Hayes, Rutherford B., 167

"Hedgehog and the Foxes, The," 106–21. *See also* leadership

Herndon, William Henry, 235: describes Lincoln's thinking, 107

Hicks, Thomas, 126

Historians: employment alternatives, 202; employment prospects, 202; research on Congress, 193; research techniques, 194. *See also* scholarship

History of American Foreign Policy, 17

Hofstadter, Richard, 5

Hooker, Joseph, 165

House War Contracts Committee of 1861, 198

Hunter, David, 60–61, 138

Hyman, Harold, 13–14

Illinois Central Railroad, 246–47

Jackson, Andrew, 233

Jackson, Claiborne F., 134

Jefferson, Thomas, 36, 51n6

Johnson, Andrew, 178: supported by Frederick Douglas, 78

Johnson, Ludwell, 9

Johnson, Lyndon, 94

Joint Committee on the Conduct of War, 198

Kansas-Nebraska Act, 116–17: Lincoln's reaction to, 236

Kentucky, 101; alienation of Unionists, 132; black soldiers, enlistment of, 64, 133; colonization, 37; Confederate Army's invasion, 131; John C. Fremont's proclamation, 131; neutrality, 23, 130–31; reaction to Emancipation Proclamation, 142–43; secession senti-

ment, 129; status as border state,
123
Keyes, Erasmus D., 165
Know-Nothings, 66n2, 173
Kock, Bernard, 35, 46
Krug, Mark, 5
Ku Klux Klan, 243

Lane, James H., 61
leadership: assessment, Lincoln's,
102–3, 171, 218, 225; assessment,
Lincoln's border policy, 126, 129,
133, 134, 138, 143, 148–49; assessment, Lincoln's first one hundred days, 102–3; decisiveness vs.
effectiveness, 97; "hedgehog vs.
foxes," 106–21; as incremental
process, 91, 99; Lincoln's single
central vision, 106–8; qualities,
90–91. *See also* Lincoln's first one
hundred days
Lee, Robert E., 220
Lester, Julius, 245
Liberator, The, 78
Lincoln, Mary Todd, 12
Lincoln, Thomas (father of Abraham), 210–11
Lincoln compared to Washington,
89
Lincoln-Douglas Debates, 5, 6, 37,
158: in Peoria (1854), 116; political expediency, 7; in Springfield,
38
"Lincoln factor, the," 171
Lincoln legacy, 231–52
—misuses of to account for contemporary societal turmoil, 248–49;
to allege Lincoln as racist,
244–45; to bolster economic system, 246–47; to claim Lincoln as
Southern patriot, 244–45; to support anti-communism, 247; to

support Equal Rights Amendment, 247–48
—use of, 243
Lincoln's first one hundred days,
98–99: actions, listed, 97; "Anaconda Plan," 98; assessment of
leadership, 102–3; border states,
101; comparisons with other presidents, 89–90, 94, 101, 111; Congressional inaction, 93; defensive
vs. offensive strategy, 98–100;
expansion of presidential power,
92–93; firing on Fort Sumter, 94,
95; foreign intervention, 101; military actions, 99–100, 112; military preparedness, 93; pressures
on, 95–96; raising an army, 96, 98;
reliance on Simon Cameron, 98;
secession policy formation,
98–99; southern forts, 93
London Times, 97
Lothrop, Thornton, 173, 177
Louisiana and gradual emancipation, 28–29
Louisiana Purchase, 236

McClellan, George B., 78, 164, 186,
198, 231
McCrary, Peyton, 14
McCulloch, Hugh, 29, 164
McDowell, Irvin, 100, 164
McGinnis, Ralph, 246
McLain, William, 44
McLaughlin, Andrew C., 243
Magoffin, Beriah, 129, 131
Malcolm X, 245
Martin, Edward, 249
Maryland, 101: arbitrary arrests,
127–28; control of Unionist Party,
127–29; federal interference with
elections, 127–28; importance of
Baltimore, 126; loyalty oath,